JESUS

FIRST-CENTURY RABBI

RABBI DAVID ZASLOW
with JOSEPH A. LIEBERMAN

PARACLETE PRESS
BREWSTER, MASSACHUSETTS

In Memory of

Rabbi Zalman Schachter-Shalomi

for a lifetime of promoting
interfaith understanding

2015 First Printing Paperback Edition
2014 First Printing Hardcover Edition

Jesus: First-Century Rabbi

Copyright © 2014 by David Zaslow; foreword copyright © 2015 by David Zaslow

ISBN 978-1-61261-644-5

The Library of Congress Cataloging-in-Publication has catalogued the hardcover edition of this book as follows:
Zaslow, David, author.
  Jesus : first-century rabbi / Rabbi David Zaslow with Joseph Lieberman.
    p. cm.
  Summary: "This bold, fresh look at the historical Jesus and the Jewish roots of Christianity challenges both Jews and Christians to re-examine their understanding of Jesus' commitment to his Jewish faith"—Provided by publisher.
  ISBN 978-1-61261-296-6 (hardback)
1. Jesus Christ—Historicity. 2. Jesus Christ—Jewishness. 3. Judaism—Relations—Christianity. 4. Christianity and other religions—Judaism. 5. Judaism (Christian theology) 6. Christianity—Origin. I. Lieberman, Joseph, author. II. Title.
  BT590.J8Z93 2013
  232.9'06—dc23 2013027637

10 9 8 7 6 5 4 3 2 1

Published by Paraclete Press
Brewster, Massachusetts
www.paracletepress.com
Printed in the United States of America

CONTENTS

I
The Jewishness of Jesus

II
Judaism as Jesus Might Have Known It

III
Theo Logos: Knowing God

IV
Theological Misunderstandings

V

Troubled Past and Hopeful Future

FOREWORD TO THE PAPERBACK EDITION

I T IS DIFFICULT TO IMAGINE THAT THERE WOULD HAVE BEEN MUCH OF a readership for this book thirty years ago. Books about the "historical Jesus" seem to lie deep in the past, the realm of Albert Schweitzer and others a century ago.

But in the 1960s, things began to change. The proliferation of Jewish Studies departments at major universities opened an avenue for Jews to pursue graduate studies (and undergrads to take courses) in fields that included first-century Judaism and early Christianity. By the 1980s we saw the first Jewish scholars publishing books not only about Jesus, but also about the Apostle Paul. Then, of course, we witnessed a whole new wave—some have called it the "third wave"—of deep and lasting interest in the historical Jesus throughout the 1990s. Now, for the first time in history, large numbers of Jewish scholars are studying the New Testament.

Maybe we're at a moment in history that fulfills the prophesy in Isaiah 43:19 where God says, "I am about to do a new thing; now it springs forth, do you not perceive it? I will make a way in the wilderness and rivers in the desert."

When I arrived in Oregon in 1970 to complete my graduate studies, I had already given up on "organized religion" as a young man. My faith in Jewish cuisine was strong enough that I believed bagels, lox, pastrami, and kugel came from recipes handed down to Moses on Mt. Sinai, and I retained the Jewish worldview of wanting to make the world a better place, known in Judaism as *tikkun olam*. But if you had asked me if I was religious I'd have said, "No, but I'm spiritual."

On the West Coast at that time new, hip, spiritual, musically exciting Christian movements were forming in living rooms, and a small, vocal band of my twenty-something contemporaries were having born-again experiences. When they asked if I had been reborn or if I was saved, I had no idea what they were talking about. Born again? Saved? These were not questions my Italian or Irish Catholic friends had asked me in Brooklyn. Yet these hipsters were tossing out Bible verses left and right, trying to prove I'd go to hell without Jesus in my life. When they cited an Old Testament verse to demonstrate Jesus was the messiah, I felt called to respond to their attempts to convert me. I'd look up the verse, study the passage in Hebrew in its proper historical context, and then answer them. By the 1980s the notes I wrote down about those Biblical passages became the basis for this book. I began giving talks about Judaism and Israel in local churches and on the local Christian radio station. I had become convinced that Jesus still had something to say to Jews, as well as to Christians.

I realized that I not only had a unique perspective on the roots of Christianity and Jesus's life as a Jew, but that I was also honored to represent this new understanding to Christians. At the same time, I knew there were Christians who sincerely worried for my soul and status in the afterlife if I didn't accept Jesus as my personal Lord and Savior. After all, they argued, there was no forgiveness, no remission of sins, outside of Jesus. Although I was appalled by such a narrow, triumphalist theology, it was the sincerity of these friends that helped stimulate my own return to organized Judaism. The friends whose view of salvation was so black and white gave me the opportunity to realize people can be spiritually awake even if their theology is somewhat misguided. Suddenly I found myself praying for the people who were praying for me. Out of my rivalry with missionaries something positive emerged. My own faith had been strengthened, and I not only made a full return to the Judaism of my ancestors, but I entered into a training program to become a rabbi as well.

Since the publication of *Jesus: First-Century Rabbi* I've been invited to lecture in dozens of synagogues and churches. The greatest surprise to attendees of my talks is that Jesus lived and died as a religious Jew. People find it easy to say that "Jesus was Jewish," but they usually mean that he was Jewish in the way that Einstein or Freud were Jewish—culturally. Most believe that Jesus discarded his religious practices (i.e., observing the Sabbath, keeping kosher, etc.) in order to create a new and more universal religion. A primary goal of this book is to help the reader see Jesus in his historical context as a religious, Torah-observant Jew who lived and worked among many other great teachers in his era. This historical fact, though, does not diminish the theological Jesus of the Church who is seen as messiah, Son of God, and the incarnation of God to Trinitarians.

On closer examination of the Judaism of Jesus we also learn that words like *messiah* and *salvation* had different meanings in the first century than in modern translations of the Bible. For example, on what is known as Palm Sunday, Matthew 21:9 reports, "The crowds that went ahead of him and that followed were shouting, 'Hosanna to the Son of David! Blessed is the one who comes in the name of the Lord! Hosanna in the highest heaven!'" What the crowds (Jewish crowds) meant by chanting "hosanna" (Hebrew for "save us") was a desperate plea for physical rescue from the oppression of the Roman Empire.

These citizens of Judea represented the wishes of the majority of Jews living under the domination of Rome. They weren't looking for a new way to get to heaven, to gain eternal life, or to be saved in the spiritual sense. Rather, they urgently prayed to be saved from the earthly, physical suffering they endured economically and politically. The chant reflected their fervent, messianic desire that this seemingly anointed man named Yehoshua (Joshua in English and Jesus in Greek) would indeed be crowned King of the Jews—the political and spiritual ruler of Judea. Jesus's greatest threat to the Romans was not his theological teachings, nor his thoroughly Jewish gospel of love, compassion, and forgiveness. He was a threat because his rise as the people's possible choice to rule the government of Judea would challenge the authority of Rome. This is why the Romans crucified him along with thousands of other Jews in the first century who were perceived as threats to their authority.

Growing up in New York City in the 1950s, I was aware of the complex web of rivalries that surrounded me. My beloved Brooklyn Dodgers were rivals to the New York Giants, and both teams wanted to beat the Yankees. There were also rivalries between Irish, Italian, Jewish, Black, and Puerto Rican cultures, and the internal religious competition between Irish and Italian Catholics, or between German and Russian Jews. Of course, there were also competitions regarding food. We argued heatedly about where to get the best Italian food. Who made the best pizza or the best bagels? Which Chinese restaurant was best? Everyone had an opinion, and New Yorkers still do. Rivalry still shapes the character of New York, and it probably improves the menu. Of course, if you're from Boston, Chicago, Texas, or even the West Coast, you'll have different opinions, all part of the larger web of rivalries that help shape our nation.

We often overlook how competitive groups have a positive impact upon each other. When the Dodgers and Giants left New York after the 1958 season, we fans were brokenhearted, but the Yankees' fans were saddened as well. After all, they'd lost their main rivals, and with that, the tension and exhilaration of a competition that helped make them a top-notch team. Similarly, one thesis of this book is that the theological rivalry between Christianity, Judaism, and Islam for that matter, have had significant, positive impacts on each faith, although this is rarely acknowledged except by scholars and courageous theologians.

Since the construction of Solomon's Temple around 832 BCE until the destruction of the second Temple in 70 CE, Judaism had been a religion based upon bringing offerings that would be distributed to the family of the offerer, the poor, the priests, and the Temple workers. First-century teachers, Jesus among them, were part of a movement that had begun approximately two hundred years earlier by sages who realized Jerusalem's Temple was in jeopardy because of foreign invaders. They worked to establish new religious practices that would ensure Judaism's survival apart from the Temple, and yet remain true to the commandments of the Torah.

The transition from the Temple system into what would later be called Rabbinic Judaism was nothing less than extraordinary—and Jesus was at the center of that transformation. In his lifetime Judaism was on the verge of being changed from a religion based on offerings of grains, fruit, and animals at the Temple to a religion of fixed prayers and blessings that could be offered anywhere. The kind of liturgical prayers and blessings that we are familiar with today in synagogues, churches, and mosques was, in part, an innovation of the sages during the early centuries of the common era—all of which is recorded in the Talmud. When Jesus instructed his followers to say what is sometimes called "The Lord's Prayer" (Matthew 6:9), he was doing what many of his colleagues were doing—composing liturgical masterpieces that would eventually replace the Temple offerings. The motto of these sages could have been the verse from Psalm 19:14: "Let the words of my mouth and the meditation of my heart be acceptable to you, O LORD, my rock and my redeemer." Words were replacing sacrifices, and local synagogues would eventually replace the Temple itself.

The emerging rabbinic movement proposed specific blessings for foods before and after eating, and for seeing rainbows, mountains, and dozens of other earthly phenomena. There were blessings for traveling, wearing an article of clothing for the first time, smelling fragrant flowers, even going to the bathroom—blessings that continue to be said by religious Jews throughout the world today. It is highly probable that Jesus, his family, and his disciples said many of these same blessings every day of their lives.

From the second through the fifth centuries, Christianity rose from a small sect within Judaism to becoming heir to what remained of the Roman Empire. The Jewish focus on sanctification of this world was steadily losing ground to the Christian theology of spiritual salvation and the condition of the soul after death, rather than merely the consecration of earthly activities. To the early Church, the question "Are you saved?" no longer meant "Are you being rescued from physical harm?" but "Are you assured of your place in the world to come through the blood of Jesus who died and was resurrected as the only means of atonement for your sins?"

By the fifth century, when Judaism was forced to respond to the competition from the Church, there emerged innovative notions of messiah, the end of days, angels, and the world to come, none of which had previously been emphasized in the Jewish Scriptures or theology. Just as the competition between the Dodgers and Yankees in the 1950s was mutually beneficial, the rivalry between Christianity and Judaism has caused each faith to blossom in response to the other. Today, thank God, we are just beginning to acknowledge and express gratitude for the gifts that have risen from that rivalry.

With all of my work around *Jesus: First-Century Rabbi*, I am more dedicated than ever to continuing the essential interfaith effort to lower the surface tension between Christians and Jews. We have so much more in common than the few theological ideas that differentiate us, and these differences clearly strengthen each of our traditions. So, if we liken Christianity and Judaism to the Yankees and the Dodgers, we'd be wise to remember that there would be no game without teams. These two rival teams are part of a much larger league of the world's religions, where all teams interplay to make a complex, fascinating game.

—Rabbi David Zaslow
Asara B'Tevet 5775 / New Year's Day, 2015

OY, AS WE SAY IN YIDDISH. OY! THE ACHE OF SADNESS, THE ACHE of joy. The ache of praying for what seems impossible. The ache of hoping for the fulfillment of God's promise to us all. The time seems to have arrived when Christians and Jews are beginning to have a new understanding of each other. Old notions and prejudices are rapidly being discarded, making room for what the Holy One might have had us understand all along. After the Holocaust, it's time to ask as the great first-century sage Hillel did, "If not now, when?" In March 2008, *Time* magazine cited "Re-Judaizing Jesus" as one of "10 Ideas That Are Changing the World." I think I know why.

There are several books published with the goal of teaching Jews how to respond to Christian missionaries. The biblical citations that missionaries like to use (Daniel 9, Isaiah 7:14, Isaiah 9:5–6, Isaiah 53, etc.) are responded to in a respectful manner, but not one of the books understands the historical Jesus. The tone of the books is defensive, and the comments about Christianity are usually as inaccurate as comments I read about Judaism from some Christian sources. Do we need to criticize each other's faith in order to explain or exalt our own faith? I hope not. Do we need to "spin" descriptions of our own beliefs when comparing them to each other's beliefs? I hope not. The word of God in each of our great religions needs no interpretative spin.

What we need are more passionate, joy-filled discussions and dialogues with an underlying celebration of what we have in common. When members of one faith community define the beliefs of another faith community, there is a tendency to "one up" the group being defined. For example, if a Jewish person describes the notion of God's unity in Judaism and then compares it to the Trinity, there may be a tendency to "spin" the comparison in order for the Jewish idea to sound better than the Christian belief. The same tendency is evident when some Christians define Jewish beliefs.

A good ground rule for interfaith encounters would be for members of each faith tradition to self-define their own beliefs. Members of each respective faith can then agree to discontinue relying upon what they *think* the other believes, and to rely on the new definitions. I am honored to have compiled this book for Christian friends who wish to learn and study the Jewish roots of their faith, and for my Jewish brothers and sisters who often lack accurate information about first-century Jewish beliefs and religious practices. On a personal level, I feel a bit like the theologian and philosopher Martin Buber when he wrote,

> "From my youth onwards I have found in Jesus my great brother. That Christianity has regarded and does regard him as God and Savior has always appeared to me a fact of the highest importance which, for his sake and my own, I must endeavor to understand. . . . My own fraternally open relationship to him has grown even stronger and clearer, and today I see him more strongly and clearly than ever before. I am more than ever certain that a great place belongs to him in Israel's history of faith and that this place cannot be described by any of the usual categories."[1]

Herein lies the mystery of the Jewish-Christian encounter. To a Jew, Jesus can at most be a brother: a fellow Jew at the highest spiritual level who was martyred like millions of other Jews; a *rebbe* (an endearing Yiddish term for rabbi) of a group of *hasidim* (pious disciples) who wanted to see the prophetic dream of peace and justice fulfilled in this world; a healer and miracle worker in the lineage of Elijah and Elisha before him; a mystic like the Baal Shem Tov after him; an incredible *maggid* (preacher and evangelist) in the tradition of the Pharisees. He was a good son, a good Jew, and what we in Judaism call a *mensch*—someone who lived up to his total human potential.

And yet to a Christian the above can never, and should never, be enough. To a disciple and *talmid* (student), Jesus is so much more. He is one with his father. He is the anointed one, the Messiah who was spoken of in the Jewish prophetic writings, and he is the Savior, the great Comforter, and the Redeemer. Without him, salvation had not been accessible to the citizens of the ancient empires. Through Jesus, a personal, covenantal relationship with the God of Israel now seemed possible without having to convert to Judaism. Through him hope was given to the Gentile world for the coming of the Kingdom of God, both in this world and in the world to come. Through Jesus, the non-Jewish world became "those who have received a faith as precious as ours" (2 Peter 1:1). They joined the Jews who had been keepers of this covenant since the time of Abraham.

So herein lies the mystery and the riddle: one Jesus, two understandings. Once free of missionary pressure, the Jewish people may learn to see the historical Jesus as he was—a Jew who observed the commandments of the Torah, a great teacher, rabbi,[2] and *tzadik* (a saintly person). But a Christian's relationship is not solely based on the historical Jesus. It is primarily with the theological Jesus—the Jesus who is beyond time and space—to the Christ who is mysteriously one with the Father and the *Ruakh HaKodesh* (the Holy Spirit). How can these two positions be reconciled? Do they even need to be reconciled? I do not think they can be, nor should they be.

Our contemporary, commodity-based mindset does not hold onto subtleties and contradictions very well. We don't have much room in our minds for mystery, riddle, and paradox as we once did. We want answers. We pose our questions in black and white, either/or. An evangelical pastor once said to me, "Either Jesus is the Savior or he is a fraud." I asked, "Why? Where did you come up with such a clear either/or choice? Maybe he is Savior to you and great rabbi to me, and we're both right."

Can we learn to live with the anxiety of an unanswered mystery? Can we actually celebrate the mystery and shake our heads in wonderment at the infinite wisdom of the Creator? I don't propose to minimize Jewish and Christian differences in this book. On the contrary, I think it is time to celebrate our differences. A healthy ecosystem is one where there is eco-diversity. I sense that the same principle holds true for our faiths as well. Judaism needs the broad spectrum of its various movements. Christianity needs its broad spectrum of denominations and movements. And both faiths, I believe, in a most profound and mysterious way, need each other. Jews and Christians have theologies that differ when it comes to the nature of Jesus. But we also have an identical moral passion for justice and equality based on the prophets. We have parallel problems and challenges that face us both. And we love and serve the same God.

I hope this book helps imprint a Jewish face on a Joshua whose name and identity was Hellenized and changed to Jesus, whose title is often changed to Lord instead of Rabbi so that he would appeal to the non-Jewish world, whose native country was called Palestine by the Romans in order to remove the identification with Judaism that Judea implied. It's my personal hope that this book helps place the martyrdom of Rabbi Joshua in context to the tens of thousands of other rabbis and lay people who also died on the cross at the hands of the Romans. Finally, I hope that God will bless the faithful within our various denominations and movements to study more together, cele-brate more together, and dare to pray together more often. The Bible teaches us that there is a "time to break down, and a time to build up" (Ecclesiastes 3:3). Many Jews and Christians sense the time for building up has arrived between Church and Synagogue. We will both have to leave some of our differences at the door, live with God's mystery, and shout "Halleluyah" for that which we have in common.

INTRODUCTION

WHILE I WAS COMPILING THE MATERIALS FOR THIS BOOK, I was uncertain whom to address my comments to: Catholics, mainstream Protestants, spirit-filled evangelicals, Southern Baptists, Seventh-day Adventists, Eastern Orthodox, Mormons, or to missionaries who believe that the "great commission" must extend to Jews who need to be "completed." I decided that I am not writing this book to any one particular denomination or movement. I am writing it with a focus on my Christian friends, but it is also for Jews who want to learn about the Jewish roots of Christianity. Many of the questions raised in this book come from conversations that I have had with well-meaning missionaries who usually know very little about Judaism, and who have approached me with the Christian gospel over the past forty years. I hope that the responses are useful to mainstream and evangelical Christians, as well as to Jews who want to respond intelligently to missionaries.

My goals are beyond the scope of what I can possibly achieve in a single volume, and I hope you will read some of the materials I refer to in this book. From a Jewish perspective, *A Rabbinic Commentary on the New Testament* by Samuel Tobias Lachs is a scholarly and well-researched demonstration of the roots of Jesus's teachings within first-century Judaism. I cannot speak highly enough of the anthology entitled *Christianity in Jewish Terms* published by Westview Press. It's a cutting-edge collection of essays by leading Jewish and Christian scholars who bring to light the parallels of the two religions. *The Misunderstood Jew* by Amy-Jill Levine is a rare gem because of the author's scholarship and hopeful tone. Finally, *The Jewish Annotated New Testament* that Dr. Levine coedited with Dr. Marc Z. Brettler is the first comprehensive study of the New Testament by Jewish scholars. This book is a must for any serious student of the New Testament.

I am not an academic. Borrowing the Christian term, I am more of what Christians might call an evangelist (a good news giver) or what Jews call a *maggid* (storyteller and expositor of Torah), and I have some "good news" to share with both Christians and Jews. This good news is equally shocking to religious members within each community. Let me begin by explaining to you, my Christian readers, what you may have already discovered: Jews have a knee-jerk, defensive reaction to the gospel. The "New" Testament has been badly misused over the past two thousand years, and this misuse has led to events like the Crusades, the Inquisition, and the terrible anti-Semitism of the twentieth century throughout Europe. To most Jews the good news of the Christian gospel has not been good. In fact, it has been horrible news. History has shown us that the way the gospel was taught meant that we were being asked to convert, forced to convert, forced to leave our homes, beaten for being "Christ-killers," or killed for clinging to our covenantal relationship with God.

Anti-Semitism is a virus that is sometimes difficult to isolate. It's not always as overt as the hatred expressed by Nazism or Stalinism. Sadly, at times, anti-Semitism has even taken on the disguise of the gospel. Prejudice has robbed Christians of a collegial partnership and relationship with Jews for two millennia. Xenophobia and internal church politics have contributed to anti-Semitism over the past two thousand years. Later in this book you will read how replacement theology (the doctrine that asserts that the new covenant of Christianity has replaced the old covenant of Judaism) was embedded in the writings of almost all the early church fathers, and how it inadvertently continues to be perpetuated in Bible translations, and in the sermons of well-meaning teachers and pastors.

After two thousand years, the residual hatred and distrust of Jews emerges in a variety of ways. There continue to be synagogue and cemetery desecrations, as well as local acts of vandalism targeting Jewish communities around the world. Some Jewish people will defensively lump all Christians together, and our reactions to the simple and profound message that underlies Christianity may take the form of reactionary prejudice. When a missionary approaches a

Jew who is already living a life in service to God, the idea of being told we are "incomplete without Jesus" is insulting even though the missionary may mean well. Being told we are "loved" but "without salvation" in the same breath is arrogant and displays an ignorance of the Jewish faith. On the other hand, the Jewish people acknowledge and are very grateful for Christian support of Israel. Also, in the past few decades, local churches in the Unites States are the first to come to the aid of Jewish communities after synagogue desecrations.

Within Judaism there remains plenty of hypocrisy, arrogance, and haughtiness concerning the nations of the world—issues that we have been dealing with internally for three thousand years. The writings of the prophets, in fact, are some of the best self-critical religious writings ever written. But when a religious Jew hears a Christian quoting the Jewish prophets as proof of Jewish theological inadequacy, Jews take it as condescending and hypocritical. At those moments the Jew might want to quote Jesus by saying, "Why do you see the speck in your neighbor's eye, but do not notice the log in your own eye?" (Matthew 7:3). Jesus's rhetorical question was, in fact, right in line with the teachers and sages of his era. Rabbi Natan taught the classical maxim, "Remove the chaff from yourselves, then remove it from others. . . . Reproach not your neighbor for a blemish that is yours" (Talmud: Baba Metzia 59b).

This book is not a refutation of Christianity. It isn't about Christian theology or its conception of Jesus. It's not a debate or refutation of the notion of Trinity, original sin, Jesus as the Son of God, Jesus as one with the Father, or Jesus as a mediator between people and God. It's not about Christianity's methodologies for confession leading to forgiveness, or its theological notion of salvation by grace. This book isn't about baptism, the Christian understanding of the remission of sin, or the various denominational communion rituals. It's not about the origins of Christmas, Easter, Pentecost, or any of the sacred Christian festivals. This book isn't about the miracles of the New Testament: the virginal conception, Jesus walking on water or raising the dead, Jesus's resurrection, or his after-death appearance to his disciples.

Instead, this book will clarify aspects of the life of the historical Jesus, the Jewish Jesus, the first-century Rabbi Jesus. My goal is simply to put his words and teachings into their proper cultural and religious context. The subject of this book has to do with the teachings within Judaism that were most likely studied and believed by the historical Jesus. This book does not focus on the Christian's faith in the theological Jesus—the Jesus worshiped by the church is the province of Christians. To a Christian he is seen as both Messiah and Savior. To a Jew, the messiah is an anointed person, and God is the Savior. On these points some of us will probably always differ. But the historical Jesus—Jesus the man, the Jewish man, the rabbi—he belongs to both of us. The focus of this book is on the notions, ideas, theology, scriptural passages, and eschatology that Jesus the Jew, Jesus the rabbi, the historical Jesus believed. What writings by other rabbis did Rabbi Joshua study during the first thirty years of his life? Who did he study with? Who were his favorite teachers? What prayers did he chant each morning and evening? What parts of the Jewish oral tradition did he quote or refer to that are recorded in the Gospels?

In this spirit, I come to you with the excitement of a fellow believer who has good news to share with you. It amazes me how much I know about Jesus's daily spiritual life simply because I practice Judaism. I know what prayers he might have said each morning; I know what Torah portions he studied each Sabbath; I know how he celebrated the holidays and what issues recorded in the Oral Torah were being debated during his lifetime. I remember looking at Matthew 14:19 for the first time, reading about Jesus holding up the loaves and fishes and making a blessing. The words in English would have been, "Blessed are You, Holy One our God, King of the universe, Who brings forth bread from the earth." I realized it was ironic that every religious Jew today knows the blessing that Jesus might have spoken, but very few Christians do. I cannot imagine a Christian whose Christianity would not be greatly enhanced by deepening his or her knowledge of the historical Jesus, the Jewish Jesus, and about the religion of Judaism that has flourished just as much in the past two thousand years as it did for the two thousand years before Jesus. The time is ripe for Christians to delve into the powerful teachings that grew out of the pre-Rabbinic Judaism that Jesus was a part of, and that brought the world such great wisdom in the past two thousand years. Simultaneously, it seems to be the right time for Jews to reclaim Jesus as an authentic Jewish teacher and native son.

Now seems to be the time for both Jews and Christians to move forward. We each need to correct any remaining misrepresentations that we make about each other's faiths as quickly as possible. With God's help, and through the work of many courageous scholars and teachers, I have faith that every nuance of replacement theology is on its way out. I have faith that a new understanding of the historical Jesus is on its way in. More and more Christians of every stripe and color are awakening to the possibility of new relationships and interfaith opportunities with their Jewish brothers and sisters. As a Jew, I am watching in awe. God's footprints are everywhere. Let us follow.

Setting the Scene for Interfaith Encounters

Interfaith gatherings between mainstream Christians and Jews are now commonplace. In the past thirty years both mainstream and evangelical churches have also started studying and celebrating the Jewish roots of their beliefs. I personally hope that Jews and Christians will come together in prayer more often to celebrate our Creator. Naturally I hope that the distraction of evangelism to my people can end quickly so we can get on to the greater work of serving God. There is much we can do together once Jewish people stop feeling threatened by missionaries whose goal is to convert "incomplete" Jews to Christianity.

A first step might be to realize how closely linked we are. Once a Jew or a Christian starts out on the road to study the historical roots of Christianity, he or she is startled by the exact same set of facts: (1) Jesus was Jewish; (2) Jesus kept both the moral and ritual *mitzvot* (commandments) of the Torah, and instructed his Jewish students to do the same; (3) Christianity has much more in common with its parent religion than it has ever acknowledged until recently; (4) Judaism has much more in common with the teachings of Jesus than it has ever acknowledged until recently; and (5) the historical attempts of missionaries to convert Jews hurts the Jewish people and ultimately goes against God's will.

Generalities are always flawed, so I ask the reader for a bit of poetic license in my descriptions of Judaism and Christianity as I try to shed some light on our differences so that we might ultimately be able to celebrate our commonality. Judaism generally sees the world through a collective lens, starting with a national focus on all of Israel, and then leading back to each individual. Christianity generally starts with a focus on the salvation of each individual, which would then lead to the redemption for the whole world. While the Jew's focus is usually on the messianic vision of world redemption first, the Christian's focus is usually on personal salvation first.

It's easy to utter the words *Jesus was Jewish*, but more difficult for members of either faith to actually imagine this as an historical reality. Many Christians think of the Jewishness of Jesus in the same way they think of the Catholicism of Martin Luther—in other words, he was Catholic but broke away from many of the theological doctrines of the Church at that time. Jesus, however, never left Judaism. Along with the other great sages and teachers that Jews study and revere (Judah the Prince, Hillel, Shammai, Akiva, Yokhanan Ben Zakkai, etc.), Jesus was critical of hypocrisy of some within the Temple priesthood led by the Sadducees. But Jesus never left Judaism, even when he was critical of hypocrisy. He never abandoned the practice of fulfilling the Torah's commandments (i.e., observing the Sabbath, keeping the kosher dietary laws, observing the festivals, etc.).

For the Jew, imagining a thoroughly Jewish Joshua chanting *tehillim* (psalms) and praying in Hebrew each morning with his *talmidim* (disciples) while each wears *tzitzit* (ritual fringes) on his garment and dons *t'fillin* (phylacteries) is contrary to two thousand years of Christian art that sought to de-Judaize Jesus and the disciples. Classical European painting and sculpture depicted Jesus, his family, and his friends as looking like anything but

Mediterranean Jews (e.g., Michelangelo's famous sculpture of David who is not even circumcised). Lamentably, the only Jewish-looking people in most of this art are the opponents of Jesus—Judas, the High Priest, the Sadducees, and angry mobs. In reality, however, the religion of Jesus was Judaism, and ethnically he must have looked like a million other young men of Judea who lived near the Mediterranean.

For a Christian to imagine the scene of a Jewish Jesus is startling. What, no Eucharist? No walking to the local ecclesia on Sunday? No Communion? The average Christian has been raised to believe that Jesus left his native religion to begin a new faith. Or that Paul began a new faith as Jesus would have wanted him to do. For a Jew the scene may be equally as startling. You mean Jesus quotes wisdom sayings from the rich Jewish tradition of his day, and repeats classic parables? Jesus was invited by other religious Jews to teach in synagogues? The Our Father prayer and the Beatitudes are Jewish in origin, and their content was familiar to most of the Jewish people who heard Jesus recite them? Really? Almost all the Jews who heard him teach loved his teachings because they were so rooted in the emerging movement that soon would come to be known as Rabbinic Judaism.

New Testament scholar Dr. Brad Young places Jesus squarely within the context of the Jewish heritage, culture, and religion that he never abandoned. He writes:

Although Jesus was Jewish, his theology is sometimes treated as if he were Christian, but Jesus never attended a church. He never celebrated Christmas. He never wore new clothes on Easter Sunday. His cultural orientation was rooted deeply in the faith experience of his people. His teachings concerning God's love and the dignity of each human being were based upon the foundations of Jewish religious thought during the Second Temple period. The more we learn about this fascinating period of history, the more we will know about Jesus. Jesus worshiped in the synagogue. He celebrated the Passover.

He ate kosher food. He offered prayers in the Temple in Jerusalem. The Jewish religious heritage of Jesus impacted his life in every dimension of his daily experience.[3]

Isaiah 52:13–53:9, the famous suffering servant allegory, is literally a description of the nation of Israel as the suffering servant. Yet to the Church, the servant has been reinterpreted as Jesus. In a simple and logical gesture of our mutual love for the Almighty, isn't it time for us to simply move over and make room for each other's interpretation? Does Isaiah 53 have to be read with only one "correct" interpretation? To the Jew this passage will always be about the people and nation of Israel: "But you, Israel, are my servant, Jacob whom I have chosen" (Isaiah 41:8). To the Christian this passage's simple meaning is extended to Christ (1 Peter 2:24). Let us all hear the admonition and instruction of the prophet: "Have we not all one father? Has not one God created us? Why then are we faithless to one another, profaning the covenant of our ancestors?" (Malachi 2:10).

The miracles written about in the New Testament vary little from the miracles that God demonstrated in the *Tanakh* (Old Testament). And, of course, the church wholeheartedly adopted the moral underpinnings of Judaism. The infrastructure of the prayer service arose from Judaism, and to this day Jewish and Christian service structures bear an unmistakable similarity to each other. Christianity has had an equally positive influence on Judaism: on our liturgical music, synagogue architecture, congregational decorum, and on the implementation of social justice and civil rights projects. The Reformation was the basis for the formation of Protestant denominations, but it also had a beneficial influence on Catholicism. The same Reformation was also good for Judaism, and the diversity that is evident within modern Judaism was, to a large degree, inspired by this ultimately good upheaval within the church.

In the past fifty years Christianity has courageously repented for many of the theological positions that contributed to the Holocaust. The sincerity of the Catholic Church and various evangelical groups in the work of reconciliation has been extraordinary. Mainstream Christian groups (Methodists, Presbyterians, Lutherans, Episcopalians, and others) had already been making bold efforts at reconciliation throughout the twentieth century, and especially since the end of World War II. Following the Six-Day War in 1967, evangelical Christians have shown unprecedented levels of financial, emotional, and spiritual support for the State of Israel. There are many of us in both faiths who believe that God has a special purpose for healing the divisions between Synagogue and Church—to get to work on our common mission of ushering in the messianic age of peace and justice into the world.

Another step in resolving the mystery might be to admit that we simply do not understand each other's faith. Many years ago I was teaching an "Introduction to Judaism" class in my synagogue. When I attempted to define Christianity, there was almost a riot in the class. You see, I was using concepts about the church that I had learned from my extensive contact with the Irish and Italian Catholic kids I grew up with in Brooklyn. As I tried to redefine what I was saying, I realized I was only digging myself into a deeper hole. If I said something that was appealing to the Lutheran in the class, it was incorrect to the evangelical in the class. If I said something that was appealing to the Baptist in the class, it was inaccurate to the Methodist.

Oy, what a lesson! I learned that I would never again try to define someone else's faith. The next year I brought in representatives from several Christian denominations. Differences in doctrine became clear and my yearly lecture on Christianity improved since I was no longer trying to define Christianity through my own childhood biases and filters, no matter how well-intentioned. Just as I made many unwitting errors in attempting to portray Christianity, most Christians make these same unwitting errors when they try to define Judaism. When it comes to issues of the remission of sin, atonement, forgiveness, the afterlife, and salvation, I have heard the oddest explanations by Christians about what Judaism supposedly believes. I have also heard the oddest "definitions" of Christian beliefs from fellow Jews about doctrines like resurrection, the virgin birth, vicarious atonement, the Trinity, and salvation.

Statements about the parallels between the Old and New Testaments come from scholarly research published mostly during the past fifty years or so. Courageous twentieth-century pioneers of interfaith dialogue have inspired my own editorial statements about the overlap in our theologies. My editorial goal has been to try to uncover what I believe to be artificially contrived separations between our theologies. For example, Jews certainly do not define the notion of mediator, son of God, vicarious atonement, Trinity, and original sin in the same manner as Christians—but functionally speaking, Judaism does in fact have all five of these elements within our faith.

I realize I risk offending some within my own faith community by "minimizing the differences" between these two great faiths. I'm willing to take that risk. We have all maximized the differences for too long. Although I don't want to minimize important differences, I no longer wish to defend what I sincerely believe to be contrived distinctions, especially those based on false stereotypes. Rev. Dr. Clark Williamson, one of the pioneers in the modern interfaith dialogue movement, sadly affirms that the "Christian stereotype of Judaism as arid, legalistic, grace-less, and devoid of faith is familiar." But in his critique of a particular Jewish scholar's inaccurate description of Christian theology, he warns of "the other side of the stereotype: Christianity is individualistic, other-worldly, unconcerned with doing good works, focused entirely on truth, and exclusivist with regard to salvation."[4]

I am not the first to have noticed that Christ to a Christian is functionally similar to what Torah is to a Jew. Of course, Jews don't worship Torah, but it is clear that both Torah and Christ are connecting points, or portals, to God. It could be said that whereas Trinitarian Christians worship Christ, Jews simply revere the Torah. When the Torah is taken out of the ark, Jews stand and give it a gentle kiss as it is carried around the congregation. We listen to the Torah with the expectancy of a direct and personal encounter with the Divine. In this sense, the Torah is a mediator—an intermediary between God and the people. For Jews the Torah is simply the most dependable way that we can know what God wants from us. Do we read and listen to the Torah as the living word of the Holy One? Yes. Mediation simply means that something (Torah for Jews, Christ for Christians) aids two parties (God and us) to have accurate and intimate communication. Words like redemption, sin, law, repent, commandment, and Lord may have uniquely different meanings within each of our faiths, but that's the beauty of an interfaith relationship—to learn how the same Living God has revealed identical concepts to us in unique ways.

Theologically, Jesus is seen as God incarnate, who entered the world as a man so that humanity could be redeemed by identifying with his suffering, death, and resurrection. Christianity teaches that Jesus entered the world as the final sacrifice for the nations of the world. Jews, on the other hand, look to Sinai both as a moment in history and as the primal, spiritual event that is linked to the journey of every individual: a journey from slavery to freedom, from the enslavement that led to the revelation at Sinai, and from revelation to the Promised Land. At the same time, the suffering of ancient Israel in Egypt has been an unending model for many minority groups—pilgrims, Mormons, and the leaders of the civil rights movement, for instance—to renew their sense of hope in the face of despair.

Christians tend to focus on their Messiah's suffering, which expiates the sins of every believer. This leads every individual to empathize with the suffering of others. Jews start the other way: we tend to see the suffering of every child, and every righteous person, as having the potential to bring a certain degree of atonement to the world. Although the analogy is not perfect, it seems that to some degree, at least, what the Torah is to a Jew, Christ is to a Christian. Christians see Jesus as the Son of God whereby everyone may enter the kingdom of heaven, while Jews see every person as a son or daughter of God, whereby everyone may enter the Kingdom of God right here on earth. Christians focus on the death and resurrection of Jesus. However, both Jewish and Christians await a universal resurrection and share the dream that the messianic era will be marked by worldwide peace and justice.

The Torah is the story of a people, and Sinai is the story of the revelation of God's word to that people. The life of Jesus is the story of a person, the model for all people, and the Logos made flesh. Every Jew leaves Egypt at Passover; every Christian goes to Calvary each Easter. Israel is the suffering servant; Jesus is the suffering servant. At Sinai millions received the revelation at one time; at Pentecost each Christian receives the blessings of the Holy Spirit, one at a time. From a historical perspective, Jesus was crucified by the Romans, and was perceived to be a political threat to the Empire. From a Christian theological perspective, Jesus died at Calvary to atone for the sins of humanity.

Rabbi Dr. Nancy Fuchs-Kreimer, who teaches at the Reconstructionist Rabbinical College, reminds us of our common history of misrepresentation: "We Jews and Christians have made a lot of noise over the centuries, drawing boundaries in the wrong places and reducing subtle dialectics that exist in both faiths to dichotomies that allegedly divide one from the other. When our traditions have tried to paint pictures of the other, they have hardly been at their best."[5] When we enter an interfaith discussion, let us permit spiritually committed Jews to define Judaism and spiritually committed Christians to define Christianity. We all need to be as spin-free and objective as we can when it comes to history, especially the history of two thousand years ago when record keeping and documentation wasn't at the same level as it is today.

A further step might be to admit that there's nothing to resolve—that God has given each of our faiths separate, parallel, but uniquely different missions. Arising out of decades of prayer, study, and interfaith conversations, I believe that first-century Christian theology was never intended for Jews who already had a gospel of their own. Although there is contradictory evidence, it is possible that Paul might have intended for the good news primarily to be "proclaimed among Gentiles" (1 Timothy 3:16). This might have been seen as a fulfillment of Isaiah's words: "I will give you as a light to the nations, that my salvation may reach to the end of the earth.'" (Isaiah 49:6). Also, it may have been that when Jesus sent his disciples "to the lost sheep of the house of Israel" (Matthew 10:6), he was doing the same kind of outreach that all rabbis do—reaching out to Jews whose connection to God is severed because of bad teachers or assimilation.

The underlying critique that informs my writing has to do with the way that some Christian teachers, preachers, and scholars continue to misrepresent Judaism. Needless to say, distorted teachings about Christianity by Jewish leaders have also contributed to keeping us apart, but distorted teachings about Judaism by Christians have had disastrous consequences for Jews, including vandalism, persecution, forced conversions, violence, pogroms, exile, and massive numbers of deaths. Christianity, our daughter religion, represents two billion followers, whereas Judaism, a nonmissionary religion, rarely sought the kind of growth that the Christian church sought. In every generation we struggle to maintain our own small population in the face of prejudice, assimilation, secularism, anti-Semitism, anti-Zionism, and missionary encroachment.

Along with most Jews, I have been deeply moved by the extraordinary rate of positive change, acts of repentance, revision of prejudicial liturgy, songs, Passion play texts, and ideas within the church toward the Jewish people especially since the end of World War II. I also recognize that fewer and fewer American Christians subscribe to the kind of replacement theology analyzed in this book. This is not, however, always true.

The sense of reproof and rebuke that underlies some of my commentary cuts both ways. Some Jews and Christians may choose to spend another two thousand years criticizing each other's rituals, theological dogmas, and beliefs, but I believe that God would be better served if we were to look into the mirror and correct the errors within our own religions and denominations first. In the eighteenth century, one of our saintly teachers, the Baal Shem Tov, said, "If a person sees something wrong with someone else, this is a sign that he himself has a similar fault. He sees himself, as it were, in a mirror: if the face he sees is not clean, it is his own which is dirty." Or as the rabbis in the Talmud wisely observed, "He who continually declares others unfit is himself unfit. With his own blemish he stigmatizes others as unfit" (Kiddushin 70a).

Christians from various denominations who just a few decades ago didn't ever talk with each other are now in ecumenical dialogue with each other. More and more they're talking with Jews as well. This is a moment in history that should not be taken for granted. Something much greater than all of us is at work here. May God bless us with the courage that each of us will need to take the risk to continue our dialogue, study, and prayer together. The cross in Constantine's dream turned into a sword raised against the Jews and other non-Christians in what remained of the Roman Empire. Now, let us ask God together to turn Constantine's sword into a pruning hook! Measure for measure, trust for trust. As this happens, I believe the Jewish people will be able to study and celebrate the Jewishness of the historical Jesus.

In a world where all religious beliefs come under scrutiny, some may ask, what can God's purpose now be for the Jewish people? Many modern philosophers and scholars, both religious and secular, have tried to answer this question. Judaism, and the survival of the Jewish people, seems to have defied the laws of history and probability. Just as Christianity has its own special mission and covenant with the Creator, so too the liberation of the Israelites from slavery in Egypt has always been a beacon of light and hope to all downtrodden minorities who need to cling to their faith in God in the face of oppression and hopelessness.

The same principle of a unique but distinctive destiny holds true for Christians. The word *christ* comes from the Greek word meaning "anointed." Maybe it's the destiny of Christians to recognize and anoint all that is good in the world—not to convert the world to Christianity, but to "christen" the beauty of all that God has created. The Jewish people may have endeavored to be a light unto the nations (Isaiah 42:6), but Christianity has brought that light to the world in a way that Judaism could never have done. This partnership between Jews and Christians has rarely been acknowledged, let alone celebrated, by leaders of either faith. Maybe now is the time to acknowledge and express gratitude for each other's divinely guided spiritual paths. God, Torah, Israel; Father,

Son, Holy Spirit—two triads, two paths, two religions, one God, one goal! Could it really be so simple? I think so.

About Language

Words like law, sin, repent, salvation, and redemption have very different meanings in Hebrew than they do in English. I've attempted to deal with each of these key theological terms in word studies throughout this book, but I haven't retranslated them into English. For example, I would have preferred using the term *return* instead of *repent* in parts of this book, since that's a more literal translation of the Hebrew. But I want the English reader to be comfortable studying the biblical texts they love. Another example would be the word *law*, a poor translation of the Hebrew *Torah*, which more accurately and literally means "teaching."

The reader will note that I have used Jewish abbreviations for dating: BCE, the abbreviation of "before the Common Era" is used in place of BC. CE, the abbreviation for "Common Era" is used in place of AD. When I include a citation from a book of the Bible, you will see the citation at the beginning or end of a quoted verse (e.g., Genesis 1:1). I have done the same with the Talmud, midrash, and other writings in the rabbinic tradition (e.g., Mishnah: Avot 1:1). I realize that some readers are not familiar with books from the rabbinical tradition, but those who wish to study and research further will at least have the correct source for each citation and quote.

When quoting from the Bible, I have used the NRSV (New Revised Standard Version) translation, except when noted, or when I quote someone who uses a different version. Many of the barriers that separate Jews and Christians are due to mistranslations, misinterpretations based on poor translations, and the non-Hebraic features of all English renditions of the Bible. The Tanakh (Jewish Scriptures in Hebrew) is a Middle Eastern text, written in a Middle Eastern language, and directed at a Middle Eastern audience. It uses a Middle Eastern grammar that is distinctively different from Greek, Latin, or English. The New Testament is written in Greek, which has its own nuances and is difficult to translate into modern languages. It seems odd to say, but the Tanakh is not the same as the Bible we know in English. The Bible is a translation of the Tanakh, and there are fundamental linguistic differences that can only to be bridged by good teachers with accurate Bible commentaries.

The first centuries before and after the common era were some of the most fertile periods in Jewish history. New theological concepts were emerging, along with new modalities for Jews to express their relationship with the Creator. Jesus lived in the middle of that era, and was part of the creative process that saw the emergence of a "new" Judaism by the fourth and fifth centuries. This new, or more accurately "renewed," Judaism has been called Rabbinic Judaism, and the period of time is known as the Rabbinic Era. Throughout this book, I refer to the writings of the sages and rabbis of this period by a number of somewhat synonymous and overlapping terms: the rabbinic tradition, oral tradition, Rabbinic Judaism, Oral Law, Oral Torah, rabbinic writings, rabbinic commentaries, and rabbinic literature. The relationship between the Written Torah (the Five Books of Moses) and the Oral Torah (key rabbinical writings) will be discussed in its own chapter.

As we know, Judaism did not stop growing when the temple in Jerusalem was destroyed two thousand years ago. Judaism changed as much in the last two millennia as it did in its first two thousand years. Judaism has not been replaced, but it has been renewed. The "old" Testament is still a "new" Testament to Jews. My own rabbi and teacher, Rabbi Zalman Schachter-Shalomi, has proposed that we use the terms Elder Testament and Younger Testament, which I use in much of this book. First of all, the word *elder* is a term of respect that the Jewish Scriptures deserve. And second, these terms tend to bring a smile to almost everyone who hears them—after two thousand years of disputation, we all need to smile a bit more.

I
The Jewishness
of Jesus

ONE

Shared Roots

IT STRIKES ME AS NOTHING LESS THAN EXTRAORDINARY THAT BOTH Christianity and modern Judaism were born of two separate catastrophic events that happened within a few decades of each other, within only a few hundred meters from each other, and brought on by the same ruthless Roman Empire. The crucifixion of Jesus took place just outside the Jerusalem city walls somewhere around 36 CE, and the destruction of the Temple occurred within those very walls in 70 CE. Somehow each religion has transformed these catastrophes and what seemed to be failure into compelling stories of hope, renewal, and redemption.

Christianity as a religion emerges from the hope brought on by an inspired theology that connects Jesus's death to the resurrection—the story told each Easter. A lesser-known fact is that the rebirth of ancient Judaism into modern Judaism was also catalyzed and symbolized by a single event—the destruction of the Jerusalem Temple. It was after that terrible event that Judaism was forced to accelerate the transformation of its religious practices from an offering-based religion centered around the Temple to a prayer-based religion centered around individual homes and synagogues—in essence, the Judaism we are familiar with today.

This transformation actually began a few hundred years before the events of 70 CE, and culminated in the fourth and fifth centuries with the compilation of the Jerusalem Talmud. But it was the Temple's destruction that forced the hand of Jewish theology whose scriptures are clear and specific about offerings being made at the Temple in Jerusalem. It was the explosive growth of Christianity and its absorption by Constantine into what remained of the Roman Empire that forced the sages of Judaism to intelligently and creatively respond to Christianity's exclusive claims.

Although the fruits of modern rabbinical Judaism did not fully ripen until centuries after Jesus's lifetime, it seems clear that Jesus was part of the paradigm shift that was transforming his native religion. How do we know this? Because throughout the Younger Testament, Jesus not only quotes the Torah and the prophets, but his teachings parallel the emerging oral tradition that existed in his lifetime. As you will learn throughout this book, Jesus often seems to be quoting directly from the Jewish oral tradition that was extant in his lifetime. We can further infer from the synoptic Gospels (Matthew, Mark, and Luke) that Jesus taught in synagogues by invitation, and that scribes and Pharisees came willingly to hear him teach.

As a mainstream congregational rabbi in America, I would not waste the time of my congregation with guest lecturers and out-of-town teachers unless they really had something special to add to our understanding of Torah. Religious leaders in the past were no different. It seems implausible for Jesus to have been reading aloud the words of the prophets and teaching in synagogues without some kind of invitation, permission, and blessing of the synagogue leaders. In Luke 4:16, Jesus was the reader of the weekly prophetic portion. This act is considered an honor in Jewish worship services. It seems unlikely that this could have happened without an explicit invitation.

Many teachers and rabbis in Jesus's day used parables to teach difficult subjects. Jesus lived on the cusp between biblical and rabbinical Judaism, and it's striking how many of his statements, phrases, expressions, and style of argument come from the oral tradition that began to be written down in the first century BCE. Whether or not Jesus was quoting from his contemporaries and the sages who came before him, it's clear his teachings are firmly rooted in the Judaism in which he was raised. Knowing this opens up immense possibilities in understanding the historical Jesus's day-to-day behavior and activities, what he believed, how he prayed, and even what his intentions may have been with regard to the gospel.

Further, placing Jesus firmly within the rabbinic tradition adds a new dynamic to Jewish-Christian conversation. Sometimes Jesus speaks on his own authority, yet the realization that most of his teachings were in line with those of his rabbinic colleagues will permit Jews to discover a new level of esteem for this native son of Judaism. On the other side, understanding the historical Jesus can only enhance a Christian's faith and help eliminate anti-Semitism stemming from misinterpretation of the Younger Testament regarding Jesus's Jewishness. How do we know that Jesus was on the leading edge of the most creative transformation of Judaism in his day? We can't be certain, of course, but from the anecdotal evidence in the Younger Testament it seems that Jesus was recognized by at least a few synagogue leaders and rabbis as an inspired teacher. Consider these passages:

> **Matthew 4:23** Jesus went throughout Galilee, teaching in their synagogues and proclaiming the good news of the kingdom and curing every disease and every sickness among the people.

> **Mark 5:22** Then one of the leaders of the synagogue named Jairus came and, when he saw him, fell at his feet.

> **Luke 4:16** When he came to Nazareth, where he had been brought up, he went to the synagogue on the sabbath day, as was his custom. He stood up to read. . . .

For most of the past two thousand years, the uncertainty about Jesus's fidelity to Judaism has been a rational, survival-based response by many Jews to the attitude of Christians toward Judaism. In the name of Jesus, terrible brutality has been aimed toward Jews for stubbornly holding fast to the commandments of the Mosaic covenant. Is it any wonder that Jewish people have a negative reaction to the idea of embracing Jesus as an authentic rabbi?

The Jewishness of a rabbi named Joshua has been mostly suppressed until recently. The Jesus of Christian theology has too often been portrayed as someone who wanted to replace the "old" covenant with a "new" covenant. Recognizing Jesus for what he was—a religious Jew—it becomes far less likely that he ever intended supplanting the Mosaic covenant with any "new covenant" spoken of by the prophet Jeremiah. We know with certainty that Jeremiah also never considered the possibility that any future covenant would replace any of the existing covenants. Dr. Brad H. Young writes:

> The religion of the Jews in the first century is the root, which produced the fruit of Christian faith. Faith in Jesus, however, has sometimes made it difficult for Christians to understand and appreciate the faith of the Jews. The religion of Jesus and his people was Judaism. Christian faith in Jesus sometimes has alienated Jesus from ancient Judaism and exiled him from his people. . . . Theologians have read the Gospels as Christian literature written by the church and for the church. When Jesus is viewed among the Gentiles, the significance of Jewish culture and custom is minimized or forgotten altogether. But when Jesus is viewed as a Jew within the context of 1st century Judaism, an entirely different portrait emerges.[6]

Jesus must be understood as a Jewish theologian. His theology is Jewish to the core. The tragic history of the relationship between Judaism and Christianity makes it difficult to hear his forceful voice. The attacks of the church against the synagogue have stripped Jesus of his religious heritage. Many Christians have been taught wrongful prejudices about Jews and Judaism. Hatred of the Jewish people has erected a barrier separating Jesus from his theology. Ethnically he may be considered a Jew, but religiously he remains a Christian who failed to reform the corrupt religious system of the Jews. Such an approach fails. Jesus is Jewish both in his ethnic background and in his religious thought and practice.

In line with most first-century teachers, Jesus was critical of religious hypocrites, and there were plenty of them back then, just as there are today in churches, synagogues, mosques, and ashrams. When Jesus warns the people in Matthew 5:19 about breaking "the least of these commandments," he seems to be talking about upholding both the ritual and moral mitzvot of the Torah. In Matthew 23:1–3 when Jesus instructs his followers to "do" and "follow" whatever the leaders tell them, he seems to be referring to the rulings that were part of the prerabbinic judgments and rulings of his day.

In Matthew 5:23–24 Jesus is likely basing his remarks on the well-known rabbinic tradition of his day that requires a person to reconcile with a neighbor before bringing an offering to the Temple. In Acts 20:16 it is written that Paul observed the Jewish festival called *Shavuot* (literally "the Festival of Weeks"). Even after the resurrection, when some Christians say that sacrifices were no longer necessary, Paul offers a sacrifice, as reported in Acts 21:26, in order to demonstrate that he, like Jesus before him, upheld the Torah. Paul said, "Do we then overthrow the law by this faith? By no means! On the contrary, we uphold the law" (Romans 3:31).

Renowned New Testament scholar, Dr. David Flusser, adamantly places Jesus as a religious Jew who lived, taught, and died as a Torah-observant Jew, and who instructed his fellow Jews to keep the commandments of the Torah as well. He wrote:

> Jesus regarded the Torah . . . as a world complete in itself, on which the existence of the real world depended (Matthew 5:17–20). And he was therefore faithful to the Torah in its entirety. Like many members of the school of Hillel, Jesus gave the Torah a humanitarian explanation, at the same time taking the view that the smallest commandment weigh as heavily as the greatest. . . . Jesus's position is made clear in the fifth chapter of Matthew. There he speaks of keeping the Torah. . . . Anyone transgressing against the least commandment will not enter the kingdom of heaven, and anyone who keeps the "minor" commandments and teaches others to keep them shall be called great in the kingdom of heaven. He emphasizes that the righteousness of his disciples in keeping the commandments must be greater than that of the scribes, or else they shall not enter the kingdom of heaven. . . . The Christian sources, of course, provide us with the contrast between Jesus and the Jewish law. Matthew presents the

views of Jesus as opposed to the views of the sages. The truth of the matter, however, is that there is no difference between the views of Jesus and authentic Jewish tradition.[7]

Contemporary scholars have a clear sense of what caused the rift between Christianity and its mother religion soon after the first century was over. One variable was the explosion of the Pauline doctrine, and the increased number of Gentile believers who had no ancestral allegiance to the Torah's ritual commandments. When faced with Jesus's powerful and consistent allegiance to even the "least" of the commandments, and the oral tradition as well, Christian theologians faced a dilemma—how to reconcile Jesus's allegiance to the *mitzvot,* and Paul's demand that Gentiles be "free" of such obligations. Dr. Flusser assesses the situation as follows:

It would be a mistake . . . not to recognize the unease experienced by many Christian thinkers and scholars. They have felt obliged to deal with the fact that the founder of their religion was a Jew, faithful to the law, who never had to face the necessity of adapting his Judaism to the European way of life. For Jesus there was, of course, the peculiar problem of his relationship to the law and its precepts, but this arises for every believing Jew who takes his Judaism seriously.[8]

In the Gospels, we see how Jesus's attitude to the law has sometimes become unrecognizable as a result of "clarification" by the evangelists and touching up by later revisers. Nevertheless, the synoptic Gospels, read through the eyes of their own time, still portray a picture of Jesus as a faithful, law-observant Jew. Few people seem to realize that in the synoptic Gospels, Jesus is never shown in conflict with current practice of the law.

The Younger Testament is filled with explicit and implicit statements indicating that Jesus, his family, and *talmidim* were in the mainstream of Jewish life. There are contradictory passages as well, so it's impossible to make a blanket statement and say that Jesus fully observed Jewish law. But the general sense is that Jesus and his followers honored Sabbath, kosher dietary laws, laws of modesty (e.g., outside of the family, men and women do not touch each other), and the purity laws (e.g., washing hands, using a *mikvah* for ritual bathing). Again, consider what Scripture says:

Mary and Joseph have Jesus circumcised as commanded by Torah:

> **Luke 2:21** After eight days had passed, it was time to circumcise the child; and he was called Jesus, the name given by the angel before he was conceived in the womb.

Mary immerses herself in the ritual bath as commanded by Torah:

> **Luke 2:22** When the time came for their purification according to the law of Moses, they brought him up to Jerusalem to present him to the Lord.

Jesus and his family observe the Passover as commanded by both Torah and the Oral Law:

> **Luke 2:42** And when he was twelve years old, they went up as usual for the festival.

Jesus wore *tzitzit*—religious fringes on his garment as commanded by the Torah:

> **Matthew 9:20** Then suddenly a woman who had been suffering from hemorrhages for twelve years came up behind him and touched the fringe of his cloak.

Jesus instructs his followers to keep the commandments of the Torah:

> **Matthew 19:17** If you wish to enter into life, keep the commandments.

Jesus instructs his followers to bring a Temple offering as commanded by the Torah:

> **Matthew 8:4** Go, show yourself to the priest, and offer the gift that Moses commanded, as a testimony to them.

Jesus celebrates Hanukkah:

> **John 10:22–23** At that time the festival of the Dedication took place in Jerusalem. It was winter, and Jesus was walking in the temple. . . .

Why did they do these things? Because Jesus and his family were religious Jews, dedicated to fulfilling the Torah's commandments, just as religious Jews do today. If the Last Supper was a Passover seder, it's important to know that Jesus was celebrating the festival using a form (*matzah*, wine, seder meal, etc.) that comes from the oral tradition, and not the Torah. Even after the resurrection, we see his disciples fulfilling commandments, bringing offerings to the Temple, and living in accordance to Judean social and religious culture.

When Jesus talks of a "new commandment" to his Jewish students, he clearly seems to imply that this new mitzvah is in addition to, not in place of, the other mitzvot: "I give you a new commandment, that you love one another" (John 13:34). When the synoptic Gospels are read without historical context, most readers focus on points of disagreement that Jesus had with his contemporaries, rather than seeing those disagreements as the leading edge of constructive, insider debates within first-century Judaism.

Dr. Amy-Jill Levine offers an example: "The popular push to depict Jesus as a Galilean and see Galilee religiously and ethnically distinct from Judea winds up conveying the impression that 'Judaism,' with its Temple and its leadership, is quite distinct from the Galilean Jesus. . . . Worse, the lingering view that Jesus dismissed basic Jewish practices, such as the Laws concerning Sabbath observance and ritual purity, turns Jesus away from his Jewish identity and makes him into a liberal Protestant."[9] In reading the Younger Testament, it's as important to "read between the lines" to truly understand what is actually written. In other words, much is implied rather than explicitly stated. For example, attending synagogue services and reading the words of the prophets as he does in Luke 4:16 is a "custom" of rabbinic Judaism that Jesus follows.

=====

As Christians become more familiar with the basic tenets of Judaism, many of Jesus's teachings will reveal their Jewish roots. There are dozens of examples in the Younger Testament that express the connection between Jesus's teachings and teachings recorded in later centuries that are part of the Oral Torah. As one more example (among many), Jesus's opinion about healing on the Sabbath was in line with the emerging Jewish consensus of his day. Similarly, Jesus was a miracle worker in the tradition of Elijah and Elisha, and his teachings were in line with the powerful words of the prophets.

T W O

A Jewish Gospel

THE WORD *GOSPEL* COMES FROM AN OLD ENGLISH TRANSLATION OF a Hebrew word meaning "good news," first spoken of by Isaiah: "How beautiful upon the mountains are the feet of the messenger who announces peace, who brings good news, who announces salvation" (Isaiah 52:7). The notion of a gospel is Jewish in origin, even though Jews are reluctant to use that term because of its connotation within Christianity. What is the Jewish good news? God so loved the world that he gave his only Torah at Sinai. It is a Torah of redemption, revelation, forgiveness, and hope for humanity. It's a gospel of joy about serving God and being part of the holy work to repair and sanctify our broken world. Then, when monotheism branched out in novel ways through Christianity and Islam, each new religion brought its own version of "good news" to billions of new adherents.

As God has grafted Christians onto the olive tree of Israel (Romans 11:17), they abide by their "new" covenant, which grew out of the earlier covenants. Many sincere Christians have asked me over the years why Jewish people don't accept the gospel. Answering a question with a question, Jewish people ask, "Why don't some Christians accept the reality that the Jewish people already have a gospel?" As Jesus said, "Salvation is from the Jews" (John 4:22). A clear goal of many of the biblical prophets was to remind the Jewish people to fulfill their part of the covenant, and to spread the good news of the existence of a God of love and justice. In Malachi 1:11, God says, "For from the rising of the sun to its setting my name is great among the nations, and in every place incense is offered to my name, and a pure offering . . . says the Lord of hosts."

There's no question that Gentile followers of Jesus were instrumental in helping to spread the Torah's principles of ethical monotheism, albeit packaged in a new form, to people around the world. However, the question of whether a Christian is under the law, under some of the law, or free from the law has been debated within Christianity since the beginning. From a Jewish reading of the Younger Testament, it certainly seems that there are universal commandments that must continually be fulfilled by all people. John does not appear to be abrogating the commandments of the Torah when he explains the two "love" commandments in the Torah: "The commandment we have from him is this: those who love God must love their brothers and sisters also" (1 John 4:21). Judaism also teaches that under the covenant of Noah (Genesis 9:3–9), all humanity is obliged to fulfill the same moral commandments.

The psalmist assures us, "For the LORD will not forsake his people; he will not abandon his heritage" (Psalm 94:14). And Paul does the same in the Younger Testament: "I ask, then, has God rejected his people? By no means! I myself am an Israelite, a descendant of Abraham, a member of the tribe of Benjamin" (Romans 11:1). Speaking about the Jewish people Paul says, "As regards election they are beloved, for the sake of their ancestors" (Romans 11:28). Finally Paul warns his Gentile students not to become arrogant concerning Jews who are not followers of Jesus. Using an exquisite metaphor of Israel as an olive tree, he teaches: "But if some of the branches were broken off, and you, a wild olive shoot, were grafted in their place to share the rich root of the olive tree, do not boast over the branches. If you do boast, remember that it is not you that support the root, but the root that supports you" (Romans 11:17–18).

For most of two thousand years, it's been difficult for many Jews to see Jesus even as a wonderful rabbi since his name was associated with the most terrible forms of prejudice. When Jesus is presented as someone who left Judaism, he is seen as someone who betrayed Judaism. Most Jews respect Christian theology as long as it is separated from coercion and the notion of exclusive salvation, and backed up by the force of the Crusades and pogroms. Martin Buber put it this way:

> God is our help in all need and none outside of him. But this was also—of this I am certain—the faith of Jesus himself. I do not believe in Jesus, but I believe with him. I firmly believe that the Jewish community, in the course of its renaissance, will recognize Jesus; not merely as a great figure in its religious history, but also in the organic context of a Messianic development extending over millennia, whose final goal is the Redemption of Israel and of the world. But I believe equally firmly that we will never recognize Jesus as the Messiah Come, for this would contradict the deepest meaning of our Messianic passion. . . . Standing, bound and shackled, in the pillory of mankind, we demonstrate with the bloody body of our people the unredeemedness of the world. For us, there is no cause of Jesus; only the cause of God exists for us.[10]

The idea that Israel is to be a light unto the non-Jewish nations (Isaiah 42:1; Isaiah 42:6; Isaiah 60:3) is a recurring metaphor to the prophet Isaiah, whom Jesus quotes so often. An excellent example of this is Isaiah 49:6: "[The Lord] says, 'It is too light a thing that you should be my servant to raise up the tribes of Jacob and to restore the survivors of Israel; I will give you as a light to the nations, that my salvation may reach to the end of the earth.'" In the Younger Testament, Isaiah's image of Israel as the servant is allegorically extended to Jesus. Jesus recognized a covenantal duty to help bring the Jewish message of God's unity, ethical monotheism, and redemption to the non-Jewish world.

Matthew seems to support the notion that the gospel was *from* Israel and not *to* Israel. Concerning Jesus, he writes, "This was to fulfill what has been spoken through the prophet Isaiah: 'Here is my servant, whom I have chosen, my beloved, with whom my soul is well pleased . . . and he will proclaim justice to the Gentiles'" (Matthew 12:16–18). Paul seems equally clear that the newly emerging Christ covenant was for Gentiles since Jews already had an intact covenant between themselves and God. Paul writes, "In Christ Jesus the blessing of Abraham might come to the Gentiles, so that we might receive the promise of the Spirit through faith" (Galatians 3:14). Within Judaism, Paul's "promise of the Spirit" was never based on the profession of a creed or membership in a particular religion—it is based solely on God's mercy. Paul's teaching about salvation is universal. He never imagined Jews leaving their native Judaism and converting to another faith.

The destruction of the Temple in Jerusalem by the Romans in 70 CE accelerated the transformation of the sacrificial system into the rabbinic Judaism that is practiced today. As will be explained later in the book, the commandments regarding grain, fruit, monetary, and animal offerings were brilliantly interpreted by the rabbis to apply to personal, family, and synagogue rituals. Many of these rabbinic innovations directly influenced Christian rites as well. Throughout the Gospels, Jesus is clearly teaching from within the world of an emerging rabbinic Judaism.

Echoes of Torah

Hanging above our fireplace at home is a hand-painted, eighteenth-century ceramic plate from Italy. The painting is of Miriam standing next to Pharaoh's daughter as she takes baby Moses from his basket on the Nile. I cannot count the number of people who want to know what a painting of baby Jesus is doing hanging in the home of a rabbi. Explaining that it is baby Moses always elicits amazed smiles from our friends. Yet in all the years we have owned this ceramic painting, it never occurred to me until recently that there was a parallel between the birth stories of these two great Jewish men.

Anyone reading the biblical texts will discover unmistakable overlaps within the birth narratives of Moses and Jesus. There are also echoes within the betrayal stories of Jacob's son Joseph and Jesus—both are acts of duplicity done for silver by those who were supposed to have loved them. There are even overlaps in the miracle stories of Jesus and the early prophets Elijah and Elisha. Finally, there's an echo in the death stories of Moses and Jesus: neither lived to see his dreams fulfilled in this world. Both died with a great "promise" in front of them.

Judaism and Christianity are unique, distinctive, and different religions, but for too long the differences were emphasized while the far greater territory of their similarities has been ignored, suppressed, or simply unknown. If you try holding the stories of Isaac, Joseph, Moses, Elijah, Elisha, and Jesus in your mind at the same time, you might experience what a Jew in the time of Jesus may have felt as he or she heard some of the stories in the Younger Testament being told—similarity, echo, overlap, emulation, and an identical moral imperative.

The master stories within Judaism and Christianity are, of course, uniquely different, but there are exquisite resemblances and contrasts in their details. While the Joshua of the Elder Testament is a warrior hero and leadership heir to Moses, the Joshua of the Younger Testament is a spiritual warrior claimed by Christianity as their Messiah. Jesus's mother's Hebrew name is Miriam, and Moses is rescued and protected by his big sister Miriam. Elijah and Elisha are miracle workers who are used by God to heal the sick, raise the dead, float an axe head on water, and multiply food. The miracles of Jesus echo the earlier Hebrew prophets (e.g., compare Luke 7:11–17 to 1 Kings 17:17–24). Finally, just as Jesus dies and is resurrected, there's a parallel midrash about Isaac being sacrificed by Abraham and then being resurrected.

Beyond these larger themes, there are many other parallels between the Testaments. In Exodus 1:22 Pharaoh orders the death of every Hebrew male baby through drowning in the Nile, and in Matthew 2:16 Herod orders a massacre of all Jewish babies in Bethlehem under two years of age. When Herod's murderous decree goes out, the Younger Testament (Matthew 2:18) quotes the lamentation from Jeremiah 31:15, "A voice is heard in Ramah, lamentation and bitter weeping, Rachel is weeping for her children; she refuses to be comforted, because they are no more." Could the first-century

Jewish followers of Jesus make a link between Rachel's son Joseph (Genesis 30:25) and Mary's husband Joseph?

In Exodus 2:15 Pharaoh wants to kill the adult Moses, who fled for his life from Egypt to Midian. In Genesis 37 we learn that Joseph, the son of Jacob, was a dreamer. In Matthew 2:13–14 an angel appears to Joseph in a dream and tells him to flee to Egypt to save his life. Dr. Amy-Jill Levine points out, "Matthew 1:16 lists Joseph's father as Jacob and so connects Jesus' adoptive father to that earlier Joseph, son of Jacob."[11] Listen to the echo in the stories of when Moses is told to return to Egypt (Exodus 4:19), and when Joseph (Mary's husband) is told to return to Judea (Matthew 2:19–20).

The coming of the messiah in Judaism is to be foretold by the miraculous return of Elijah. The prophet Malachi says, "Lo, I will send you the prophet Elijah before the great and terrible day of the Lord comes" (Malachi 4:5). In the Younger Testament, some priests and Levites ask John the Baptist if he is the reincarnation of Elijah: "And they asked him, 'What then? Are you Elijah?' He said, 'I am not'" (John 1:21). When John the Baptist says he's not Elijah, he's asked to identify himself (John 1:23). His response is to quote from Isaiah 40:3, "A voice cries out: 'In the wilderness prepare the way of the LORD.'"

In Genesis 37:26 it was Judah who saves his brother Joseph's life by suggesting to his other brothers that they sell him into slavery for twenty pieces of silver. The other brothers were ready to leave him to die. In Matthew 26:15 it was Jesus's disciple Judas who betrays his rabbi for thirty pieces of silver. The stories of the final moments in the life of Jesus (Matthew 27:50) and the death of Moses (Deuteronomy 34:5) are both so sad.

Finally, many of the rituals, modes of worship, and liturgy within Christianity are variations of Jewish spiritual practices. The Tree of Life images used in Proverbs 3:17–18 and Revelation 22:2 have an almost identical function in linking the Creator to the creation. The image of the Church as God's bride in Revelation 22:17 is taken from Hosea 2:19 where Israel is called God's bride. The notion of the election of the Church is taken from Deuteronomy 14:2–3, when God chose Israel.

Here is a look at just a handful of hundreds of parallels in the Younger Testament that have been drawn from the Elder Testament. Using Paul's metaphor of roots and branches, I use the term *Root* to refer to Jewish sources (Jewish Scriptures and Oral Torah) for these passages, and *Branch* to refer to verses on the Younger Testament.

Parallel Miracles of Moses, Elijah, Elisha, and Jesus

Multiplying oil and food

Root:

2 Kings 4:43–44 "How can I set this before a hundred people?" "So he [Elisha] repeated, "Give it to the people and let them eat, for thus says the LORD, 'They shall eat and have some left.'" He set it before them, they ate, and had some left, according to the word of the LORD.

Branch:

Matthew 15:36–37 He took the seven loaves and the fish; and after giving thanks he broke them and gave them to the disciples, and the disciples gave them to the crowds. And all of them ate and were filled; and they took up the broken pieces left over, seven baskets full.

Healing infertility and infection

Root:

2 Kings 4:8–17 The woman conceived and bore a son at that season, in due time, as Elisha had declared to her.

2 Kings 4:40–41 While they were eating the stew, they cried out, "O man of God, there is death in the pot!" They could not eat it. He said, "Then bring some flour." He threw it into the pot, and said, "Serve the people and let them eat." And there was nothing harmful in the pot.

Branch:

Matthew 4:23 Jesus went throughout Galilee, teaching in their synagogues and proclaiming the good news of the kingdom and curing every disease and every sickness among the people.

Resurrection of the dead

Root:

2 Kings 4:34 Then he got up on the bed and lay upon the child . . . and the flesh of the child became warm.

1 Kings 17:22 The Lᴏʀᴅ listened to the voice of Elijah; the life of the child came into him again, and he revived.

Branch:

Luke 7:15 The dead man sat up and began to speak, and Jesus gave him to his mother.

Healing the body

Root:

2 Kings 5:14 So he [Na'aman] went down and immersed himself seven times in the Jordan, according to the word of the man of God [Elijah]: his flesh was restored like the flesh of a young boy, and he was clean.

Branch:

Matthew 8:6–7 "Lord, my servant is lying at home paralyzed, in terrible distress." And he [Jesus] said to him, "I will come and cure him."

Appointing Disciples

Root:

Numbers 11:25 Then the Lᴏʀᴅ came down in the cloud and spoke to him, and took some of the spirit that was on him and put it on the seventy elders; and when the spirit rested upon them, they prophesied. . . .

Branch:

Luke 10:1 After this the Lord appointed seventy others and sent them on ahead of him in pairs to every town and place where he himself intended to go.

Matthew 10:1 Then Jesus summoned his twelve disciples and gave them authority over unclean spirits, to cast them out, and to cure every disease and every sickness.

Miracles with water

Root:

Exodus 14:21 Then Moses stretched out his hand over the sea. The Lᴏʀᴅ drove the sea back by a strong east wind all night, and turned the sea into dry land; and the waters were divided.

2 Kings 6:5–6 His axe head fell into the water . . . he [Elisha] cut off a stick, and threw it in there, and made the iron float.

Branch:

Matthew 14:29 He said, "Come." So Peter got out of the boat, started walking on the water, and came toward Jesus.

Quotes, Parallels, and Echoes from the Bible and Oral Law

Most of the teachings of Jesus were quite familiar to his fellow citizens. There are literally hundreds of instances when a speaker in the Younger Testament quotes directly from the Elder Testament. Whenever you read, "as it is written" in the Younger Testament, it is a quote from the Elder Testament. Jesus seems to cite directly, or create variations of, the teachings of the sages before and during his lifetime. Some of the Jewish teachings below were known before Jesus's lifetime; others were contemporaneous, and some were first recorded centuries later, but were possibly known in oral form during the first century. Although it cannot be proven that Jesus was quoting from his contemporaries or the sages who preceded him, it's also difficult to deny that his teachings are in line with normative first-century rabbinic pedagogy. As Christianity was developing and gaining a foothold in the Roman Empire, it is likely that the rabbis were influenced and inspired by Jesus's teachings and particular aspects of Christian theology. We cannot dismiss the reality of Christian influence on the rabbinic writings.

When I quote from the Talmud (first published as a unified text in the fifth century), it's simply intended to return Jesus's teachings to their Jewish theological context. Jesus is obviously not quoting from a text written hundreds of years after his lifetime. Regarding such teachings, Rabbi David Wolpe makes an astute observation: "Today . . . Christian scholars are beginning to understand that much of what Judaism preserved is what Jesus would have known. It may be that a fifth or sixth-century rabbinic *midrash* perpetuates a tradition that Jesus would've taken for granted in a world of oral transmission."[12]

Jesus maintained his observance of the Torah's mitzvot until the end of his life, when he was murdered along with tens of thousands of other Jews who died at the hands by the Roman Empire. The following selections place Jesus's teachings squarely within the rabbinic tradition during the centuries before and after his lifetime.

The Golden Rule

Root:

Talmud: Shabbat 31a Hillel said, "What is hateful to you, do not to your neighbor. That is the whole Torah—the rest is the commentary thereof. Go learn it."

Mishnah: Avot 2:10 Rabbi Eliezar said, "Let the honor of your friend be as dear to you as your own."

Targum Pseudo Jonathan on Leviticus 19:18 Love your neighbor, for whatever displeases you, do not to him!

Branch:

Matthew 7:12 In everything do to others as you would have them do to you; for this is the law and the prophets.

The Greatest Commandment

Root:

Jerusalem Talmud: Nedarim 9:4; Midrash: Genesis Rabbah 24:7 Rabbi Akiva taught, "Love your neighbor as yourself" **(**Leviticus 19:18**)** is the great principle of the Torah. Ben Azzai said that the verse "This is the book of the descendants of Adam . . . him whom God made in His likeness" (Genesis 5:1) displays a principle even greater.

Branch:

Mark 12:30–31 "You shall love the Lord your God with all your heart, and with all your soul, and with all your might" [Deuteronomy 6:5]. And the second [commandment] is this, "Love your neighbor as yourself" [Leviticus 19:18]. There is no other commandment greater than these.

Pride

Root:

Mishnah: Avot 1:10 Hate positions of authority over others.

Branch:

Matthew 23:8 But you are not to be called rabbi.

Adversaries and Enemies

Root:

Proverbs 25:21 If your enemies are hungry, give them bread to eat; and if they are thirsty, give them water to drink.

Exodus 23:4 When you come upon your enemy's ox or donkey going astray, you shall bring it back.

Midrash: Avot de-Rabbi Natan 23 Who is the mightiest of the mighty? He who turns his enemy into his friend.

Branch:

Matthew 5:43–44 You have heard it said, "You shall love your neighbor and hate your enemy." But I say to you, "Love your enemies and pray for those who persecute you."

Sabbath

Root:

Talmud: Yoma 85b Rabbi Jonathan bar Joseph said, "The Sabbath is committed to your hands, not you to its hands."

Midrash: Mekilta de Rabbi Ishmael/Exodus 31:13 Sabbath was made for man, not man for the Sabbath, so that man is master over the Sabbath.

Branch:

Mark 2:27 The sabbath was made for humankind, and not humankind for the sabbath.

Reconciliation

Root:

Talmud: Yoma 85b The Day of Atonement does not procure forgiveness until he is reconciled with his neighbor.

Branch:

Matthew 5:23–24 So when you are offering your gift at the altar, if you remember that your brother or sister has something against you, leave your gift there before the altar and go; first be reconciled to your brother or sister, and then come and offer your gift.

Measure for Measure

Root:

Talmud: Sanhedrin 90a All measures of punishment and reward taken by the Holy One, blessed be He, are done in accordance with the principle of "measure for measure."

Talmud: Shabbat 127b Our Rabbis taught: "He who judges his neighbor favorably is himself judged favorably."

Branch:

Matthew 7:1–2 Do not judge, so that you may not be judged. For with the judgment you make you will be judged, and the measure you give will be the measure you get.

Vows

Root:

Talmud: Baba Metzia 49 Rabbi Judah said, "Your 'yes' shall be true, and your 'no' shall be true."

Branch:

Matthew 5:34, 37 Do not swear at all. . . . Let your word be "Yes, Yes" or "No, No."

Spiritual Laborers

Root:

Mishnah: Avot 2:15–16 Rabbi Tarfon said, "The day is short, the work is great, the laborers are lazy, the reward is great, and the Master of the house is insistent. . . . Faithful is your Employer to pay you the reward of your labor."

Branch:

Matthew 9:37–38 Then he [Jesus] said to his disciples, "The harvest is plentiful, but the laborers are few; therefore ask the Lord of the harvest to send out laborers into his harvest."

Adultery/Lust

Root:

Midrash: Leviticus Rabbah 23:3 Resh Lakish expounded, "You must not suppose that only he who has committed the crime with his body is called an adulterer. If he commits adultery with his eyes he is also called an adulterer."

Branch:

Matthew 5:28 But I say to you that everyone who looks at a woman with lust has already committed adultery with her in his heart.

Reproof and Self-criticism

Root:

Talmud: Arakhin 16b Rabbi Tarfon said, "I wonder if there is anyone in this generation who is able to give reproof. For if anyone says to another, 'Take the chip from between your teeth,' the other retorts, 'Take the beam from between your eyes.'"

Midrash: Ruth Rabbah 1:1 Woe to the generation whose judges are in need of being judged. When a judge would say, "Remove the toothpick from between your teeth," the man would reply, "Remove the beam from between your eyes."

Branch:

Matthew 7:3–5 Why do you see the speck in your neighbor's eye, but do not notice the log in your own eye? Or how can you say to your neighbor, "Let me take the speck out of your eye," while the log is in your own eye? You hypocrite, first take the log out of your own eye, and then you will see clearly to take the speck out of your neighbor's eye.

By Their Fruits

Root:

Philo[13] **On Curses 6** God judges by the fruit of a tree, not by the roots.

Branch:

Matthew 7:19–20 Every tree that does not bear good fruit is cut down and thrown into the fire. Thus you will know them by their fruits.

The Presence of God

Root:

Mishnah: Avot 3:2 Rabbi Hanina said, "When two sit together and there is between them words of Torah, the Shekhinah [Divine Presence] dwells between them."

Branch:

Matthew 18:20 For where two or three are gathered in my name, I am there among them.

Weightier matters

Root:

Talmud: Hagigah 14a Those to whom weighty matters appear as light ones will come to behave insolently against those to whom light matters appear as weighty ones.

Branch:

Matthew 23:23 For you . . . have neglected the weightier matters of the law: justice and mercy and faith. It is these you ought to have practiced without neglecting the others.

Sacrifices

Root:

Psalm 51:17 The sacrifice acceptable to God is a broken spirit; a broken and contrite heart, O God, you will not despise.

Talmud: Berakhot 32b Rabbi Eleazar said, "Prayer is more efficacious than offerings."

Branch:

Mark 12:33 "To love him with all the heart, and with all the understanding, and with all the strength." and "to love one's neighbor as oneself,"—this is much more important than all whole burnt offerings and sacrifices.

The Meek

Root:

Psalm 37:11 But the meek shall inherit the land.

Branch:

Matthew 5:5 Blessed are the meek, for they will inherit the earth.

Humility

Root:

Lamentations 3:30 Give one's cheek to the smiter, and be filled with insults.

Branch:

Matthew 5:39 If anyone strikes you on the right cheek, turn the other also.

Salvation

Root:

Joel 2:32 Then everyone who calls on the name of the Lord shall be saved.

Branch:

Romans 10:13 Everyone who calls on the name of the Lord shall be saved.

Giving in Secret

Root:

Talmud: Baba Batra 9b He who gives charity in secret is greater than Moses.

Branch:

Matthew 6:2 So whenever you give alms, do not sound a trumpet before you.

Born Again

Root:

Talmud: Yevamot 48b Rabbi Jose said, "One who has become a proselyte is like a child newly born."

Branch:

John 3:3 Jesus answered him, "Very truly, I tell you, no one can see the kingdom of God without being born from above."

High and Low

Root:

Leviticus Rabbah 1:5 Hillel said, "My humiliation is my exaltation, my exaltation is my humiliation."

Branch:

Matthew 23:12 All who exalt themselves will be humbled, and all who humble themselves will be exalted.

New Wine

Root:

Mishnah: Avot 4:26–27 Rabbi Yosi bar Judah of Kefar ha-Bavli asks, "He who learns from the elders, what is he like? He is like one who eats ripe grapes and drinks old wine. Do not look at the container, but look at what's inside. One can have a new flask that is filled with old wine, or an old flask that does not have even new wine."

Branch:

Luke 5:36–39 He also told them a parable. . . . "And no one puts new wine into old wineskins; otherwise the new wine will burst the skins and will be spilled, and the skins will be destroyed. But new wine must be put into fresh wineskins. And no one after drinking old wine desires new wine, but says, 'The old is good.'"

Mercy

Root:

Midrash/Mekhilta de Rabbi Ishmael on Exodus 15:2 Be merciful, even as your Father is merciful.

Branch:

Luke 6:36 Be merciful, just as your Father is merciful.

Judging Another

Root:

Mishnah: Avot 2:5 Judge not your neighbor until you have stood in his place.

Branch:

Luke 6:37 Do not judge, and you will not be judged.

The Our Father Prayer & The Beatitudes

Jesus knew both the Bible and the oral tradition that were already ancient in his lifetime. The Our Father prayer is another example of an elegant compilation of words and phrases that would have sounded familiar to any religious Jew who heard Jesus chant this supplication. I have placed together the phrases from Jewish sources to demonstrate what Jesus might have been thinking when he composed this piece. For example, when Jesus says, "Give us this day our daily bread," he might have been creating a variation of Jeremiah 37:21: "So King Zedekiah gave orders . . . a loaf of bread was given him daily."

By reading Jesus's words next to those of the prophets and the rabbis, we get a sense of how really rooted Jesus was in his Judaism even when the "Source" was written after Jesus's lifetime. The "Jewish Root" citations are a patchwork created for this demonstration, whereas Jesus transformed source material into an exquisite prayer. The Our Father prayer is an excellent example of the rabbinical creativity that emerged and developed in the centuries before and after Jesus's lifetime. I have used the popular King James translation for the words of Jesus.

Jewish Root	Source	Christian Branch
Our Father Who art in heaven	**Talmud: Yoma 85b**	Our Father which art in heaven,
exalted and hallowed be Thy great Name	**Siddur/Kaddish**	hallowed be thy name.
Thine is the Kingdom	**1 Chronicles 29:11**	Thy kingdom come.
In accordance with His will	**Siddur/Kaddish**	Thy will be done
Heaven and earth are one . . .	**Talmud: Pesakhim 87b**	in earth,
All that is in heaven and earth is Yours	**1 Chronicles 29:11**	as it is in heaven.
Feed me with the bread allotted to me	**Proverbs 30:8**	Give us this day
You will rain bread from heaven	**Exodus 16:4**	our daily bread.
Every creditor . . . shall release the debt	**Deuteronomy 15:1**	And forgive our debts,
God . . . bestows goodness to debtors	**Siddur/Rescue Prayer**	as we forgive our debtors.
Bring us not into the grasp of temptation	**Siddur/Goodness Prayer**	And lead us not into temptation,
The Lord will deliver us in the day of evil	**Psalm 41:2**	but deliver us from evil;
For Thine, O Lord is the greatness, and the power, and the glory and the victory, and the majesty. . . .	**1 Chronicles 29:11**	For thine is the kingdom, and the power, and the glory forever. Amen!

A Jewish Exegesis on the Our Father Prayer

Matthew 6:9, Our Father which art in heaven, Hallowed be thy name.

Calling out to God for help requires humility. We are admitting that we cannot solve our problems by ourselves. True to Jewish liturgical tradition, Jesus instructs his disciples to begin this prayer as a communal supplication with the words *Our Father* rather than as a personal prayer. Calling God in the first person plural ("Our Father" rather than "My Father") is humbling since it is an implied admission that we are each part of something greater than ourselves—a community. If the first step in the prayer is "calling," the second step might be called "affirming." Jesus instructs his students to take a second step by affirming God's hallowed nature.

Matthew 6:10, Thy Kingdom come. Thy will be done in earth, as it is in heaven.

Dr. Brad Young teaches, "Jesus' words could be better translated 'May you continue establishing your Kingdom.'"[14] The verse suggests that God's kingdom is not just spiritual and apart from the world we live in. Implied is the idea that we are divine accomplices in seeing that God's will does get accomplished here on earth. We affirm that it is God's will that is fulfilled even as we hope that our prayers will be answered. In the Mishnah Rabbi Judah taught, "Do His will as if it were your will, so that He will do His will as it were yours" (Avot 2:4).

Matthew 6:11, Give us this day our daily bread.

The third step in this prayer is "petitioning"—asking God to satisfy the needs of ourselves, our families, and our communities. The image of "daily bread" is emblematic of all material needs. Dr. Lawrence A. Hoffman, a contemporary Reform rabbi and scholar, points out that by the first century, bread "was already a Jewish symbol of salvation that paralleled and then took the place of the paschal lamb as the primary symbol of God's deliverance of

Israel in Egypt."[15] Dr. Young points out that "Jesus often makes allusions to the Hebrew Scriptures without actually quoting the verse in full detail." He suggests that "daily bread" might be an allusion to Proverbs 30:8 where the term "the food that is needful to me" is used.[16]

Matthew 6:12, And forgive us our debts, as we forgive our debtors.

Still in the third step, we ask God to give us bread and forgive our debts. However, Jesus ties our personal petitions to specific actions—we ask to be forgiven, measure for measure, as we are willing to forgive. The rabbis affirmed that God has embedded laws of reciprocity and balance in nature. Just as modern science teaches us about this principle in Newton's Laws, so we see it expressed here in spiritual and poetic terms. As Rabbi Meir said in the Talmud, "The way one measures others, so he will be measured" (Talmud: Sotah 8b).

Matthew 6:13, And lead us not into temptation, but deliver us from evil:

After petitioning for the satisfaction of our material needs, we ask for protection and deliverance from evil. Jesus's words are in line with the Hebraic concept that good and evil are not to be understood through the lens of dualism. The prayer implies that when we've been led into temptation, there is a way back. The Hebrew word for "temptation" shares the same root as the word for "test." We could translate this verse as, "And lead us not to where we will be tested." Finally, Jesus echoes the psalmist, "The Lord delivers them in the day of trouble" (Psalm 41:1). The word *trouble* is literally "evil" in Hebrew.

Matthew 6:13, For thine is the kingdom, and the power, and the glory, forever. Amen.

The fourth and final step in this prayer is "acknowledging." We acknowledge God as the sole source of power and glory. In conclusion, Jesus quotes directly from the Elder Testament (1 Chronicles 29:11). The Hebrew word *amayn* comes from the word meaning "faith." When a person who hears a prayer responds with *amayn,* it is implied that the witness affirms his or her faith in the veracity of the prayer. The prayer ends here, but is followed by some further explanation by Jesus. The infrastructure of this prayer follows the orderly pattern of prayer typical of the sages who preceded and succeeded Rabbi Jesus.

> **Matthew 6:14,** For if you forgive men their trespasses, your heavenly Father will also forgive you.

The prayer was complete in Matthew 6:13, but we can imagine Jesus asking his disciples if they have any questions. One of them asks Jesus to share more about the phrase "Forgive us our debts as we forgive our debtors." So Jesus restates the law of reciprocity in more detail. The Talmud (Rosh Hashanah 17a) teaches, "He who waives his right to retribution is forgiven all his sins. . . . Whose sin does God forgive? The one who forgives transgression."

> **Matthew 6:15,** But if you forgive not men their trespasses, neither will your Father forgive your trespasses.

Jesus states the law of reciprocity first in the positive and then in the negative just to make sure his students understand. The notion of "measure for measure" is a central concept in rabbinic Judaism. As you do to others, so it shall be done to you; as you respond to God, so God responds to you. It is God's grace that fills in the disparity between our imperfect actions to each other and our less than perfect responses to God's will. The rabbis taught, "As you withhold mercy so the Holy One will withhold mercy from you" (Midrash Tahuna 15:11).

Turning to the Beatitudes

The Beatitudes (Matthew 5:3–12) are another excellent example of how rooted Jesus was in the moral tone of Jewish Scriptures and the oral tradition. These passages contain many quotes, echoes, and rabbinic-like restatements of biblical verses that would have been familiar to his Jewish listeners. The Beatitudes is a magnificently crafted teaching-chant. Biblical and Talmudic verses cited here are intended to show what Jesus might have been thinking of when he was preparing this part of his quintessential sermon—The Sermon on the Mount (Matthew 5, 6, & 7). The opening verses utilize the rhythmic shape of poem-chant found in many spiritual traditions where a word or phrase is repeated for emphasis and beauty. Since it is probable that Beatitudes were first uttered in Hebrew or Aramaic, the same word (*ashrey* in Hebrew) often translated as "blessed" in the opening is rendered as "fortunate, praiseworthy," and "happy" in other biblical verses.

Root: Bible and Talmud	Jewish Source	Branch: Words of Jesus
One who is lowly in spirit Will obtain honor.	**Proverbs 29:23**	Blessed are the poor in spirit, for theirs is the kingdom of heaven.
He heals the broken-hearted, and binds up their wounds.	**Psalm 147:3**	Blessed are those who mourn, for they will be comforted.
But the meek shall inherit the land	**Psalm 37:11**	Blessed are the meek, for they will inherit the earth.
For you bless the righteous, O LORD; You cover them with favor as with a shield.	**Psalm 5:12**	Blessed are those who hunger and thirst for righteousness, for they will be filled.
Whoever has mercy upon creatures will be granted mercy from heaven.	**Talmud: Shabbat 151b**	Blessed are the merciful, for they will obtain mercy.
Who shall ascend the hill of the LORD? And who shall stand in his holy place? Those who have clean hands and pure hearts	**Psalm 24:3–4**	Blessed are the pure in heart, for they will see God.

Seek peace, and pursue it. Aaron loved peace and pursued peace and made peace between person and person.	**Psalm 34:14** **Talmud: Sanhedrin 6b**	Blessed are the peacemakers, for they will be called children of God.
A person should always try to be among the persecuted rather than the persecutors.	**Baba Kamma 93a**	Blessed are those who are persecuted for righteousness' sake, for theirs is the kingdom of heaven.
A person should always try to be among the persecuted rather than the persecutors.	**Baba Kamma 93a**	Blessed are you when people revile you and persecute you
Those who are insulted but do not insult . . . act through love.	**Talmud: Shabbat 88b**	and utter all kinds of evil against you falsely

The teachings and parables of Rabbi Jesus emerged in the context of an already ancient Jewish wisdom tradition: Torah, the prophets, and the sages who preceded him. His role as the Anointed One, the Messiah within the Church ought not negate who he was historically: a Jew whose genius arose from the Judaism that he practiced and loved. And we can see the evidence of that genius and divine inspiration in the Our Father prayer, the Beatitudes, parables, and in his other teachings. To those whose hearts, minds, and souls are open, the historical Jesus and the theological Jesus actually complement each other.

II
Judaism
as Jesus Might
Have Known It

THREE

Two Torahs

ONE OF THE MAJOR UNDERLYING DIFFERENCES BETWEEN JUDAISM and Christianity is that every Jewish denomination is in some way engaged with an ancient oral tradition in addition to written Scripture. Religious Jews everywhere study the stories and follow, to varying degrees, the ritual and moral commandments of the Torah, the five books of Moses. But in addition to this, Jews study the stories, laws, and commentaries that are found in what's called the Oral Torah.

Although the Mishnah (the first major collection of writings by the rabbinic sages) was not redacted until the third century CE, it reflects debates and discussions that took place more than a hundred years before Jesus's lifetime. A way for Christians to understand this Oral Torah is to imagine a collection of the widest range of Christian writings during the first thousand years of nascent Christianity, including the passionate theological disagreements and debates that took place between the early church leaders.

In a way, we can think of some of the books in the Younger Testament as a kind of Christian Oral Torah—a commentary on the Bible and Judaism. The way the Younger is linked to the Elder is parallel to the way the Oral Torah is written in relationship to the Jewish Bible. It is in this sense that Notre Dame professor Dr. Michael A. Signer writes that the "documents of the New Testament present an extended meditation on the meaning of the Hebrew Bible that is analogous to the process used by the rabbis in Talmud and Midrash. . . . For example, the infancy narratives in the gospels of Matthew and Luke were composed in the same style as the genealogies in Genesis and Chronicles."[17]

On a spiritual level, Jews experience the revelation of the Torah given to Moses at Mt. Sinai as if it were a contemporary and ongoing event that occurs through our participation in the study of the sacred literature. This simple fact cannot be overstated enough to Christians who want to understand Judaism. Jewish study is not the rote memorization of an ancient creed, dogma, or collection of interpretations. Study for the spiritually involved Jew is an active and participatory encounter with the Divine. This idea is expressed in Catholicism as *Lectio Divina*—study, debate, and prayer intended to foster an intimate connection to the Divine. This encounter is rooted in the notion that the human relationship with God is covenantal—humans have obligations and God has obligations. God keeps the universe in proper order. In return, we are to live moral lives and to sanctify the material world. When we fail, as we will, our sages have given us an elegant process for repentance called *teshuvah*, the way of return.

There is a great deal of misinformation about the rabbinic tradition within Christianity. The sense when reading some Christian theologians is that the Torah may have been given by God, but the rabbinic tradition is an example of legalistic thinking in ancient Judaism. I hope to clear up such incorrect perceptions. First, let's look at how the oral tradition ended up being written down in the first place. When the Torah was given at Mt. Sinai more than 3,300 years ago, the details of how to fulfill the commandments were transmitted orally from generation to generation. Approximately 2,200 years ago, the ceaseless occupations of ancient Judea threatened Jewish survival to such an extent that leaders felt that the already old oral tradition should be collected and written down to insure Judaism's continuity.

There was a general sense that writing down these traditions might rigidify Bible interpretation, whereas the direct transmission of wisdom from teacher to student kept Judaism vital and creative. Another concern was that of translation. Since biblical Hebrew was oriental in nature and Greek was occidental, the scribes were concerned that word meanings and theological ideas would get lost in translation, and people would start claiming that they understood the "single" or "true" meaning of biblical verses. Due to the grammar and structure of biblical Hebrew, Judaism has always celebrated the multiple meanings and interpretations that can be derived out of a single scriptural word, verse, or story.

Historically, Jesus lived at the height of when this oral tradition was being collected and written. There is little doubt that the core teachings of Jesus were shaped by this creative oral tradition. Throughout the Gospels, Jesus and the other rabbis of his day refer to and quote from the Oral Torah that was extant during their lifetime. You can see how their teachings intersect and might have influenced each other. For example, as cited earlier, Hillel was a renowned rabbi who taught in the generation just before Jesus. He taught, "What is hateful to you, do not to your neighbor. That is the whole Torah—the rest is the commentary thereof. Go learn it" (Talmud: Shabbat 31a). This, of course, becomes the basis for the Golden Rule that Jesus repeated: "In everything do to others as you would have them do to you; for this is the law and the prophets" (Matthew 7:12).

A few centuries later these newly written oral traditions would be published in the Mishna (220 CE), Gamara (500 CE), and in various collections of Midrash. The Mishna is written in a kind of shorthand, and contains interpretations, examples, and applications of Torah law. Almost immediately after its publication, additional commentaries, discussions, anecdotes, and stories were collected for a few hundred more years and named the Gamara. Talmud scholar Jacob Neusner maintains that the creativity and innovation contained in this latter body of writing was made, in part, as a response to the explosive growth and challenges coming from Christianity. Historically, Jewish ritual innovations, particularly those noted in the Oral Torah, were the basis for the Eucharistic rites, some Christian holidays, notions of the afterlife, and Christian liturgical infrastructure.

Jesus, Hillel, Gamliel, Shammai, Akiva, Yokhann ben Zakkai, Shimon bar Yochai, and Judah HaNasi (among other great sages during the first centuries of the Common Era) were in the midst of one of the major paradigm shifts in Jewish history. Judaism was slowly morphing from Temple-based spiritual practices to synagogue and home-based practices. To accomplish this feat, the rabbis needed to tie every prayer and every ritual they innovated to the Temple rite itself.

In other words, what Judaism calls "tradition" is not just an entertaining song chanted by Reb Tevya in *Fiddler on the Roof*. Nor is following tradition sentimentally doing what your fathers and grandfathers did in past generations. Rather, tradition can be thought of as a spiritual connection—an energetic transfer—between what is old and what is emerging—all under the spell of divine inspiration. For example, where Jews once lit fires in the Temple in Jerusalem, candles are now lit on Sabbath evening. Where fruit, grain, animal offerings, and charity were once brought to the Temple along with personal prayers, Jews now offer prayers and charity wherever they are.

After replacement theology had already taken root within Christianity, the rabbis wrote how their worst fears about writing down the oral tradition had been realized. In one midrash it is reported, "Rabbi Judah HaLevi son of Shalom said, 'Moses wanted the *Mishna* to be given in writing. God, however, foresaw that the nations of the world would translate the Torah and read it in Greek and proclaim, "We are the true Israel"'" (Midrash-Exodus Rabbah 47:1). Jewish sages accomplished a transfer of the Temple practices into rituals that have helped the Jewish people survive to this very day. Jesus's teachings indicate that he, along with the other rabbis and sages of his era, was at the forefront of the innovations that made it possible for Judaism to endure.

The Talmud was first printed in book form in 1520, designed by an inspired Christian named Daniel Bomberg, on behalf of the Italian Jewish community. Whereas the Written Torah tells us what the laws are, the Oral Torah tells us how to keep them through traditions developed over a thousand years. As each blessing and ritual in the oral tradition became formalized, it was subject to the consent, critique, and revisions of the people. The Written Torah is a set of divine imperatives written in shorthand (e.g., Don't steal, love your neighbor, keep the Sabbath, etc.). There are 613 such commandments in the Pentateuch, and most lacked specific detail about how they were to be carried out. The Oral Torah provides those details. Written Torah is the starting point, whereas the other books of the Bible are commentaries, interpretations, and practical applications of the Torah to new situations. Oral Torah complements Written Torah, and contains commentary and detailed laws on all aspects of Jewish life.

Over hundreds of years, what Jews metaphorically call the "white space" of the Torah was filled in with interpretations and novel applications. When these interpretations take on the form of stories, homilies, and parables, they are called midrash. Jesus, along with his fellow rabbis, often used midrash as a means of teaching. Although midrashic interpretations are not necessarily intended to be taken literally, many are considered to be divinely inspired. They have been studied, disagreed with, added on to, adapted, and passed on for thousands of years. In the following example, the words of God are taken directly from Genesis 22:2, but the responses of Abraham are midrash, or imagined responses that literally help us to read between the lines in order to gain a deeper understanding of the text:

God: Take now your son.
Abraham: I have two sons. Which one do you mean?
God: Your only son.
Abraham: Both are only sons. Isaac is the only son I have from his mother, and Ishmael is the only son I have from her who is his mother.
God: The son whom you love.
Abraham: Master of the universe, are there separate compartments in one's inmost self for love? I love both of them.
God: Very well, then—take Isaac. . . .[17]

Studying the practical and theological wisdom in the Oral Torah is itself an act of devotion, and trains the mind to think Hebraically. Further, it teaches the student to respect opposing opinions, thereby preventing the faith from following a simplistic literalism where discussion and disagreement are not permitted.

As Rabbi Maurice Harris wrote, "A religious tradition is a living entity, and in order to stay healthy its boundary needs to be permeable so that it can live in an interconnected and interpenetrating relationship with the world around it."[19] In many rabbinical writings, Jews are taught to respect what is called "controversy for the sake of heaven." Each of us today continues to participate in this process known as "living Torah." Some would claim that this love of open-minded debate and creative interpretation is one of the main reasons that Judaism has survived. Perhaps Saint Augustine understood this when he wrote, "It is indeed a remarkable fact that the tribe of the Jews has not abandoned its laws, not under the rule of pagan kings nor under that of Christians. Neither emperors nor kings who found them in their land were able to prevent the Jews from maintaining their distinctiveness from the family of other nations through their observance of their own law."[20]

I have often heard the criticism that Judaism is a legalistic religion. However, in ancient Judea, religious law and civil society were part of a single fabric, lacking a strict separation of "church and state." Judaism is no more prone to legalism than any other organized religion. Ancient Judaism was not innately legalistic; it simply combined both spirituality and the day-to-day business of the people. Likewise, the Talmud isn't a collection of legalistic arguments that try to impose man-made rules upon the people. Rather it is an extraordinary collection of biblical interpretations, parables, and prayers mixed together with the most practical issues of civil law. The Talmud reveals a very vital, ancient culture that dealt with metaphysical questions as well as issues pertaining to everyday life: marriage, divorce, manners, business, and property disputes.

Judaism is both a religion and a civilization made up of many cultures. What we call the Jewish people is really an anthology of subcultures representing every race and nationality upon the planet. Each unique subculture appends its own special customs to what we call the religion of Judaism. This was true also in the time of Jesus, and the Oral Torah takes that into account.

Christianity's Influence upon Modern Judaism

Regarding the documents that would later be incorporated into the Talmud and other key rabbinic writings, Rabbi Dr. Jacob Neusner notes:

> Each of the important changes in the documents first redirected at the end of the fourth century responded to a powerful challenge by the triumph of Christianity in the age of Constantine. On that basis I maintain that the Judaism of the dual Torah (the Written and Oral Torah) took as its set of urgent questions the issues defined by Christianity as it assumed control of the Roman Empire, and that it provided as valid answers a system deriving its power from the Torah, read by the sages, embodied by sages, and exemplified by sages.[21]

It's reasonable to propose that the destruction of the Temple in 70 CE was the single most important causative event that unified the diverse Jewish population, forcing them to make major revisions to Jewish ritual practices in the early centuries of the Common Era. But as Neusner points out, it was the need to respond to this new religion called Christianity that forced Jewish sages to create the intellectual framework that would clearly define the theology of salvation and Jewish messianic expectations later expressed in the Gemara and various collections of midrash. He writes:

> The Judaism that was portrayed by the final document of late antiquity—the Talmud of Babylonia—at the end laid equal emphasis on sanctification in the here and now, and in salvation at the end of time. That shift represents only one chapter in the sages' restatement

of the Judaism of the dual Torah in the confrontation with triumphant Christianity. [22]

In other words, it was the need to answer the new Christian claims that forced Jewish theological innovation to rise to a new level. The first five centuries of the Common Era became one of the most inspired and creative periods in both Jewish and Christian history. By the fifth century, the paradigm shift that had been taking place in Judaism for several hundred years before Jesus's lifetime was almost complete. To borrow a Christian term, Judaism was born again with new life, new form (synagogue and home worship), and new content (the rabbinic writings and liturgy).

To say that the Jewish sages were inspired by Christian theology is stretching the point, but we cannot underestimate its profound influence on Judaism, a fact rarely acknowledged by either Christian or Jewish theologians. Though we cannot say that there's a Christian root to modern Judaism in the same way we can say there's a Jewish root to Christianity, it's accurate to say that the emerging power of the Church after Constantine accelerated the development of some of Judaism's most eloquent theological concepts, which became the foundations of the Judaism we have today. The sages may not give credit to Christianity for inspiring them, but Judaism's competition with the Church certainly inspired innovations in Jewish theology.

In the early centuries it seems that as Christian theology emphasized spiritual salvation and the afterlife, Jewish sages responded with added emphasis on sanctification in this world. By the third century it became clear that Judaism needed a clearer definition of its messianic expectation and the end times. Added emphasis was put on the coming of a final messiah that had not existed to that degree within Judaism. By the fifth century the sages of the Talmud, partially in reaction to the extraordinary influence of Christianity, had given Judaism a new lease on life.

Concurrent to this surge in Jewish creativity was the creativity of the early church. While Christ, the suffering servant of the church, would eventually become heir to the Roman Empire under Constantine, the Jewish people continued to fulfill Isaiah's prophesy by remaining a suffering servant among the nations. Each, it would seem, had a unique destiny to fulfill. Jesus likely would have rather seen the messianic era of swords turning into plowshares rather than experience the unbearable suffering of the cross. Given the choice, Jews would have never agreed to two thousand years of relentless anti-Semitism, mass murders, and the genocide of the Holocaust even for the noble purpose of bringing ethical monotheism to the world.

For two thousand years, neither religion has talked much to the other, except in a few instances where it was mutually beneficial. The church and its leaders usually despised Judaism (tolerated it at best), and Judaism pretty much did all it could to avoid and ignore Christianity along with its Romanized, Prometheus-like conquering Christ. While the church was busy constantly trying to convert the Jews, the Jews found themselves perpetually on the run from missionaries and "soldiers of Christ" who followed Constantine's vision of the cross turned into a sword.

But just as we cannot drive a car by constantly looking in the rearview mirror, so memory can only be made holy when it directs us to what's in front of us—a future filled with hope and new beginnings. Both religions will fail to fulfill their respective and unique missions as long as prejudice, resentment, patronization, triumphalism, jealousy, avoidance, and contempt continues. Certainly some denominations within Christianity have failed miserably in their continuous missions to convert Jews. Certainly Judaism has failed by surrendering any claim to Jesus—Joshua, Yehoshua, a native son of Judea—as one of our greatest teachers by not acknowledging the influence of the best parts of Christian theology on modern Judaism and the world.

FOUR

Meet the Sects

DURING THE FIRST CENTURY CE, THERE WERE A NUMBER OF major social, political, and religious sects among the Jews of Judea, along with dozens of smaller subsects, and numerous social and political groups. Only a few of the larger sects will be discussed here. Naturally, brief descriptions necessitate generalizations, and it's important to know there was much overlap and exchange between these groups. For example, there were major distinctions between the two largest sects within first-century Judaism: Sadducees and Pharisees. However, at the fringes of each group, there were Sadducees and Pharisees who had lots in common with each other.

Learning about the unique viewpoints of the major sects will shed new light to any student of the Younger Testament. Terms like *Sadducee* and *Pharisee* almost sound synonymous to the uninformed modern reader. Understanding the actual differences between these groups will help in making the Gospels and writings of Paul, in particular, more meaningful and three-dimensional. I have ordered the description of these sects and groups by their level of influence within the Jewish world in the first century.

Not one of the sects ever represented a majority of the Judean population, since most Jews during the first century were independent, nonsectarian thinkers and probably participated in the activities of different sects during the year. In general, however, the Sadducees had a high social status due to their priestly duties. They were theologically more conservative than the Pharisees, and more literalistic in their interpretation of the Bible. With no means of stopping the Roman occupation, by the first century CE, many

Sadducees were reluctantly willing to live with the status quo whereby the Temple could remain under Jewish administration. The Pharisees, by contrast, were more populist, eclectic, and democratic in their approach to theological innovations and decision making. Meanwhile, the Essenes were an apocalyptic and mystical sect, and the Zealots were religious nationalists highly involved in political activism and uprisings against the Roman occupation.

Sadducees Their name derives from Zadok the priest, a descendent of Aaron. This is the sect that maintained the Temple in Jerusalem and admin istered local government under the watchful eye of the Roman Empire. They believed they were the authentic heirs to biblical Judaism. They were priests and administrators and generally fit into what we would call today the mid- dle and middle-upper classes of Judean society. Theologically, the Sadducees typically took a fairly literalistic approach toward the interpretation of the Torah. Their noble aim was to bolster support for the sacrificial system that was crumbling under the weight of the Roman occupation.

Wanting to maintain the status quo in order to preserve the Temple, they were somewhat compliant, pragmatic, and compromising concerning their relationship to the various empires (Greek, Syrio-Greek, and Roman) that ruled Judea. Most of what we know about the Sadducees comes from the writings of Josephus and the sages and rabbis of the Talmud who considered them to be rather boorish, unwilling to recognize the changing times, and unresponsive to the spiritual needs of the people for a more decentralized relationship to God through personal religious practices.

Pharisees From the Hebrew word meaning "the ones who separate." This sect was the most popular in Judea since their leadership arose from the working class. They were comprised of intelligentsia, artists, theologians, scholars, and craftspeople. They might have taken the name Pharisees because they saw themselves as "separated" from the aristocratic leaders of the Temple, or "separated" from the influences of Hellenism and popular Roman culture. For over a hundred years before Jesus's lifetime, they were at the cutting edge of redefining and renewing Judaism so that it could survive the onslaught of one ruling empire after another. They adopted a flexible approach toward interpreting the Bible, and believed that their innovations were the authentic continuation of the revelation of the Torah.

The Pharisees gave authority to both the Written and Oral Torah, seeing them as intimately linked together. They were the forbears of the Talmud, and helped preserve the vast collection of homiletical interpretations of the Bible that we are heirs to today. They are credited with continuing the development of the prayers and rituals we're familiar with in synagogues— innovations absorbed by Christianity and Islam as well. Pharisees had many theological differences with Sadducees, especially concerning concepts of life after death, immortality of the soul, eschatology, and the resurrection of the dead.

After the destruction of the Temple in 70 CE, the Pharisees got the lion's share of credit for helping to develop modern, rabbinic Judaism. They contributed the most toward Judaism's survival even after the forced expulsion of Jews from Judea following the failed Bar Kokhba revolt in 135 CE. Josephus indicates that of all the sects, Pharisees garnered the most support and respect from people. Judaism saw some of its greatest intellectual and creative flowering in the rulings, religious practices, poetry, and theological writings of the Pharisees. If not exactly a Pharisee, Jesus certainly had much in common with this sect and seems to have drawn directly from their insights, innovations, and wisdom.

Theological and ritual innovations that the Pharisees supported included new fixed prayers and liturgy to complement the recitation of psalms that were already part of the Temple service. In addition, they helped foster congregational worship in local synagogues, new ideas about the afterlife, and the resurrection of the dead—ideas that weren't well developed in the Tanakh.

Essenes These were a diverse group of people who came from many sects and strata of society. In general, they were an apocalyptic and mystical sect, and mostly apolitical. Some members of the Essene community were ascetic and did not marry. One of their defining beliefs was in the imminent expectation of the messianic age, and they anxiously anticipated the Kingdom of God here on earth. They were a semimonastic community, living and eating communally, and had a major library and center of learning near the Dead Sea in Qumran. They had many of the same theological beliefs as the Pharisees except that they saw themselves as the new elect, the remnant of true Judaism, and the ones who would lead the way to the coming of God's kingdom brought about by the messiah.

The eschatology of the Essenes was that their current age was coming to an end, and a glorious new kingdom was at hand. It was the Essenes who developed a sophisticated notion of not just one messiah whom God would anoint, but two. They spoke of a Messiah son of David who would successfully lead a war against outside occupation and be declared king of the Jews. However, they also spoke of a Messiah son of Joseph who would be a suffering servant of the Holy One in his attempt to restore the Jewish priesthood. Like the Pharisees, Essenes rejected the hypocrisy of the Temple's administrators. Leaving Jerusalem to "prepare a way for the LORD" was a powerful statement against the Sadducees and an invitation for others to help them usher in the Kingdom of God here on earth. Like the Pharisees, Essenes too had been in existence for more than 150 years before Jesus's lifetime. It seems as though John the Baptist was probably influenced by the Essenes.

Zealots The Zealots saw themselves as heirs to the political legacy of the Maccabees, famous for leading the uprising that defeated the Syrio-Greeks who ruled Judea in the century before the Romans came to power. According to Dr. David Flusser, the Zealots were a diverse religious group who "believed that armed struggle against Rome was divinely ordained."[23]

Some citizens of Judea who weren't formally affiliated with the Zealots nevertheless supported the kind of aggressive, sometimes violent, tactics they advocated. Zealots believed that activism, nationalism, and guerrilla warfare were necessary components for liberating Judea and making it a free and independent nation once again. During the first century, Zealots had an ongoing campaign to convince the population not to bow to the authority of the Romans by avoiding Roman taxes. The majority of Pharisees, first- and second-century rabbis, and Essenes opposed the aggressive tactics of the Zealots, though they might have agreed with their goal of liberating Judea.

Herodians A political party that represented a diverse group of Jews who identified themselves by their support for the Herodian Dynasty. Herod the Great was the Judean king in the century before the Common Era. He was a client king of the Roman Empire, and was responsible for many major public work projects that included a major remodeling of the Temple in Jerusalem. Nevertheless, he was an authoritarian despot responsible for the murder of many Jewish leaders. Herodian Jews might have included contractors, crafts-people, and local rulers whose employment was enhanced under Herod's rule. The Herodian Dynasty lasted from 37 BCE through 92 CE.

First-century Followers of Jesus Historically, Jesus and his disciples might not have thought of themselves as a sect at all. Rather, they likely saw themselves as an innovative movement within Judaism squarely in line with other cutting-edge sages and rabbis in that era (such as Hillel, Rabban Gamliel, and Rabbi Akiva). Most of their beliefs were in line with those of the Pharisees, and some of their beliefs were similar to the Essenes.

The earliest followers of Jesus were all Jewish, so at first there was no particular term for their sect. In general, they were known as "Nazarenes" (see Acts 24:5), meaning followers of the teacher from Nazareth. The term *Christian* is first used in Acts 11:26. The followers of Rabbi Jesus believed the Messiah had come in his person, and that his crucifixion and resurrection were signposts of his imminent return to earth to declare the Kingdom of God. Later, they were referred to as *Notzrim*, a Hebrew word from Isaiah 11:1 meaning "branch." The Notzrim were followers of the one they believed to be "the Branch," a poetic appellation for the Messiah.

In general, the Nazarenes did not support active resistance to the Romans, since they were certain that the Messiah would be returning any day. "Why risk life with political resistance," they might have argued, "when the Kingdom of God at hand?" This placed the followers of Jesus in direct opposition to the activism of the Zealots and to those who actively opposed the Empire. As the second century progressed, the Nazarenes were becoming less and less of a Jewish sect, and this fact certainly shaped the tone of the New Testament as it was being redacted. By the second and third centuries, Nazarenes were increasingly considered informers who would betray their fellow Jews to protect themselves from Roman persecution. Even more than their belief in Jesus, this seems to have been the major variable in the split between Judaism and Christianity.

A culture is like any living system in nature. It has many parts that interact and influence each other. First-century Jewish culture was no different, and the various sects and movements had more exchange with each other than we are led to believe by reading short, generalized descriptions of them. Today, for instance, the normative Jewish community looks askance at Jews who follow Jesus while also proclaiming some degree of allegiance to Judaism. It is simply not appropriate to merge two different and unique religions. But this was not the case in the first century regarding the mainstream Jewish community and the followers of Rabbi Jesus.

At first, Jesus's followers were practicing Jews, and even in the book of Acts it is difficult to ascertain what they called themselves. For sure, many of Jesus's followers were affiliated with the progressive pharisaic movement, while others were more aligned with the apocalyptic, mystical visions of the Essenes. Some were Zealots involved in politics, while others were not. Some were Herodian and more supportive of maintaining peace with Rome, while others were not. Just as in our culture today, many citizens of Judea in the first century fell between the lines of simple classifications.

Taking a Second Look at the Pharisees

Most scholars agree that the Younger Testament was compiled and edited under highly stressful political conditions. For example, the words "Roman" or "Romans" are mentioned only twelve times in the Christian Scripture, and in most of these citations they are portrayed in a neutral light. On the other hand, the words "Jew" and "Pharisee" are mentioned hundreds of times in the Younger Testament, and are mostly used in a negative or critical light. From what was originally a progressive Jewish sect, similar to the Pharisees, the followers of Jesus became estranged from their Jewish roots within the first few centuries. This is especially true as the work of Pauline followers brought larger numbers of Gentiles into the Church. These early Christians had no familial or sentimental attachment to Judaism, the Hebrew language, Jewish rituals, or the culture of Judea. The split between the Jews and the early followers of Jesus took several hundred years. The "divorce" between Judaism and Christianity was made under the command of Constantine at the Council of Nicaea in the year 325 CE.

Rabbis today have a broad spectrum of beliefs within the various Jewish denominations (Orthodox, Hasidic, Conservative, Reform, Reconstructionist, and Renewal), and there are many levels of spiritual practice regarding the performance of ritual mitzvot. These levels range from the most lenient to the most strict, from the most traditional to the most modern, from the most rational to the most mystical. Yet each one of the religious leaders shares the title of rabbi or cantor. Two thousand years ago, members of the Pharisaic movement were among the most progressive, cutting-edge teachers, sages, scribes, and rabbis of their day. Yet within this group were what we would today call liberal, conservative, traditional, strict, lenient, old-fashioned, and modern thinkers.

Among the Pharisees were saints, geniuses, scholars, and hypocrites too. This diversity among the rabbis seems to be reflected in the varied statements made by Jesus and the other rabbis about the Pharisees. Some of Jesus's statements are very supportive of this sect, and some are very critical. If you speak with rabbis today, you'll find that they too are both critical and supportive of different theological positions within the various movements to which they belong. Most scholars now agree that Jesus's teachings and personal religious practices (kosher eating, daily worship, fulfillment of ritual commandments, etc.) were generally parallel to those of the Pharisees. David Flusser writes:

> Although Jesus was apparently indirectly influenced by Essenism, he was basically rooted in universal non-sectarian Judaism. The philosophy and practice of this Judaism was that of the Pharisees. . . . Although not really a Pharisee himself, he was closest to the Pharisees of the school of Hillel who preached love, and led the way further to unconditional love—even of one's enemies and of sinners.[24]

A disciple of Flusser, Brad Young, adds:

> The theology of Jesus was actually almost identical to that of the Pharisees. In contrast to the Sadducees, Pharisees believed in the oral interpretation of the Torah, the resurrection of the dead, the messianic idea, Angels, Demons, and the devotion to God who is actively involved in the affairs of creation . . . His sharp criticism of the hypocrisy of some Pharisees is far different from an attack against the theology of Pharisism.[25]

The Pharisees get a bad rap when the Younger Testament is taught without proper commentary and historical context. Pharisees certainly had their fair share of hypocrites, just as all modern religions do. But without their innovations, Judaism and Christianity wouldn't be the same today. For the past two thousand years, rabbis have drawn from the wisdom of the Pharisaic movement. Jesus seems to have challenged the Pharisees as an insider with a kind of healthy self-criticism of the movement he was so close to. His words against some Pharisees are in line with what other Pharisees later wrote, which were collected and published in the Talmud.

Unfortunately, the general impression one gets from the Gospel accounts is that Pharisee equals hypocrite. Sadly, if you look up the word *Pharisee* in most dictionaries, you'll find that "hypocrite" and "phony" are definitions arising from misinterpretations in the New Testament. Equating "Pharisee" with "hypocrite" is as inaccurate as equating rabbi, priest, or pastor to "hypocrite" today. There certainly are rabbis, priests, and pastors who are hypocrites, but we know that the foolishness of a few people shouldn't define the greater good of the majority of religious leaders.

How do we know that Jesus was criticizing Pharisees as an insider, as a rabbi who loved Torah and observed the mitzvot, and as a colleague who respected his fellow rabbis? We cannot be certain, but when we read Jesus's words about Pharisees, we see statements that are both positive and negative. We also see that he tells his students to support and obey them. It would seem that he was talking about different groups of Pharisees at different times during his ministry. For example, in Matthew 5:20 Jesus says, "Unless your righteousness exceeds that of the scribes and Pharisees, you will never enter the kingdom of heaven." Yet in Luke 11:42, he criticizes Pharisees in that they "tithe mint and rue and herbs of all kinds, and neglect justice and the love of God." At the same time, he admonishes his followers to "obey them and do everything they tell you."

Jesus, along with many of his rabbinical colleagues, was critical of those Pharisees who did not practice what they preached. For example, Talmudic rabbis such as Yehoshua used to say, "A foolish pietist . . . and the plague of the Pharisees bring destruction upon the world" (Sotah 20a). Another passage in the Jerusalem Talmud (Sotah 3:4) declares, "What is the plague Pharisee? He who gives advice to orphans in order to benefit from the widow." Statements from the historian Josephus about Pharisees tended to be positive, on the other hand. He said that they "live plainly and despise delicacies in diet, and they follow the conduct of reason; and what that prescribes to them as good for them, they do. . . . The cities give great attestations to them on account of their entirely virtuous conduct, both in the actions of their lives, and their discourses" (*Antiquities*, Book 18 1:3). In another passage, Josephus compares them favorably to the Sadducees:

> The Pharisees simplify their standard of living, making no concession to luxury. . . . They show respect and deference to elders, nor do they rashly propose to contradict their proposals. . . . The Pharisees are affectionate with one another, and cultivate harmonious relations within the community. The Sadducees, on the contrary, are, even among themselves, rather boorish in their behavior, and in their intercourse with their peers are as rude as to aliens. (*War of the Jews* II 8:14)

Of course, the Sadducees had their own criticism of the Pharisees. In Avot de-Rabbi Natan 5 it is written, "It is a silly tradition of the Pharisees to subject themselves to austerity in this world for in the world-to-come they will possess nothing at all." One Talmudic source was very specific indeed regarding different types of Pharisees. The Talmud (Sotah 22b) reports that there were Pharisees who looked over their shoulders to see whether anyone was observing the good deeds they were about to perform. Such internal criticism still goes on today between various sects in all religions.

There are actually many passages in the Younger Testament that portray the Pharisees in a positive light. For example, Rabbi Gamliel was a Pharisee who is highly regarded in Acts 5:17–42. Paul also found sympathetic Pharisees in Acts 22:30–23:10. As students of the first century, we would all be wise to read each part of the Bible in its proper cultural and historical context.

Jesus and Paul ought to be seen as active members of the Jewish community. Otherwise, inaccurate information will continue to be perpetuated about what was really said about the Pharisees.

FIVE

The Sacrificial System

EGINNING WITH THE DEDICATION OF THE FIRST TEMPLE (possibly in 953 BCE) right up until 70 CE when the Romans destroyed the second Temple, this incredible place of worship served as the focal point for the Jewish people. The Temple rituals brought the Israelites together and bound them together as a people for almost one thousand years. Our contemporary minds cannot begin to imagine the excitement, joy, and inspiration associated with this ancient center of worship. Even when the Temple was destroyed the first time in 586 BCE by the Babylonians, the dream of rebuilding it helped bind the Jews together until Cyrus of Persia came to their aid.

Why was this "dwelling place for God" so special, and what made it so different from any other place in the Jewish imagination? With all the internal self-criticism of Israel's hypocrisy concerning the sacrificial system, why did the prophets love the Temple so much that they risked their lives to criticize some of its leaders? Why did the rabbis of the first century, including Jesus, love the Temple so much that they too carried on the struggle started by the prophets to keep the Temple free from corruption and hypocrisy? Why do religious Jews look forward to the rebuilding of the Third Temple to this day?

From our knowledge of Jewish history, and extensive rabbinic writings on the subject, we see that the sacrificial system had many purposes. Although it was not necessary to offer a sacrifice to be reconciled with God, the public nature of the Temple system was used as a demonstration that the penitent's confession was accepted. Unlike what some Christians have been taught, the sacrificial system was not instituted as the exclusive, or even the primary, means for the remission of sin. Offerings were brought to the Temple only after confession, repentance, and restitution took place. Plus, Temple offerings were only efficacious for minor, inadvertent sins, and not for premeditated sins or criminal behavior. Unintentional sin included what we call today sins of omission rather than sins of commission. Some examples are unconsciously withholding testimony, rashly making a verbal oath, saying things in anger that we don't really mean, or inadvertently eating prohibited foods.

The elaborate rituals that were part of the daily Temple system of offerings were inspiring to Jewish and non-Jewish pilgrims. The dramatic ceremonies they witnessed encouraged gratitude for all that God provided. Additionally, offerings supported both the priesthood and the poor who had no other means of making a living. Offerings also created a sense of vicarious atonement resulting from the compassion elicited for the animals that were sacrificed. After a sinner performed the sacrificial rites in the Temple, it was hoped that he or she would be less likely to commit the same sin again.

Finally, Temple rituals built a strong sense of community, binding the people together with a common sense of purpose, mission, and national pride. They were a mechanism for building family unity, and bringing everyone into a closer relationship to God. The Israelites thought of Solomon's Temple as the actual intersection of heaven and earth. Like the great cathedrals of Europe, the Temple in Jerusalem gave people a sense that they were part of something much greater than themselves.

In the twelfth century, Maimonides suggested that the Temple rites were an intermediary stage that God created in order to wean people away from the human sacrifices that were routine in Abraham's era. He also suggested that animal, grain, and incense offerings were an in-between step leading to the more portable system of prayer-as-offering that became the greatest innovation of rabbinic Judaism.

It's important for both Jews and Christians to get a sense of why sacrificial offerings were so important for thousands of years, and how Temple sacrifice played a role in the lives of the most important characters in the Gospels of the Younger Testament. Surely Jesus, Joseph, Mary, and the disciples brought offerings to the Temple throughout their lives. Paul and the disciples continued to practice them after Jesus's death. Unfortunately, today many people have incorrect information regarding Jesus's attitude toward the Temple sacrifices, and most Jews know very little about them.

Keep in mind that these sacrifices were not used for forgiveness of criminal sins, moral sins, or sins against person or property. These could only be vindicated by a court judgment or by the personal apologies and reparations made by the perpetrator to the aggrieved person, or the victim of a crime. In addition, the prophets, priests, and rabbis had always taught that Temple sacrifices were outward signs of inward changes; the offerings themselves were physical representations of feelings, thoughts, and words.

The pilgrimage to Jerusalem during the festivals was understood metaphorically as going from a lower to a higher state of spirituality. Walking up the hill toward the Temple in Jerusalem, and then ascending the steps of the Temple itself while chanting David's Psalms of Ascent, the pilgrims had the sense that they were actually walking from the earthly realm into the heavenly realm—to the very place where heaven meets earth. Bringing and then making an offering requires a renunciation of something material: money, jewelry, grain, fruit, or animal. This is where we get the idea of "making a sacrifice." The real sacrifice, however, is giving one's self to God, and sacrificing one's very self.

In the case of a sin offering, a transfer of the sin is procured from the sinner to the animal through the spiritual process known as *s'mikha* or the "laying on of hands." Spiritually, the animal is sacrificed in place of the repentant individual. This must have been a very emotional and transformative process for a sincere penitent to experience. Returning to family was one of the final stages in the penitent's offering process as he or she shared the details of the experience, especially how the ritual brought him or her closer to God. Finally, there was the partaking of the newly sanctified food and sharing the sacred meal with loved ones. This became the basis of the sacrament in Christianity, and of the weekly Sabbath meal in Judaism.

The Extended Meaning of Offerings

The well-known verses about the suffering servant in Isaiah 53 are literally about the suffering of the Jewish people and the atoning power of Jewish martyrdom throughout history. Many Jews apply this same spiritual principle today when trying to understand the martyrdom of those who were murdered in the Holocaust. The word *holocaust*, in fact, comes from the Greek meaning "burnt offering," which itself came from the Hebrew *olah*, meaning "whole" burnt offering. The extension of the sacrificial system to prayer began when the prophets fearlessly told the people that simply going through the motions of making offerings was devoid of meaning and hypocritical.

By the time the Temple was destroyed by the Romans, the system for transferring the spiritual power of a physical offering to prayer was already being developed. By the middle of the second century, under the inspired leadership of Yokhanan Ben Zakkai, the survival of Judaism was assured, as the entire sacrificial system had been accurately transferred to charitable giving, synagogue worship, home Sabbath observance, Torah study, and various festival rituals. Christians made the same extension of the sacrificial system in the way they understood Jesus as the final sacrifice, primarily building upon the writings of Paul.

Paul expected every believer to personally participate in the sacrifices themselves. He wrote: "I appeal to you therefore, brothers and sisters, by the mercies of God, to present your bodies as a living sacrifice, holy and acceptable to God, which is your spiritual worship" (Romans 12:1). Based on the rabbinic tradition, Macy Nulman writes, "The study of the Torah is an atonement like the offering of sacrifices."[26] The Talmud teaches, "Whosoever occupies himself with the study of Torah does not need a burnt offering, a meal offering, a sin offering, or a guilt offering" (Talmud: Menakhot 110a).

Just the act of studying the sacrifices with a full heart was seen as akin to actually making or bringing offerings. Having knowledge of the Temple is akin to building the Temple. These novel applications of the Temple system help save Judaism from complete destruction after 70 CE.

There are many ways that the rites of the ancient Temple are replicated in modern Judaism: The morning prayer service in Judaism is called the *shakharit* just like the morning offering at the Temple. The afternoon service is called *minkha* to commemorate the grain offering in the Temple. There is an additional synagogue service on the Sabbath to correspond to the additional offering that was made in the Temple. The eternal light in every Synagogue is called the *ner tamid,* and represents the daily *tamid* offering. The Friday night Shabbat services in Jewish homes include candles, wine, and *challah* (special Sabbath bread). The *challah,* representing the showbread (Exodus 25:30) in the Temple, is sprinkled with a dash of salt to fulfill the commandment "You shall not omit from your grain-offerings the salt of the covenant with your God; with all your offerings you shall offer salt" (Leviticus 2:13). The tablecloth at the Sabbath table represents the beautiful fabric where the bread offerings were brought in the Temple, and the table itself represents the altar. In essence, every Jewish home and synagogue became a miniature Temple.

Temple Hypocrisy

Since the time of the prophets, a unique quality of Judaism has been the consecration of self-criticism. In ancient Israel, there was an ongoing desire for national, religious, and personal self-improvement. No one was more critical of religious hypocrisy in the Temple than the prophets, priests, sages, and rabbis. But they made this criticism as insiders dedicated to improving the amazing system of offerings, and not to replace it. No institution, no matter how great, should neglect awareness of internal corruption or hypocrisy—not the Temple, not the Vatican, not national governments, not our local synagogues and churches. In the Talmud Rabbi Gamaliel proclaimed,

"No disciple whose inner self does not live up to his acceptable exterior self may enter the house of study" (Berakhot 28a).

When Jesus singled out the money changers for rebuke at the Temple, he did so in the tradition of a long line of insiders, beginning with the prophets, who wanted to safeguard, reform, or improve their beloved Temple. Regrettably, this story as reported in the New Testament, and its subsequent misinterpretation by the Church Fathers, led to a distorted view of the Temple. Reading the story of Jesus overthrowing the moneychangers (John 2:13–17) in its proper historical context, it becomes clear that Jesus was not giving a signal for the overthrow of the Temple. Nor was he criticizing the system of offerings. Rather, Jesus was displaying righteous anger against what he judged to be a defilement of the Temple. He demands that people stop selling cattle, sheep, and doves when he says, "Stop making my Father's house a marketplace."

After Jesus's disciples saw him turn over the money changers' tables (John 2:17), they quoted the words of David who said, "It is zeal for your house that has consumed me" (Psalm 69:9). The disciples seem to have understood that Jesus's action was in the tradition of the prophets who preceded him in their criticism of religious hypocrisy. During the early decades of the first century, many Jewish leaders understood that some of the Temple administrators, judges, and priests (i.e., Joseph Caiaphas as reported in the New Testament) were steadily being corrupted as they were appointed by the Romans. It's likely that Jesus would have enjoyed support from many of the religious leaders in his time.

Post-Temple Sacrifices in Judaism and Christianity

Just as the rabbis justified the evolution from material sacrifices to the "sacrifice" of prayer, so early Christians took this same theological step in their growing understanding of Jesus's sacrificial death. Over the centuries, Christian thinkers made the same intellectual leap that the rabbis made. They transferred the meaning of Jesus's sacrifice directly to the Eucharist.

Dr. Lawrence Hoffman, professor of liturgy at Hebrew Union College, explains it this way:

> *Tefillah* [prayer] was likened to the ancient *Tamid*, the public sacrifice offered daily, mornings and afternoons. . . . Prayer was called "the offering of our lips." . . . In the Roman Catholic Church, the bread and wine are called *oblata*, "things offered." And even in Protestant churches, which shun much of this language, the collection plate is usually called an "offering," as are certain prayers spoken at its presentation. [27]

Dr. Robert Louis Wilken, professor of Christianity at the University of Virginia, reminds us that the Christ-resurrection story is rooted in the Jewish sacrificial system. He writes:

> From the beginning of Christianity, the death and resurrection of Christ have been understood as a sacrifice. In the Epistle to the Hebrews . . . the author writes: "But when Christ came as a high priest of the good things that have come, then through the greater and perfect tent (not made with hands, that is, not of this creation), he entered once for all into the Holy Place, not with the blood of goats and calves, but with his own blood, thus obtaining eternal redemption" (Hebrews 9:11–12). In the ancient prayers spoken over the bread and wine, the priest said: "We offer to Thee O Lord this fearful and non-blood sacrifice, beseeching Thee that Thou deal not with us after our sins nor reward us after our iniquities, but according to Thy leniency and Thine unspeakable love towards mankind overlook and blot out the handwriting that is against us Thy suppliants." It's clear from this prayer that Christian worship has deep roots in the sacrificial worship of the ancient Jewish Temple, but in Christian belief there's only one sacrifice, one offering—the offering of Christ's life. [28]

When I read those beautiful words in the prayer spoken over the bread and wine, I think of an ancient prayer found in Jewish prayer books, and chanted during the morning services: "Master of all the worlds: it is not because of our righteousness that we bring our prayers before You, but because of Your abounding mercies." This prayer is recited just before the study of passages in the Torah (Exodus 30:24–36) and Talmud (Jerusalem Talmud/Yoma 5:5) that recount the burnt offerings and the incense offerings. When Christians participate in the Eucharist, they are spiritually participating in Christ's sacrifice in the same way that Jews participate in the Temple offerings by recounting them. In both religions, prayer and ritual are efficacious substitutes for Temple offerings.

Virtual Sacrifice and Making the Past Present

Dr. Ruth Langer of Boston College uses a novel comparison to explain how reading biblical or Talmudic passages can be understood in our technological age. Just as the Internet has opened up the world of virtual reality, so certain rituals in Judaism and Christianity can be thought of as virtual reenactments of religious history. In a profound and mysterious sense, these reenactments actualize and make present the events in the past that they recall. This idea seems parallel to Augustine's idea that a sacrament is a visible form of an invisible grace. Wilken explains:

> In a sacrament, a spiritual reality is conveyed through a material object. . . . In the Christian Eucharist, the bread and wine are visible forms that convey an invisible blessing. What one sees is bread and wine, but what one receives is Christ. . . . The language of sacrifice comes directly out of Jewish tradition, and the prominence of a term such as "lamb of God" has broad symbolic links to Jewish practices at the time of the Christian beginnings. In calling the Eucharist a sacrifice, Christians wish to say that their liturgy is not a memorial meal recalling what happened centuries ago, but a re-presenting of

what happened once for the benefit of the present community. . . . In the Christian liturgy, the term "remembrance" means re-presenting, re-actualizing, making present what happened in the past.[29]

Rabbinic Judaism, in the first century and today, promotes a very pure notion of forgiveness by God's grace. This forgiveness does not come as the result of the profession of a dogma, religious belief, the enactment of a ritual, or by bringing an offering to the Temple. God, not the priests of ancient Judaism, instituted the system of rituals that would allow the sinner to have physical evidence that his or her inadvertent sins had been forgiven. Several decades after Jesus was crucified, the Romans destroyed the Temple in Jerusalem, and yet the spiritual mechanism for the remission of sin had not changed.

Jesus, as the New Testament attests, was not starting a new religion. Rather, he was at the epicenter of the shift from Temple Judaism to Rabbinic Judaism. The rabbis knew that Judaism was vulnerable as long as the religion centered around one particular place. They understood that if the Temple were destroyed (as it had been in 586 BCE), then Judaism would be in jeopardy. Through novel applications of the mitzvot relating to the Temple, religious leaders from many different sects and movements began formulating what we now call congregational worship. Their intention was not to replace the Temple, but to reinterpret the commandments relating to offerings. Their genius was in shifting the focus from the Temple to the home and synagogue, from a Temple in space to Temple in time—the Sabbath. Without such forethought and divine inspiration, it's unlikely that the Jewish religion would have survived the crucifixions, mass murders, ethnic cleansing, and destruction of the Temple by the Romans.

By Jesus's lifetime, the Pharisees believed they had God's approval to shift the focus from actual offerings to personal and communal prayer. The idea that even martyrdom, under some circumstances, can be symbolically understood as a sacrificial offering was well known and accepted by the rabbis. In a midrash it's written, "Moses said to God, 'Will not the time come when Israel shall have neither Tabernacle nor Temple? What will happen with them then?' The Divine reply was, 'I will then take one of their righteous men and retain him as a pledge on their behalf, in order that I may pardon all their sins'" (Exodus Rabbah 35:3).

As stated earlier, Paul echoed this idea when he wrote, "Present your bodies as a living sacrifice" (Romans 12:1). I can imagine that many Jews would have understood his intent and symbolism. His injunction seems to be a continuity of the prevailing Jewish view. We also see evidence in the New Testament that praising God was understood as a form of sacrifice. When the New Testament says, "Let us continually offer a sacrifice of praise to God, that is, the fruit of lips that confess his name" (Hebrews 13:15), it's paraphrasing what the prophet Hosea said: "Take words with you and return to the Lord; say to him, 'Take away all guilt; accept that which is good, and we will offer the fruit of our lips'"(Hosea 14:2–3).

Prayer as a form of sacrifice is not a Christian innovation or improvement over the "old" system in Judaism. Rather, applying the idea of offerings to other forms of expression (prayer, good deeds, charity, etc.) is central to the prophetic and rabbinic traditions. The destruction of the Temple was a national tragedy, but it did not have any impact on the way that Jewish people received forgiveness. As a religious Jew, it seems impossible that Jesus would have wanted his people to give up fulfilling the ritual mitzvot. As Paul says in Romans 3:31, "Do we then overthrow the law by this faith? By no means! On the contrary, we uphold the law." On the other hand, there certainly are passages in the Younger Testament indicating that Paul might have intended a substitution of an "old" covenant for a "new" covenant, certainly for Gentile believers (Galatians 4:21–31).

In all religions there are people mindlessly performing their ritual obligations with little spiritual focus or purpose. The message of the biblical prophets was clear and explicit: fulfill the ritual mitzvot, but not at the expense of confession, repentance, and doing good in the world. A thousand years later, the rabbis, including Jesus, taught the same. Today, almost three thousand years after the age of the prophets, rabbis, pastors, and priests are still delivering sermons based on this ancient prophetic wisdom.

Many prophecies in the Bible and within the rabbinic tradition indicate that offerings will be restored during the messianic era. The nature of these offerings, however, has been debated within Judaism for the past two thousand years. In one midrash, it's suggested that "in the future, all sacrifices, with the exception of the Thanksgiving-sacrifice, will be discontinued" (Vayikra Rabbah 9:7). Some theologians believe there will be a restoration of animal sacrifices, while others, such as Rabbi Abraham Isaac Kook, the first chief rabbi of what became the modern state of Israel, proposed that only the non-animal (grain, vegetable, and fruit) offerings will be restored.

His Blood Be upon Us

Some fundamentalist Christians continue to teach that there is no remission of sin without blood sacrifices in ancient Judaism. They claim this teaching is upheld by the verse in Hebrews 9:22 where it's written, "Indeed, under the law almost everything is purified with blood, and without the shedding of blood there is no forgiveness of sins." First, within Judaism two thousand years ago it just wasn't the case that "almost everything" was "purified with blood." Secondly, it was never true that "without the shedding of blood there is no forgiveness of sin." So let me suggest that Hebrews 9:22 might have other possible interpretations. Certainly, from a Jewish perspective, I don't agree with the traditional understanding of this verse.

The Hebraic way of thinking is what we might today call holistic. The Hebrew poets described an intimate relationship between the Creator and creation, between physicality and spirituality. Animal offerings were certainly the most dramatic form of offering in the Temple process for expressing gratitude for peace, reconciliation with God, and for the remission of inadvertent sins. However, the prophets, sages, and rabbis always taught that the intention of the heart was more important than ritual. The psalmist taught that confession and repentance were the central elements necessary for the remission of sin. This is affirmed by the prophets, sages, and rabbis who lived in the days of the First and Second Temples. The misleading verse in the Epistle to the Hebrews is often linked to Leviticus 17:11 where God says to Israel, "For the life of the flesh is in the blood; and I have given it to you for making atonement for your lives on the altar; for, as life, it is the blood that makes atonement."

The Hebrew word translated as "life" in Leviticus 17:11 and Deuteronomy 12:23 is actually the same word meaning "soul." From a Hebraic viewpoint, both the physical world (life) and the spiritual world (soul) were part of a single fabric. These verses teach us about the relationship between the spiritual essence of the soul that is within an animal's blood, and the great care that must be taken when slaughtering an animal for consumption. Kosher dietary law tried to insure animals were treated and slaughtered humanely. When these passages in Leviticus and Hebrews are examined in context to other passages in the Torah, it's clear that blood sacrifices were only required for the remission of the lesser category of unintentional sins. Even then, Temple offerings were not required since prayer was just as effective.

Regarding someone who is poor, grain could always be substituted for an animal offering. When no grain or animal sacrifice was possible (e.g., for Jews living far from the Temple) then prayer was seen as an efficacious offering. So long as Leviticus 17:11 is taken out of its context from the rest of the Torah, and interpreted with inaccurate knowledge of the ancient Jewish rituals, it will continue to be taught incorrectly. If you read the verse in Leviticus in its entirety and in its full context, it's clear that this passage is principally a prohibition against drinking blood, and not primarily a formula for the remission of sin.

Leviticus 17:10–12 If anyone of the house of Israel or of the aliens who reside among them eats any blood, I will set my face against that person who eats blood, and will cut that person off from the people. For the life of the flesh is in the blood; and I have given it to you for making atonement for your lives on the altar; for, as life, it is the blood that makes atonement. Therefore I have said to the people of Israel: No person among you shall eat blood, nor shall any alien who resides among you eat blood.

Paul alludes to this prohibition against eating blood in Acts 15:20 and 29 when he urges Jesus's Gentile followers to "abstain only from things polluted by idols and from fornication and from whatever has been strangled and from blood." Leviticus 17:11 does state that blood makes atonement, but the Torah also states that incense, repentance, Yom Kippur, prayer, flour, releasing a bird, releasing a goat, charitable donations, and oil may accomplish the same. During the time when sacrifices were offered, blood was seen as an important, but not exclusive, mechanism for bringing about certain kinds of atonement.

Here is a verse where the same phrase "to make an atonement for your lives" is used, and where no blood sacrifice was required: "The rich shall not give more, and the poor shall not give less, than the half-shekel, when you bring this offering to the LORD to make atonement for your lives" (Exodus 30:15). In the book of Numbers the phrase "to make an atonement for our lives" is also used, and no blood was required. The offerer was asked to donate "articles of gold, armlets and bracelets, signet rings, ear-rings, and pendants, to make atonement for ourselves" (Numbers 31:50).

There were many ways for people to reconcile themselves with God in ancient Israel. And when all of these verses are studied in their proper biblical and historical context, we see that no offering was better than sincere, heartfelt confession. As so eloquently stated in Micah 6:8, the primary means for the remission of sin is to "do justice, and to love kindness, and to walk humbly with your God." This was true in ancient Judaism and it's true today in modern Judaism. The sacrificial system of the Temple is gone, but the means for forgiveness and the remission of sin remains the same.

This role of blood in the ancient Temple has been central to the misrepresentation of Judaism down the ages, and is at the root of anti-Semitism. From the misinterpretation of Hebrews 9:22 and Leviticus 17:11 came a belief, expounded upon in the twelfth century, that Jews needed the blood of a Christian child to make *matzah* (unleavened bread) for Passover. We see this strange belief expressed in the widespread blood libels that cost many Jews their lives throughout the Middle Ages, especially around Easter. We see this in Shakespeare's characterization of Shylock in *The Merchant of Venice,* who, more than the money owed him, would rather have a pound of flesh. And we see the more benign version of this idea in the continuance of the false teaching by some preachers that ancient Judaism required blood sacrifices for the remission of sins.

It is distressingly apparent that the "blood curse" the Jews supposedly pronounced upon themselves, as told by Matthew, is the malevolent seed from which later anti-Semitism grew. Matthew reports, "When Pilate saw that he could do nothing, but rather that a riot was beginning, he took some water and washed his hands before the crowd, saying, 'I am innocent of this man's blood; see to it yourselves.' Then the people as a whole answered, 'His blood be on us and on our children!'" (Matthew 27:24–25).

Who was Matthew referring to by "the people as a whole?" All the Jewish people? Was it the same people who welcomed Jesus in the Triumphal Entry a few days earlier? Or, is it possible that the people who handed Jesus over to Pilate were not, in fact, "the people as a whole"? Rather, could they have been a tiny band of traitors who were in cahoots with the Roman government's desire to kill Jesus, along with thousands of other rabbis and Jewish leaders, who were seen as a threat to the Empire? Whatever took place on that fateful day, the issue of blood and blood sacrifices in the Hebrew Scriptures has been terribly distorted for the past two millennia.

Atonement and the Remission of Sin

J EWS IN THE BIBLICAL ERA UNDERSTOOD ATONEMENT DIFFERENTLY than most Jews and Christians think of it today. The word commonly translated as *atonement* literally means "covering" in Hebrew. Yom Kippur, for instance, is usually translated as the "Day of Atonement" in English, but from a Hebraic perspective it can be understood as "the day our sins are covered over." The concrete image of a "cover" is the etymological root of the Hebrew word for "atonement." The meaning was then extended to the secondary sense of what we think of as making amends for our sins and personal reconciliation with God.

The image of "cover" is a common theme in the Bible used to represent various forms of protection. We find the word *cover* in the word *kippa*, the traditional head covering worn by religious Jews. The root of this word is also found in the "pitch" that Noah used to cover and protect his ark (Genesis 6:14). Historically, cities on the borders of Israel often were named with the word *k'far*, meaning "village" and implying that they were intentionally located to "cover" and "protect" the rest of Israel. Capernaum, the town mentioned many times in the New Testament, in Hebrew was called *K'far Nahum* in Jesus's lifetime.

By time the Hebrew word for atonement is translated into English, only the secondary meanings are apparent. It comes out as "make amends, purge, pacify, pardon, reconcile," and the root metaphor of "cover" gets lost. All these meanings are correct to some degree, but they are extensions of the primary idea that atonement has to do with covering. The biblical notion was that our mistakes and sins would be covered over by the process of repentance required in the period around the autumn holiday of Yom Kippur. The idea of having our sins covered by God gave the penitent a sense of being forgiven from his or her wrongdoing.

We have a contrasting, and equally beautiful, metaphor for atonement in the origin of the English word. First used in the sixteenth century, atonement is a contraction of the words *at one*. The original English sense was that atonement had to do with unification, an "at one-ment" with both God and self. It was this image that was then extended to the idea of reparations made for past sins. Both images—having our sins "covered" and being "at one"—create the sense that atonement is part of a natural and life-affirming process.

The Remission of Unintentional Sins

There tends to be a lingering Christian impression that the remission of all sins, for Jews before the time of Jesus, occurred as a result of a penitent bringing offerings to the Temple. Christian theology has historically taught that through the grace ushered in by Christ's final sacrifice, the Temple sacrifices were no longer necessary. However excellent the Christian doctrine of grace is, it has historically been based on a flawed understanding of the Temple system.

It cannot be overstated that the primary purpose of the many types of offerings had nothing to do with sin. Rather, offerings were made to celebrate peace, to express gratitude, or to bring the offerer closer to God. The Paschal offering, for instance, made each Passover, had nothing to do with sin. However, when offerings were used for the remission of sin, they were never used for anything but the remission of the more minor category of unwitting, unintentional sins. Bringing an offering never replaced regret, repentance, confession, and restitution. Sincere repentance is what elicits God's grace, not the ritual offering. As reported by the prophet Hosea, "For I desire steadfast love and not sacrifice, the knowledge of God rather than burnt offerings" (Hosea 6:6). Similarly, take a look at how many times the word *unintentionally* is used in this passage that defines the atonement brought about by bringing an offering to the Temple:

> **Numbers 15:22–28** But if you unintentionally fail to observe all these commandments that the LORD has spoken to Moses . . . if it was done unintentionally without the knowledge of the congregation . . . the priest shall make atonement for all the congregation of the Israelites, and they shall be forgiven; it was unintentional, and they have brought their offering. . . . An individual who sins unintentionally . . . the priest shall make atonement before the LORD for the one who commits an error, when it is unintentional, to make atonement for the person, who then shall be forgiven.

Rabbi Jacob Milgrom, a renowned twentieth-century Bible scholar, is emphatic when he says: "Inadvertence is a key criterion in all expiatory sacrifice. A deliberate, brazen sinner is barred from the sanctuary."[30] No biblical verses summarize the Jewish view of sacrifices and the remission of sin better than the words of the prophet Micah. He states the superiority of justice, mercy, and humility to any ritual sacrifice. This is, in fact, one of the most recurrent themes in the writings of all the prophets, and later on by the rabbis of the Talmud:

> **Micah 6:6–8** With what shall I come before the LORD, and bow myself before God on high? Shall I come before him with burnt offerings, with calves a year old? Will the LORD be pleased with thousands of rams, with tens of thousands of rivers of oil? Shall I give my firstborn for my transgression, the fruit of my body for the sin of my soul? He has told you, O mortal, what is good; and what does the LORD require of you but to do justice, and to love kindness, and to walk humbly with your God?

The message of the prophets to the Jewish people was clear: fulfill the ritual mitzvot, but not at the expense of repentance and doing good in the world. The psalmist states it beautifully: "The sacrifice acceptable to God is a broken spirit" (Psalm 51:17). The prophets preached passionately about the relationship between external rituals and personal transformation. Regarding religious holidays, rituals, and sacrifices, the Holy One asks,

"When you come to appear before me, who asked this from your hand?" (Isaiah 1:12). God is, of course, asking a rhetorical question since it was God who commanded these rituals. But God never intended for these powerful spiritual practices to be carried out in a legalistic, mindless manner. In the Torah, the Holy One expects people to be conscious of the connection between rituals and the moral values they are intended to reinforce.

> **Isaiah 1:11–18** What to me is the multitude of your sacrifices? says the LORD. . . . Bringing offerings is futile; incense is an abomination to me. . . . Your new moons and your appointed festivals my soul hates; they have become a burden to me, I am weary of bearing them. . . . Wash yourselves; make yourselves clean; remove the evil of your doings from before my eyes; cease to do evil, learn to do good; seek justice, rescue the oppressed, defend the orphan, plead for the widow. Come now, let us argue it out, says the LORD: though your sins are like scarlet, they shall be like snow; though they are red like crimson, they shall become like wool.

Scripture, Talmud, and all other rabbinic sources are absolutely clear that ritual offerings were secondary to contrition, regret, and humility:

> **Talmud: Sanhedrin 43b** Rabbi Joshua Levi also said, "When the Temple was in existence, if a man brought a burnt offering, he received credit for a burnt offering; if a meal offering, he received credit for a meal offering. But he who was humble in spirit, Scripture regarded him as though he had brought all the offerings, for it is said, 'The sacrifices of God are a broken spirit' (Psalm 51). And furthermore, his prayers are not despised, for it is written, 'A broken and contrite heart, O God, You will not despise.'"

Eternal Covenants

The system of Temple offerings was based on commandments God gave the Israelites, and that are recorded throughout the Torah. The acceptance of these commandments by the Jewish people is based on Exodus 19:8 where the Israelites tell Moses, "'Everything that the LORD has spoken we will do.' Moses reported the words of the people to the LORD." This, then, becomes the basis for what is called a covenant—an agreement between two parties. In this case, the covenant is between the Jewish people and God. Understanding the nature of biblical covenants will help us understand the relationship between the Mosaic covenant and the Christian covenant.

There are covenants in the Bible between people (e.g., in Genesis 21:32, a covenant between Abimelekh and Abraham) and covenants between people and God. Some of the covenants between people and God are for all people, while others are for the Jewish people. Some Christians speak of the Edenic covenant where God tells Adam and Eve to "be fruitful and multiply" (Genesis 1:28) and to "till" the garden and "keep it" (Genesis 2:15). This is a universal covenant, and even though we're not in Eden, the rabbis teach that these commandments are still in effect.

The Noahic covenant, outlined in Genesis 9:3–9, is discussed in detail by the rabbis in the Talmud (Sanhedrin 56a). It is also universal and binding today. In Acts 15:29 and Acts 21:25, Paul seems to be referring to the Noahic covenant. The Mosaic covenant has universal commandments (the moral laws), and commandments specifically for the Jewish people (commandments regarding the Temple and festivals). This covenant is beautifully summed up in Deuteronomy 29:9–12: "You stand assembled today, all of you, before the LORD your God . . . to enter into the covenant of the LORD your God, sworn by an oath, which the LORD your God is making with you today."

There are dozens of passages in the Bible that assure the Jewish people that God keeps His promises regarding the covenants. Look at Psalm 105:8–10 where the psalmist says, "He is mindful of his covenant forever, of the word that he commanded, for a thousand generations." Regardless of how sinful or righteous the Jewish people are, God assures us that He is good for his word. God does not abrogate his covenants with us, either as a nation or as individuals. In Deuteronomy 4:40, the Jewish people are commanded by Moses to "keep his statutes and his commandments, which I am commanding you today for your own well-being and that of your descendants after you, so that you may long remain in the land that the LORD your God is giving you for all time."

There is no indication here or elsewhere in the Jewish Scriptures that the covenant of Moses is conditional. If the Jewish people fail to observe the commandments, it might not go well for the nation, or they may go into exile temporarily, but the covenant itself will never be abrogated. Adam and Eve certainly disobeyed God, but they did not lose their covenantal relationship to God. Was there a consequence and punishment for their sin? Yes. Did the Edenic covenant lose its force? No. King David committed some awful sins. Did God cancel the covenant with him? No. In fact, read Psalm 89 and see what God tells King David:

> **Psalm 89:30–36** If his children forsake my law and do not walk according to my ordinances, if they violate my statutes and do not keep my commandments, then I will punish their transgression with the rod and their iniquity with scourges; but I will not remove from him my steadfast love, or be false to my faithfulness. I will not violate my covenant, or alter the word that went forth from my lips.

Finally, Moses was not permitted to enter the Promised Land because he struck the rock in Numbers 20:11. Did the Mosaic covenant lose its force? No, an *eternal* covenant means just that—eternal, forever, and irrevocable. Even when the Jewish people disobey God (as we all do on a regular basis), we are assured by the words in 2 Chronicles 21:7 where it says, "Yet the LORD would not destroy the house of David because of the covenant that he had made with David, and since he had promised to give a lamp to him and to his descendants forever."

There certainly are verses in the Younger Testament that have been *interpreted* to mean that a new covenant has replaced the "old" covenant (see Galatians 3:10, Hebrews 8:7), and this certainly might have been the intent of some of the authors. There are also teachings by the church fathers, medieval church leaders, and by modern replacement theologians that attempt to prove that a transfer of election and authority occurred between the "old" and "new" testaments. In Judaism, however, biblical covenants were always adding to previous covenants, rather than replacing them.

The covenant given to Moses was simply a codicil, or addendum, to the covenants given to Adam, Noah, and Abraham. The same is true for the covenant given to David. Later covenants don't replace earlier covenants; otherwise God's use of the terms *eternal* or *everlasting* with each covenant becomes meaningless. The "new" covenant that will take effect in the future will fulfill the biblical prophesy of peace on earth. Jeremiah elegantly outlines its details:

> **Jeremiah 31:31–36** The days are surely coming, says the LORD, when I will make a new covenant with the house of Israel and the house of Judah. . . . No longer shall they teach one another, or say to each other, 'Know the Lord,' for they shall all know me, from the least of them to the greatest, says the LORD; for I will forgive their iniquity, and remember their sin no more.

The future covenant is also spoken of by Ezekiel (Ezekiel 37:26) who described this as a "covenant of peace," since it will usher in the messianic era. Both Micah and Isaiah assure us that warfare will end and that "swords will be turned into plowshares." Joel taught that prophesy will once again be commonplace as it was in ancient Israel (see Joel 2:28).

The religious Jewish seeker has no desire to transcend or grow beyond the laws of Moses, or the ever-unfolding interpretations of our sages and rabbis. In fact, the opposite is true. In Matthew, Jesus affirms the necessity to keep the Mosaic commandments and the oral tradition, but without hypocrisy. He says, "The scribes and the Pharisees sit on Moses' seat; therefore, do whatever they teach you and follow it; but do not do as they do, for they do not practice what they teach" (Matthew 23:2–3). A goal of Jewish spiritual practice is to find the innate joy in serving God through the fulfillment of mitzvot.

SEVEN

Akedah:
The Binding of Isaac

To FULLY UNDERSTAND JESUS ACTUALLY BEING A FIRST-CENTURY rabbi and the Jewish roots of Christianity, it's important to understand several interrelated things:

- The nature of Hebraic thinking and biblical Hebrew
- First-century history from a Jewish perspective
- The central role of Oral Torah in Judaism from before the first century up to today
- The rabbinic use of parables
- Tanakh as it's interpreted by the rabbis

Thus far we've looked at the central role of the Oral Torah in Judaism. We've learned about some of the first-century sects and gained some context about them to deepen our understanding of the roots of Christianity. However, to grasp where Jewish and Christian theology meet each other and the point at which they depart, the story of the binding of Isaac is at the crossroads of our understanding. To get new insight into the Passion of Jesus, it would be wise for us to see it in context to how religious Jews in the first few centuries interpreted the Jewish passion story—the Binding of Isaac. There are extraordinary parallels between the crucifixion story and the story of the near sacrifice of Abraham's son.

The riveting event in Genesis 22 called the *Akedah* (Hebrew meaning "binding") is one of three master stories in Judaism—the other two are the creation and Exodus stories. The Akedah is so central to Jewish theology that it's read in the weekday morning prayer service throughout the year, as well as on Rosh Hashanah, the Jewish New Year. In the Talmud, third-century Rabbi Abbahu asks, "Why do we blow on a ram's horn?" And the Holy One, blessed be He, answers, "Sound a ram's horn before Me so that I may remember on your behalf the binding of Isaac the son of Abraham, and account it to you as if you had bound yourselves before Me" (Rosh Hashanah 16a).

The Akedah has given meaning to persecuted Jews in every age, and is the prototype for understanding what Christian theology calls substitutionary atonement. Judah Goldin wrote, "So profound was the effect of this account on Jewish memory and speculation, every generation of Jews invoked it as leitmotif for its own trials and tragedies."[31] Rabbi Shlomo Yitzhaki, known as Rashi, lived in France in the twelfth century, and is considered one of Judaism's greatest Torah commentators. He taught that Isaac's willingness to give his life at his Father's command brought him the same spiritual merit as though he had actually been sacrificed. Further, Rashi restated the classic teaching that when Jews suffer, God remembers Isaac on the altar as if he had been a burnt offering.

In the twelfth century, Rabbi Efraim ben Jacob of Bonn, Germany, wrote a powerful poem about the Akedah. He finishes with these words: "Thus prayed the binder and the bound that when their descendants commit a wrong, this act be recalled to save them from disaster from all their transgressions and sins." To this day, the spiritual power of the Akedah is drawn upon when a repentant individual needs to invoke God's compassion. That one event, like the revelation at Sinai, was so powerful that it is seen as reverberating through time. It continues to have extraordinary impact upon the lives of Jews today.

Like the Passion of Christ, the Akedah challenges us to ask some hard questions. Hopefully, as people of faith, we won't settle for simplistic answers. The Passion story, for example, forces us to ask the age-old question, "Why does God permit bad things happen to good people?" The Binding of Isaac forces us to ask how Abraham could follow a command to kill his son, even if the command was from God. After all, Abraham argued with God on behalf of Sodom and Gomorrah—why not for his beloved son? Colgate University's Dr. Steven Kepnes points out that the "rabbinic interpreters give multiple reasons for God's command to Abraham to sacrifice Isaac, but one reason that clearly resonates with the theme of the High Holidays is that Abraham's willingness to sacrifice Isaac is an act of merit and atonement upon which the Jewish people could count as expiation for their sins."[32] That's well and good, and the story certainly presents an opportunity for us to sympathize and identify with Isaac. But from a Jewish perspective, we cannot avoid asking why Abraham would consent to such a plan.

In the twentieth century, Rabbi Abraham Joshua Heschel once used the story of the Binding of Isaac as an opportunity to teach an important lesson about God's angels. Rabbi Heschel said that in Poland he once knew a young religious boy who wept when he first heard the story of the Akedah. "Why are you crying? You know that the angel saved Isaac's life!" said Heschel. "But what if the angel had come a moment too late?" the boy replied. The rabbi answered, "Human beings are sometimes late, but angels never are." The Akedah, like the Passion of Christ, creates an endless number of learning opportunities, and it all begins with our questions.

Let's begin by remembering the story. It may not be as familiar as it once was, when every child learned the Bible in school. In Genesis 22 we read how God tested Abraham with the commandment to take his son Isaac and offer him as a sacrifice. Abraham and Isaac leave early the next morning and make the journey to Moriah where God commanded him to go. After three days they arrive, and Abraham builds an altar, binds Isaac upon it, and lifts his knife in preparation for the sacrifice. An angel of the Lord calls to Abraham and says, "Do not lay your hand on the boy or do anything to him; for now I know that you fear God, since you have not withheld your son." Abraham then prepares to substitute a ram in place of his son upon the altar. The angel calls out a second time and declares, "Because you have done this, and have not withheld your son, your only son, I will indeed bless you, and I will make your offspring as numerous as the stars of heaven and as the sand that is on the seashore. . . ." The story ends with Abraham returning alone to where his servants had been waiting before going on to Beer-sheba.

Looking back at an earlier story in Genesis 17:11, Abraham received the commandment from God to circumcise Isaac when he was eight days old. Thus, it's in fulfillment of this commandment to Abraham that Jews continue to perform the powerful rite of circumcision. However, it's only as an adult, at the Akedah, that Isaac makes the choice to willingly enter the covenant, as he seems voluntarily to lie upon the sacrificial altar that his father has made. When a boy is circumcised, Jewish tradition teaches, we remember Isaac's circumcision, and a shower of blessings descends from heaven upon the child. His parents are also blessed since, on a spiritual level, it's as if they've offered their son up to God as Abraham did with Isaac twice—first at his circumcision, and then at the Akedah when Isaac was an adult.

Wrestling with the Story

And yet, we wrestle with all of this, for good reasons. Along with the traditional explanations of the Akedah story within Judaism, over the millennia rabbis and Jewish parents alike have wondered how Abraham could have gone along with such a command, even knowing it was a test from God. The nineteenth-century Danish Christian philosopher Søren Kierkegaard makes a statement about Abraham's ethics that is both startling and unnerving when he writes: "What ordinarily tempts a man is that which would keep him from doing his duty, but in this case the temptation is itself the ethical . . . which would keep him from doing God's Will. Therefore, Abraham arouses my admiration. He, at the same time, appalls me."[33] Enlightenment philosopher Immanuel Kant is then in line with many rabbis and Jewish parents throughout history when he envisioned what he thinks should have been Abraham's response to God's request:

Abraham should have replied to this punitive divine voice: "That I may not kill my good son is absolutely certain. But you who appear to me as God is not certain and cannot become certain, even though the voice were to sound from the very heavens." [For] that a voice which one seems to hear cannot be divine one can be certain of . . . in case what is commanded is contrary to moral law. However majestic or supernatural it may appear to be, one must regard it as a deception. [34]

We cannot help but wonder why Abraham didn't argue with God when he was asked to sacrifice Isaac, just as he had when advocating for the people of Sodom and Gomorrah. One midrash suggests that Abraham used his silence as leverage on behalf of the future generations when he spoke with God after the Akedah: "Abraham said 'Master of the Universe, when You said to me 'take your son . . . ' I did not argue with You. I suppressed my natural feelings of compassion and was prepared to sacrifice him to fulfill Your will. Now I have something to ask of You. May it be Your will that when the descendants of Isaac commit transgressions and perform wicked deeds, that You remember the binding of Isaac, and that You become filled with compassion for them" (Genesis Rabbah 56:10).

Jesus and Isaac: Parallel Stories

From the first century on, Jesus was portrayed within the church as a "type" of Isaac. Several of the early church fathers, including the bishop of Sardis (died 189 CE) and Origen (185–251 CE), compared the story of Jesus to that of Isaac. The binding of Isaac was purposely linked to the story of Jesus's death. In many churches this linkage is evident in the Easter liturgy, the Eucharist, and in the Christian prayer for the dying. Within Judaism, the binding of Isaac, along with the suffering servant passages in Isaiah 53, have helped the Jewish people understand their suffering and persecution throughout history. The atoning power of the millions of Jews, millions of Isaacs, who died as martyrs (including Jesus) carries forward from generation to generation. In these ways and more, Jesus's story can be said to parallel Isaac's story. Dr. Leora Batnitzky, professor at Princeton University, writes:

> The themes of the death and resurrection of the beloved son (Isaac and Jesus, respectively) play crucial roles in the formation and development of both the Jewish and Christian traditions. The Christian interpretation of Isaiah 52:13–53:12 is in keeping with the Jewish interpretation of the binding of Isaac throughout the rabbinic and medieval periods. Both narratives describe the sacrifice of an innocent, beloved son who is sacrificed on account of the father's love for a God who demands such a sacrifice. [35]

Both Jewish and Christian theologians have pointed out the similarities between the stories of Isaac and Jesus. Both of their births were foretold by angels, and each is called a "son of promise." They each had a miraculous birth, and both were called an "only" son. Isaac carried wood to his sacrifice and Jesus carried the wooden cross to his. Both men were in their thirties. Both were brought to a mount (Moriah and Calvary) and went willingly to the slaughter. The story of Jesus battling Satan to overcome death itself (Hebrews 2:14) is parallel to the midrash where Abraham battles with Satan on the way to Mt. Moriah (Genesis Rabbah 56:4). As the Jewish scholar Shalom Spiegel explains:

> Already in the Epistle of Barnabas, Isaac is referred to as the prototype for the sufferings and trials of Jesus. Irenaeus exhorts Christians that in their faith they too must be on the alert to bear the cross, just as Isaac bore the wood for the burnt-offering wood. . . . Christian writers make Isaac the symbol of their faith, and so interpret the *Akedah* chapter as to have it serve as a foreshadowing of the death of Jesus. [36]

Even the image of Jesus's resurrection on the third day was told in relation to the Akedah taking place on the third day of Abraham and Isaac's extraordinary journey. The rabbis calculate that Isaac was forty years old when he married Rebecca, which would have been three years after the Akedah. Could it be that the three days Jesus spent in the tomb before his resurrection was an echo of Isaac's departure for three years between the Akedah and his resurrection or reappearance? The notion of something crucial happening on the "third day" is in fact revealed in several places in the Tanakh.

For example, the prophet Hosea taught that separation from God is a kind of spiritual death. After repentance, God will "revive" (resurrect) each person on the third day. The prophet said, "Come, let us return to the LORD; for it is he who has torn, and he will heal us. . . . After two days he will revive us; on the third day he will raise us up, that we may live before him" (Hosea 6:1–2). Joseph made his brothers wait for three days (Genesis 42:18) so that they could live. Jonah had a death and rebirth experience in the belly of the fish for three days (Jonah 1:17). Returning from exile, the Israelites waited three days (Ezra 8:32). And Queen Esther put on her royal apparel on the third day (Esther 5:1), just to name a few.

For some Christian theologians, the goal of linking Jesus to Isaac is to read back into the Torah to "prove" that Isaac's binding was merely a foreshadowing of the greater crucifixion story that was yet to come. Their aim is to show that Jesus's death was the perfection and completion of the Isaac story. But this attitude is a perfect example of the insidious influence of what is called supersessionism (also called replacement theology). This is the belief that the Christian covenant supersedes the Jewish covenantal relationship to God. The terms "old" and "new" testaments were originally intended to signify that one covenant has now replaced the other.

From a Jewish perspective, the similarities in the stories do not demonstrate any kind of completion or fulfillment. Rather, an accurate reading of history shows that Christianity was built upon the existing foundations of

Judaism, which should be celebrated by both church and synagogue. It is probable that in the early centuries after Jesus's lifetime, the message of the atoning power of Jesus's sacrifice was told in the light of the already well-known story of the atoning power of the Akedah. The reverse is likely also true—that as the atoning power of Jesus's death and resurrection became more widely taught throughout the growing Christian world, Jews found new meaning in their already ancient Isaac story.

More Specific Parallels

There are other parallel stories, too, between the Testaments and traditions. For example, the use of "son" to describe Jesus as the "son of God" is an echo of the biblical words used to describe the nation of Israel (Exodus 4:22), the people of Israel (Deuteronomy 14:1), King David (Psalm 2:7), and Isaac (Genesis 22:2). Just as Isaac is called Abraham's "only son," so Jesus is called the "only" begotten son in the Younger Testament (John 3:16). The image of Isaac as Abraham's son parallels the words describing Jesus: "This is my Son, the Beloved, with whom I am well pleased" (Matthew 3:17). The Hebrew word for "only" in the Isaac story also means "unique," and describing Jesus as a "unique" son may uncover another layer of meaning for Christians. Jesus is understood as a sacrifice who is offered on behalf of the people. Many Christians have described Golgotha in the Younger Testament as an echo of both Mt. Moriah and Mt. Sinai in the Elder Testament.

Also, there are good reasons why the image of Jesus riding into Jerusalem on a donkey on the Sunday before his crucifixion reminded people of Abraham and Isaac riding to Mt. Moriah on a donkey. As God gave Abraham a ram to be sacrificed in the place of Isaac, so Christianity teaches that Jesus was the sacrificial lamb offered in place of every Christian. The metaphor of Jesus as the "Lamb of God, who takes away the sin of the world" (John 1:29) seems to be an echo of the Akedah (Genesis 22:8), where Abraham tells his son that God will provide a lamb. Christians teach that Jesus goes willingly to the cross for all humankind. One can hear an echo of the Isaac story when

Jesus says, "For this reason the Father loves me, because I lay down my life in order to take it up again. No one takes it from me, but I lay it down of my own accord. I have power to lay it down, and I have power to take it up again" (John 10:17–18). Just as Isaac went willingly with his earthly father Abraham to Moriah (Genesis 22:6), so Jesus went willingly with his heavenly Father to Calvary.

The Torah says that Abraham and Isaac "walked on together" (Genesis 22:6). However, the Hebrew word being used means "one in purpose." When Jesus says, "The Father and I are one" (John 10:30), could he have used the word *yakhdav,* meaning "one in purpose" as an echo of Abraham and Isaac? Many of us would use that word to describe the ideal relationship between Judaism and Christianity: the two religions are not intended by God to be one in physical form, but one in purpose.

As a parallel to Genesis 22:9–11, Jesus too was laid "upon the wood" of the cross along with tens of thousands of other Jews during the first and second centuries by the Roman Empire. As the ram in the Abraham story was caught in a thorny thicket (Genesis 22:13), so Jesus wore a crown of thorns (Matthew 27:29). Christ's death is seen as substitutionary for Christians (2 Corinthians 5:21) in the same way that the ram was a substitution for Isaac. I would suggest that most first-century followers of Jesus never believed that his was a "better" version of Isaac's story. Rather, it was probably understood as one more unique application of the Isaac story.

The Death and Resurrection of Isaac

It is surprising for both Jews and Christians to learn that among many interpretations of the Binding of Isaac familiar to first-century Jews, several legends suggest that Isaac actually was sacrificed and resurrected. Some say he literally died; some say he died only momentarily; and others say he was sacrificed figuratively. While these interpretations were never the majority view within Judaism, this possibility nevertheless has persisted as an important minority opinion throughout the centuries.

One of the great sages in the Middle Ages was Abraham Ibn Ezra, who strongly disagreed with the stories of Isaac's death and resurrection. He wrote, "He who asserts that Abraham slew Isaac and abandoned him, and that afterwards Isaac came to life again is speaking contrary to Writ." In light of the Church's traditional linkage of Jesus to Isaac, it's certainly worthwhile examining the Jewish sources that suggest that Isaac was actually sacrificed. Jewish scholar Judah Goldin writes:

> When we find . . . that almost two thousand years ago . . . there was already plainly recorded a notion that the faithful patriarch did lay his hand upon the boy, did inflict wound—and more. . . . Perhaps the view that Abraham did something to the lad on the altar was an erratic and fugitive opinion. How, then shall we explain the persistence of this view, or variants thereof, in generation after generation of some of Israel's most pious souls? And those who repeat this account do so without any sense of the bizarre.[37]

The author of Hebrews may have known these stories since he appears to be referring to them; he also seems to assume that his readers knew what he was talking about when he wrote:

Hebrews 11:17–19 By faith Abraham, when put to the test, offered up Isaac. He who had received the promises was ready to offer up his only son, of whom he had been told, "It is through Isaac that descendants shall be named after you." He considered the fact that God is able even to raise someone from the dead—and figuratively speaking, he did receive him back.

Because of intense prejudice against Jews and Judaism, there's been a self-protective response by Jewish communities to keep a safe distance from the theology, rituals, and beliefs associated with Christianity. Very few Jewish people today even know how parallel the story of Jesus's sacrifice is to Isaac's sacrifice, and how one was told in relation to the other. Most Jews are not aware of the Jewish midrashim that Isaac was actually sacrificed and resurrected. Because of supersessionism, many Christians are not taught that the story of Jesus was originally understood as an analogue to the Isaac story, not as a completion of it. Nor do most Christians learn about the atoning power of Isaac's sacrifice from a Jewish perspective.

Three times a day religious Jews chant a series of powerful petitionary prayers to God regarding personal issues of strength, holiness, understanding, repentance, healing, peace, and all the key issues that relate to daily life. Jewish tradition says that Abraham, Isaac, and Jacob composed the first three of these prayers respectively. Abraham's prayer is about the Jewish people's deep connection to our ancestors. Jacob's prayer is an affirmation of holiness. But Isaac's prayer is about personal strength and the Jewish belief (adopted by Christianity) in the future resurrection of the dead. It seems possible that the rabbis associated this prayer with Isaac because of the stories that purported he was resurrected from the dead. Here is one of many accounts that try to explain how this daily blessing might have been composed:

> **Midrash: Pirkei D'Rebbe Eliezer:** Rabbi Judah says, "When the sword touched Isaac's throat his soul flew clean out of him. And the Holy One let His voice be heard from between the cherubim, 'Lay not thy hand upon the lad.' The lad's soul was returned to his body. Then his father unbound him and Isaac rose, knowing that in this way the dead would come back to life in the future, whereupon he began to recite 'Blessed are You, O Lord, who resurrects the dead.'"[38]

Now, pause for a moment. Consider again the meaning and use of midrash in Jewish tradition. The suggestion that Isaac was sacrificed is not part of a denominational creed or dogma intended to be "believed." The rabbis treated scriptural ambiguity as a spiritual tool since it inspires people to ask questions to enliven learning and strengthen devotion. The religious Jew doesn't need to believe in, or agree with, a midrash to learn something from it. Sometimes a student learns the most from midrashim, or interpretations, he or she disagrees with. To Jews the entire act of study and debate "for the sake of heaven" is elevated to a level of spiritual practice akin to prayer.

The sacred character of a midrash is not that it's true or not true, reasonable or fantastic, but that it compels the student to think and respond, thereby becoming an active participant in the *britt*. A midrash propels the imagination. It inspires the student to question someone else's "authoritative" interpretation of a biblical verse or story. It permits everyone to be partners with the Creator. One of the most elegant and unique ways Jews wrestle with God is through midrash—searching for deeper and deeper meanings in the text of the Tanakh.

Each of the following questions about the Akedah is the basis for its own midrash within Judaism. The classic midrashim continue to inspire ingenious discussions among the Jewish people as they have for thousands of years. Did God really tell Abraham to sacrifice Isaac or just to "bring him up" as it literally says in Hebrew? Was it Satan who convinced God in the first place to give Abraham such an extreme test? Was Abraham just hearing voices in his own head to even consider sacrificing Isaac? Did Abraham actually slaughter Isaac? Did Sarah actually die because she thought Abraham did slaughter her son? Did Sarah divorce Abraham after the Akedah because he did that to her son? Christian friends of mine see the candor of the midrashim as refreshing, even though the questions at first sound startling and irreverent. The rabbis were not afraid to ask extreme questions, or make inventive propositions, since they weren't looking for correct answers. They want us to think, and through thinking and debating, the Torah is kept alive.

The Haftarah and Resurrection

Every Sabbath in most synagogues throughout the world the same selection from the Torah is read. A second reading called the *haftarah* comes from another part of the Bible (often from the prophets) in order to supplement the theme of the weekly Torah reading. The Younger Testament reports (Luke 4:16) that Jesus was a reader of the weekly prophetic section of the Bible in a synagogue where he attended services.

Each autumn when the Binding of Isaac story is chanted aloud in its haunting, ancient melody, it is supplemented by the chanting of 2 Kings 4:1–37, which recounts the story of Elisha and the miraculous conception, birth, death, and resurrection of the Shunamite's son. Did the rabbis select and pair this story with the Akedah on purpose to inspire us to consider the idea that Isaac might have been sacrificed and resurrected? Did first through fourth-century Christians use the story of the Shunamite's son, as well as the Isaac story, as Christian theology was being formulated? It seems likely that when first-century Jews heard the story of the life, death, and resurrection of Jesus, it was not startling or shocking. Stories of resurrection were already well established in the Bible, in legends, and in the Jewish oral tradition.

As surprising as it may sound to Jews today, the idea that Jesus may have been resurrected, and that his martyrdom has atoning power, is not a departure from Jewish theology. That some prefer to think of Jesus as the only biblical person who was resurrected is not correct. That some describe Jesus as the only martyr whose death has atoning power is the point where Christian and Jewish theologies diverge. Concerning his own suffering and death at the hand of the Romans in the first century, Rabbi Ishmael prayed, "May I be an atonement for the children of Israel" (Mishnah: Negaim 2:1). The Talmud also teaches, "When there are righteous people in a generation, the righteous are seized by death for the sins of that generation" (Talmud: Shabbat 33b). The disciples of Jesus likely knew this teaching.

Substitutionary Atonement, the Ram, and Us

Our sages understood the suffering of Isaac as an individual, and Israel as a nation as examples of substitutionary atonement. The offering of fruit, grain, or an animal brought to the Temple in Jerusalem created opportunities for people to achieve a deep state of self-awareness through this process of substitution, or what the rabbis called "exchange." When an animal offering was made, the penitent needed to fulfill two prerequisites for the exchange to have an effect on a spiritual level. First, the person needed to feel regret for his or her transgressions. Second, the person needed to empathize with the suffering of the animal who was dying in "exchange" for his or her sins. When Abraham prayed, I imagine that he must have known what a sacrifice the ram was making, because it was a substitution for his own son. It was Abraham's deep sympathy that induced the Holy One to ratify the validity of the exchange. When slaughtering the ram, Abraham might have thought, "This could have been my son! Thank you God. God, please bless this ram!"

> **Midrash: Genesis Rabbah 56:9** Abraham prayed, "Sovereign of the Universe! Look upon the blood of this ram as though it were the blood of my son Isaac; its limbs as though they were my son's limbs. We have learned that when a man declares 'This animal be instead of this one, in exchange for that, or a substitute for this, it is a valid exchange.'"

Christianity demonstrates the substitutionary atonement provided by Jesus through verses like "For the Son of Man came not to be served but to serve, and to give his life a ransom for many" (Mark 10:45). Judaism teaches there is substitutionary atonement in the suffering of Israel and in the suffering of the innocent. The ram in the Akedah provides the spiritual exchange that permitted Isaac to live. Our empathy for both Isaac and the ram hopefully inspires us to want to better our lives. In Genesis 22:13 we read, "Abraham went and took the ram and offered it up for a burnt offering *instead* of his son." On a spiritual level, the substitution of the ram for Isaac reverberates from generation to generation, and continues to be an effectual step in the atonement process for everyone today who contemplates the story.

To many Christians, the event of Jesus's suffering and resurrection is also timeless, reverberating from generation to generation. For example, according to Paul, the resurrection is not just for the future—its power can have an impact on the life of a Christian every day. As Christians share in Jesus's sufferings, they spiritually partake of the resurrection right now. In his letter to the Philippians Paul said, "I want to know Christ and the power of his resurrection and the sharing of his sufferings by becoming like him in his death, if somehow I may attain the resurrection from the dead" (Philippians 3:10–11).

Today, modern Jews practice an elegant form of spiritual substitution or exchange. At the start of the High Holidays each autumn, the Binding of Isaac is experienced as a substitute for the sins of the people of Israel. Judaism teaches that the affliction of the righteous, the poor, the orphan, and the innocent are efficacious substitutions. This is not in any way to be understood as a justification for suffering. From a modern, psychological perspective it could be that when a person empathizes with another's suffering, there is efficacy in the empathy. Today, when there is no Temple, *tzadakah,* or charity, is seen as a form of exchange that has great efficacy. Judaism teaches that fasting during Yom Kippur, the Jewish Day of Atonement, is also a sacrifice in which the individual substitutes body fat for the elevation of the soul. On Yom Kippur, the Day of Atonement, worshipers hear Leviticus 16 chanted aloud about how the two goats were used in a profound and mysterious rite of substitution. Somehow, just by hearing about this Torah ritual, a spiritual exchange takes place; just by contemplating the scapegoat[39] story, it is as if the worshiper is participating in the ritual. On a spiritual level, empathy has efficacy in the atonement process.

The Friday night Sabbath service in Jewish homes is also a magnificent example of substitution, and this ritual became the basis for the Eucharist. Every Friday evening as the Sabbath begins, the candles, wine, and bread are substitutes for various elements in the ancient Temple's system of offerings. In Judaism, the substitutionary rites and practices of the Sabbath and the Passover seder have contributed to Jewish survival for the past two thousand years.

Rabbi Don Isaac Abarbanel, one of the leaders of Spanish Jewry during the fifteenth century, taught that in the story of the Akedah there "lies the entire glory of Israel and their merit before their Father in Heaven. And that is why it pervades our prayers every day." After the Crusades and Inquisitions, the Jews of Spain were being murdered and expelled from their homes under the edict of Ferdinand and Isabella in 1492. Don Isaac wrote, "I saw many Jews, men, women, and even young children, tortured and burned at the stake in His Holy Name and I bear witness that at that time they did not scream or utter any expression of pain, but left this world in serenity and peace."[40] Commenting on Don Isaac's words, Tzvi Freeman writes:

> This is the strength of Abraham and Isaac within us. For they opened the channel by which this power comes down to us to this day. This power not only to die, but to live as Jews. This power to remain Jews despite every adversity God could throw at us. For this is the greatest miracle: That in this day and age there remain any Jews at all, that we still have each other, our Torah and our heritage. It is a power beyond nature, beyond the ego of a created being. And with it we are eternal.[41]

Without that one ram, Isaac might not have lived to have children, and there would have been no Jacob, no Joseph, no Moses, no Elijah, no Jesus, no Jewish people, and no Christianity. Without the substitution of that one ram, the covenant could not have been fulfilled. The Talmud reports, "Since Isaac was redeemed, it is as though all Israel had been redeemed" (Jerusalem Talmud: Tannit 1:4).

A Personal Akedah Tale

Bob Dylan once sang, "God said to Abraham, 'Kill me a son.' Abe said, 'Man, you must be puttin' me on.'"[42] The phrasing may seem a bit startling, but the notion of God asking his servant to slay his son has always been seen as a startling request worthy of discussion and debate in both Judaism and Christianity. I sense that this is exactly why God might have wanted this story in the Torah—to inspire debate on the cruelty of child sacrifice and to illuminate this horrific, idolatrous practice. Yet rabbis throughout the ages have correctly wondered why Abraham would argue on behalf of Sodom and Gomorrah and then remain silent when asked to sacrifice his own son. Did Abraham simply know all along that God would never permit him to commit such a sacrifice? Abraham's silence concerning the command to offer his son has resounded throughout the ages to every father and mother who hears this story and wonders, "What would I do if God made such a request of me?"

It so happened that the Akedah was the Torah portion that the annual reading cycle required my son to chant for his *bar mitzvah* in 1997. At first I dreaded having to discuss with my "only son" all the details of child sacrifice as it was practiced in Mesopotamia. It was a privilege to teach Ari how Abraham and Sarah stood up against certain cultural beliefs and practices within their culture, yet how could I explain to my son why Abraham did not stand up to God when asked to slay his son Isaac? How could I explain why Isaac would even go along with such a preposterous plan? We discussed all the issues, and all the ins and outs of the story. In good Talmudic fashion, we even discussed the possibility that Abraham actually failed the test because he did not question God.

One evening while practicing chanting directly from the Torah scroll, my son, Ari, looked up at me and asked, "Dad, if God told you to sacrifice me, what would you do?" I thought, "Oy! Do I have to answer him?" It was almost as if Ari were an angel giving me a microcosmic, intellectual version of Abraham's test of faith. My eyes filled with tears, and the answer seemed to come from a deep place within me. I said, "Ari, if God asked me to do that, and I was really positive it was God and not my imagination; if I was one hundred percent certain it was God and that I was not just hearing voices inside my own head; if I was totally positive it was Adonai, I would say, 'God, forget about it! No way, God! I would never do that to my son. I love You and I love my son, and you already tested Abraham anyway—that's enough testing!'" Ari looked up at me surprised, delighted, and so relieved. He smiled and I smiled. He laughed and I laughed. I thought, "Thank you, God. I think I passed the test!"

III
Theo Logos:
Knowing God

EIGHT

Hebraic Thinking

THEOLOGY IS THE STUDY OF THE WAYS WE KNOW AND EXPERIENCE God. The word itself comes from two Greek roots: *theos* meaning "god," and *logos* meaning "word." In Greek philosophy the idea of *logos* was extended to also mean "knowledge." We use this root today as a suffix to describe the body of knowledge for particular disciplines such as psychology or sociology. In most of the biblical era, the Jewish people didn't have what we think of as an intellectually defined theology. They had stories, practical applications of those stories, laws, and action directives from God—what we call commandments or mitzvot. The theology of the Hebrews was rooted in a way of thinking that was holistic and unique, what has been called Hebraic thinking.

Imagine perceiving the world in such a way that past and present, time and space, nature and spirituality are seen as integrated and not separated into disconnected spheres of experience—this is the essence of Hebraic thinking. Our biblical ancestors experienced their own ancestors in a kind of present-tense state since the line between the living and the dead was somewhat blurred. In this "primitive" way of seeing the world, there was no significant distinction between what we call the animate and inanimate worlds. Modern Jews, Christians, and academic scholars alike would do well to relearn the Bible through the thought processes of the biblical characters themselves.

Indeed, I'm not sure we can really understand what Moses, the prophets, or Jesus were really saying without a clear comprehension of the Hebraic mode of thought. Understanding Hebraic thinking can give us a glimpse into the theology of our biblical ancestors, especially how they understood the interrelationship between the natural and spiritual worlds. But it also gives us insight into how they might have interpreted the original words, stories, and concepts in the Bible. Most of us learn the Bible in translation, thousands of years after the words were spoken, from an entirely different culture, and viewed through a radically different lens.

Language The Hebrew language and imagery of the Tanakh reflects the Hebraic mindset. The grammar of biblical Hebrew differs from that of Greek, Latin, or modern English. Words tend to have multiple meanings in Hebrew, and the sense of past, present, and future is often ambiguous and difficult to translate literally. Words relating to time, number, and gender are more ambiguous in the biblical Hebrew than the modern reader is used to, except in poetry. The result has been a conscious translation of biblical words to conform to European and American sensibilities, rather than to the original sense of the Hebrew. Biblical scholar Dr. Mary Ellen Chase cites an example relating to biblical grammar:

> Biblical Hebrew attests to a different way of thinking than our modern languages permit. For example, the Hebrew spoken by Moses and Jesus possessed no definite, clearly defined tenses like those common to modern, Western languages. The two forms of Hebrew verbs, the perfect and the imperfect, distinguish only between action which is completed and action which is still going on . . . a seemingly completed action is never truly completed in the Hebrew mind and imagination, but still lives and moves in the present, and that those imperishable Realities which make his present will continue to make his future as well. In this sense his patriarchal ancestors have never died, and his prophets for him still live and will continue to live in his mind as they lived in the past.[43]

As an example, the Hebrew word *ruakh* has the triple meaning of breath, wind, and spirit. The Hebraic mindset in biblical times understood the innate interrelationship between body, nature, and spirituality as expressed in this one word. In Genesis 1:2, most English Bibles translate this word as "spirit" as in "the Spirit of God moved upon the face of the waters." From a Hebraic point of view, it would be just as accurate to translate this verse as "the Wind" or "the Breath of God." Interestingly, the same holistic sense of the physical world being connected to spiritual world is found in the Sanskrit word *pranayama*, the Greek root *pneuma*, and the Latin word *spiritus*. All these words have the multiple meanings of "spirit" and "breath."

Opposites The Western, dialectical way of seeing the world tends to separate opposites, whereas the Hebraic mindset comprehends opposites (such as physicality and spirituality) in a unified, codependent interrelationship. These opposites may be in the natural world (day and night, summer and winter) or within our personal lives (birth and death, sadness and joy). The opposites may have metaphysical importance (this world and the world to come, nature and angels) or theological importance (God as immanent and God as transcendent, good and evil, God and Satan).

The Western mindset tends to see these opposites in adversarial or moral terms (birth is good, death is bad). In the Bible, opposites tend to be balance points, and are not split apart from each other. In other words, oppositional forces (life and death) and elements (earth, water, air, and fire) are in a divinely guided relationship even when there seems to be antagonism and tension between them from a human perspective. The author of Ecclesiastes lists a series of oppositional concepts that people throughout history have tried to reconcile. He wrote, "For everything there is a season, and a time for every matter under heaven: A time to be born, and a time to die; a time to plant, and a time to pluck up that which is planted" (Ecclesiastes 3:1–2).

Another example of Hebraic thinking can be seen by examining the word *shalom*. Commonly translated as "hello, good-bye" and "peace," *shalom* is etymologically derived from a root meaning "wholeness." Wholeness joins opposites together. We say *shalom* when we greet friends and when we bid them farewell. In the most opposite of situations, coming and going, we use the same word, *shalom*. When I come from somewhere I am going to some place else. When I realize this, I feel "wholeness," and that is a source of peace—the third meaning of *shalom*. This one word conveys the notion that all opposing energies are linked and part of a single whole. True peace must have wholeness as its foundation. It takes the integration of two opposing positions for there to be real *shalom*.

Sacred Ambiguity The Hebraic thinker lives with scriptural ambiguity (not to be confused with moral relativism) and appreciates the multiple meanings of words. For example, *yom,* the Hebrew word for day, has multiple meanings: a twenty-four-hour day, the daylight period of a day, an indefinite period of time, a year, a lifetime, or a thousand years. As David chanted, "For a thousand years in your sight are like yesterday when it is past, or like a watch in the night" (Psalm 90:4). This kind of scriptural ambiguity tends to limit literalism. How can I interpret the word "day" as a literal twenty-four-hour day when the Tanakh uses that same word with several very different meanings?

It's impossible for the finite human mind to truly grasp eternity, or to use biblical text to try to calculate how much time it took the Creator to create the heavens and the earth. For this reason, people who think in a Hebraic or holistic manner (regardless of religion) do not have a problem accepting a synchronicity between scientific estimates of the earth's age and the biblical script. If someone asks me if I believe the world was created in six days I can say, "Yes." And when asked if I believe the world is fifteen billion years old, I can also say "yes." It seems to me that religions are at their best when they can integrate the genius of both science and spirituality.

Time and Space When we get to the relationship between time and space, Hebraic thinking is even more wondrous. For example, the root of the Hebrew word *olam* has the multiple meanings of "world" (an entity in space), "forever" (the eternity of time), and "secret" (a hidden mystery). Unfortunately, when *olam* is translated using different English words, the reader does not know that the same Hebrew word is being used. In this single Hebrew word is a concept implying a confluence between time, space, and mystery.

To the prophets, the future can be thought of as a kind of recollection of God's own preconception. That which God predestined long ago only appears to be in the future from our limited perspective. This is what Solomon might have meant when he said, "What has been is what will be, and what has been done is what will be done" (Ecclesiastes 1:9). Maybe this is part of the phenomenon Einstein was describing regarding the time/space continuum. Dr. Chase writes:

> To the ancient Hebrews a thousand years might, indeed, be as yesterday; or each of the six so-called days in which God created the heavens and the earth might mean to them an incalculable expanse of time. Nor must the events of their history be understood as in any sense dated by them, placed in any secure niches of time. These events are forever in their consciousness, constantly in their hearts and before their eyes, in their present as well as in their remote past. In other words, the happenings of their history were timeless to them. [44]

Lawrence A. Hoffman applies this aspect of Hebraic thinking to understanding Christian Eucharistic liturgy, which he says "arises as a consequence of Jesus' command, 'Do this in remembrance of me.'"[45] Dr. Hoffman then goes on to compare Jesus's words to the practice that remains so central to Jewish home worship today on Shabbat—the sanctification of the wine called *Kiddush*. The *Kiddush* prayer is an act of remembrance or *zikarone*. He writes:

But it is hard for modern readers to grasp what remembrance meant back then. . . . Though Jews today may think of these words just as wistful glances back in time, the rabbis saw *zikarone* [remembrance] as anamnesis: making the past present. It helps to think of remembrance as a "pointer" through time, connecting the present to the past. If we adopt the notion from physics of a time/space continuum, the problem of making the past present goes away. Since time and space are actually a single unit, we can transform one into the other just by changing the metaphors in which we think. Imagine, then, that all things that ever happened coexist at different points in space.[46]

This same sense of anamnesis, time past experienced as time present, is central to the annual Passover seder, the yearly retelling of the Passover story accompanied by a festive meal in Jewish homes. In the Hagaddah, the book containing the stories and prayers to be read at the seder, it is written "In every generation a person must regard himself as if he came forth himself out of Egypt." The annual retelling of the Exodus story is accompanied by wine and foods emblematic of slavery and liberation, and has the effect of a spiritual time machine.

The King James translation of Genesis 1:1 is, "In the beginning God created the heaven and the earth." The problem with this translation, and most other Christian translations, is that the verb "creating" is translated in past tense as "created." Modern Jewish translations are closer to the Hebrew. In the Stone translation we get, "In the beginning of God's creating. . . ." The Plaut translation says, "When God began to create. . . ." And in the Hirsch translation we have, "From the beginning did God create. . . ." Contemporary Jewish translations attempt to preserve the actual sense of the Hebrew, where God's creating continues to this very moment.[47] Again, Dr. Chase sums up the Hebraic sense of the past very beautifully:

What we have to try to understand is that when the ancient Hebrew writer told of events in the past, he did not remember them as we do in the light of the present, but instead took himself back into their time, real and living, if indefinite to him. Once securely back there, the things of which he wrote might well seem uncompleted to him. The present, merely as present, meant little to him since he lived in infinity. The time to which he was sensitive was not our time, governed by an inflexible, immovable, and absolute calendar. His time knew no perceptible beginning and end, no clearly defined past, no circumscribed present, and no discernible future except that in the Infinite Mind of God.[48]

There are several examples of this transcendent sense of time in the Torah. As Moses is nearing the end of his life he says, "I am making this covenant, sworn by an oath, not only with you who stand here with us today before the LORD our God, but also with those who are not here with us today" (Deuteronomy 29:14–15). The more mystically oriented rabbis interpret this as Moses actually affirming the covenant with the Jewish people in all future generations. Moses's statement is not seen as a metaphor or rhetorical device. It is understood as a metaphysical reality that was, and remains, part of the worldview of Judaism. Many Christians recall the crucifixion, resurrection, and Pentecost with the same sense of anamnesis, or transtemporal consciousness. Rev. Dr. Clark Williamson, for instance, describes the Christian sense of redemption with a Hebraic sensibility when he writes:

> For Christians redemption has several meanings. In one meaning it points to a past event or events where redemption has already occurred. In another sense, it is a present event, insofar as people appropriate and are transformed by the meaning of the past event(s) of redemption. . . . One can sense this is precisely how Paul wanted to understand the resurrection—not as a past event, but as an event within his own life. . . . [49]

Give Ear O Heavens This brings us to the penultimate example of Hebraic thinking. When Moses chants "Give ear, O heavens, and I will speak; let the earth hear the words of my mouth" (Deuteronomy 32:1), it is likely that what we perceive as a figure of speech, he perceived as a literal reality—that the sky and the earth could actually heed his call to them to witness his words. However, it seems that our dialectical mindset has severed the link between the animate and the inanimate worlds. To the ancient Hebrews, and to other Native peoples, the creation is pulsing with the Creator's life force. At a deeper level of reality, the animate and inanimate kingdoms are inseparable.

The prophet Isaiah does the same when he requests "Hear, O heavens, and listen, O earth; for the Lord has spoken (Isaiah 1:2). Whether it is the heavens hearing Moses, or the earth hearing Isaiah, what are mere figures of speech to many people were true perceptions of reality to the Israelites. In more modern times, the nineteenth-century mystic Rebbe Nachman of Breslav taught, "How wonderful it would be if one could only be worthy of hearing the song of the grass. Each blade of grass sings out to God without any ulterior motive, and without expecting any reward. It's most wonderful to hear its song, and worship God in its midst" (*Sichot Haran* 163).

What the more rational hemisphere of brain perceives as a quaint fairytale in the book of Judges 9:8–15 was likely understood very differently by our ancestors—not exactly literally, but not as a fairytale either. There you'll find a detailed discussion among the trees and plants in their search for a king. The Hebrews took the story as a parable, of course, but that did not diminish their perception that trees were also capable of communicating on some nonverbal level. They weren't naive enough to think that trees literally spoke words, but nor were they so self-important as to believe that trees do not have their own kind of intelligence and language.

Psalm 148 is a magnificent example of the monotheistic animism that is a cornerstone of Hebraic thinking. David is literally talking to everything without regard to the arbitrary distinctions between the animate and inanimate, people and animals, angels and nature. David chants, "Let them praise the name of the LORD." Some might argue that David was just using a poetic device known as personification when he asks the sun and moon to praise God. It can be argued that he didn't really believe the sun and moon could understand him. The problem with this position is that cultures that use poetic devices (simile, metaphor, personification) name these devices, just like any physical tool. In biblical Hebrew there is a word meaning "parable" or "proverb," but no words for metaphor or personification. Why? There probably was no self-conscious use of such literary devices in biblical times. When Moses says, "Give ear O heavens," he probably meant it somewhat literally. When King David says, "stormy wind fulfilling his command," he likely meant it to be taken somewhat literally as well.

This imagination even leaves room for talking animals in the Torah. To a modern sensibility, they are figures of speech. To the Israelites it seems that they were understood neither literally nor figuratively, but, rather, somewhere in between. Our ancestors knew that snakes and donkeys didn't literally speak Hebrew. But they seemed to have known that there was some form of communication between animals that was equivalent to what we call language. Just ask any rancher or animal lover.

Dualism And then, finally, we turn to dualism. As we look at this category of Hebraic thinking, we see in fact that Moses, David, Solomon, Jesus, St. Francis, and the Baal Shem Tov might have had more in common with Native American spiritual leaders and Zen Buddhists than they would with the average twenty-first-century rabbi, minister, or priest. Why? Because our dialectical mindset has set the animate and inanimate worlds into two distinct categories. Thankfully modern physics has begun to show us that on the subatomic level, the life force—what philosopher Henri Bergson called élan vital—is imprinted in all creation. Monotheism insists that there is no need for dualism when describing the oppositional forces that we observe within creation.

Still, we're all subject to the challenges that the appearance of dualism presents. It's difficult to understand how a God of justice and love permits evil to exist, so we imagine some independent force competing with the goodness of God. But dualism is antithetical to the biblical view of a God who is sovereign and in absolute control of both good and evil. We want to say "God is love," but we have to recognize that God is also the opposite of love, even if we can't explain it in a satisfactory manner. We want to say "God is light," but a Hebraic view of the creation recognizes that God is in the darkness too. The prophet Isaiah refuses to let us off the hook by giving us a nice, dainty answer. He states what the Holy One tells him to report: "I form light and create darkness, I make weal and create woe; I the LORD do all these things" (Isaiah 45:7). However, the Hebrew is even more disconcerting than most English translators could tolerate. The King James translation is truer to the Hebrew. God says, "I form the light, and create darkness. I make peace, and create evil. I the LORD do all these things." However, the New King James Version backed off the literal translation of "evil," and translated the word as "calamity" in their revised Bible.

Yet the rabbis found that when the energy used for evil is transformed and used for good, it can lead to a positive outcome. Judaism doesn't see the existence of the inclination to do evil as an innate human flaw arising from an "original" sin. The sin committed by Adam and Eve in the garden was definitely the first sin, but according to Jewish tradition, the real sin was not that they disobeyed God, but that they didn't say they were sorry after God pointed out their transgression. From a Jewish perspective, God gave Adam and Eve the capacity to be tempted, but God also gave them the capacity to repent, which they failed to do—this was their "original" sin.

Like the Greek word *hamartia*, which means "sin" but comes from a root meaning "missing the mark," the same metaphor can be found in the etymology of the earlier Hebrew word *hayt*. Sin, of course, is wrong, but Judaism recognizes we all will miss the mark. Once we do, we have the choice to continue in sin or to repent. Once we repent, we achieve a spiritual state that's actually higher than if we hadn't sinned in the first place. Maybe this is why some of the best drug abuse counselors are recovering addicts. This idea may seem odd, and it certainly is not meant to justify sin or evil. Rather, the idea is that sin can be transformed into merit. Jewish theology acknowledges that sin and evil exist, but that God has also created a process for forgiveness. When we repent, the world is, in some mysterious way, better than it was before. The process called *teshuvah* is an elegant and profound method for the remission of sin. Each time a person rectifies his or her errors, the world is a little bit closer to perfection and the coming of the Messiah.

How does Satan fit into this Hebraic mindset? God is absolutely sovereign. All other forces, powers, and angels are created entities that are completely subservient to God. There's no room for a dualism that allows a Satan who competes for God's power, and no place for evil that operates independently of the Creator. There's much folklore in Judaism about the role and activities of Satan, but he's always seen as a subservient entity created by God to test us. Judaism does not describe Satan as a "fallen angel," and certainly not as operating outside of God's command. The Hebrew word *satan* simply means "adversary," and always the *satan* is sent by God for us to overcome. The *satan* is seen as identical to the "evil inclination" that resides in each person. When we face the choice between right and wrong, the Torah commands us to "choose life!" The best way to learn about the nature of *satan* in ancient Judaism is to read the book of Job.

Another aspect of dualism involves the role of gender. Biblical Hebrew describes God as a complex unity with metaphorical attributes that are both male and female. Since God creates both genders in his/her own image, then we have the basis for a more profound understanding of God. The masculine and feminine attributes of God as we see it in the Hebrew are actually complementary to one another. The rabbis have always understood that when God is described in human terms (e.g., having a face, speaking, etc.), the depictions are anthropomorphic. To describe God only as a king or a father limits an unlimited God. Judaism uses these metaphors but is careful not to get bound by titles or names, which, by their nature, are limiting. So it is with the notion of masculine and feminine. God is no more a man than a woman, no more a king than a queen. God is the essence of both genders, and God's imprint can be beheld throughout creation.

NINE

Comparative Theology

COMPARING ANY TWO RELIGIONS IS ALWAYS RISKY BUSINESS since there are so many different denominations and subgroups within each faith family. Judaism, in reality, is a collection of judaisms, and Christianity is made up of many christianities. A brief comparison of Judaism to Christianity is, therefore, always going to be somewhat simplified and based on generalities. My goal is not to lessen the differences between our two great faiths. In fact, I celebrate the differences! But after two thousand years many of us are asking, "Isn't it time for false differences and unnecessary barriers to be taken down?" I've tried to base my comments not on my own opinions alone, but on the conclusions of Christian and Jewish scholars who are active in their respective religions and involved in interfaith dialogue.

For many decades, I regarded the doctrinal differences between Judaism and Christianity as existing within somewhat fixed borders. After all, how can we bridge the elementary idea that Christians believe in Jesus, and Jews don't? Yet over the years my connection with both Jewish and Christian teachers has given me a more nuanced view of how members of each faith community really view these doctrines, and how these differences have been overemphasized and exaggerated. For example, regarding "believing in Jesus" I started to ask, "What is it that Christians are actually believing in? Is there a parallel to that belief within Judaism?" When a doctrine is dressed in the garb of local culture and language, it is often unrecognizable to outsiders, even though they may have a doctrine that is functionally similar to the belief of the other culture. And doctrines and rituals are always dressed in local garb.

Over the years I have been surprised to discover that many core Christian doctrines that I thought were so different from Jewish beliefs actually had their roots in ancient Judaism. Even though these doctrines look different when expressed through different rituals, they have a function that is quite similar. For example, as mentioned above, compare the Eucharist to the Sabbath ritual blessings over the candles, wine, and bread. The Sabbath blessings and the Eucharist both share at least one similar function—to bring the faithful into an intimate relationship with God. And we can say for certain that historically, the elements of the Communion (wine and bread) can be traced to their Jewish roots.

Because these doctrines were often presented in the languages of empires outside of Judea (for example, the Christian emphasis on Greek and Latin rather than Hebrew), it has been difficult for people to see the Jewish roots of many Christian doctrines and rituals. Further, with the rise of anti-Semitism in the early centuries, Jews wanted less and less to do with Christian theology, and the intellectual pursuit of "comparative religion" with their faith cousins held little appeal. Do most Jews and Christians today realize that core Christian doctrines have their roots and/or parallels in Judaism? I don't think so. Putting partisan theology aside, the differences are not as great as they appear. Let's take a look at the major theological doctrines that are generally used to differentiate our faiths.

Trinity

For a Trinitarian Christian (not all Christians are Trinitarians), the doctrine of Trinity answers the question, "Who is Jesus?" Trinity is the doctrine that the one God can be understood as three coequal persons called Father, Son, and Holy Spirit. Jews don't use the term "Trinity" to describe their own doctrines, but this too may have to do with distinguishing itself from Christianity. So let me propose that to fully understand Judaism, it's important to understand the Jewish triad. In a parallel manner, the trinity-like relationship and unity of God, Torah, and Israel is at the foundation of Judaism.

The doctrine of Trinity comes from the verse in Matthew 28:19 where Jesus instructs his students to "go therefore and make disciples of all nations, baptizing them in the name of the Father and of the Son and of the Holy Spirit." In one of the great Jewish mystical texts called the Zohar, it is written, "The Holy One Blessed Be He, Israel, and Torah are one," and the Aramaic words are chanted in many synagogues every Saturday morning. If one were to make a comparison, then, the Holy One is comparable to what Christians call the Father. Torah to the Jews is similar to the Holy Spirit for Christians; Israel is understood within Judaism to be comparable to the ways that Christians think of the Son. Although she considers the analogy a "tad strained," New Testament scholar Dr. Amy-Jill Levine agrees that to some degree, at least, "the Torah functions for the synagogue as Jesus does for the church: it is the 'word' of the divine present in the congregation."[50]

To fully understand historical and modern Judaism, it is important to understand this Jewish triad. The first person of the Christian Trinity, the Father, represents what Judaism describes as God's transcendence. The third person of the Trinity, the Holy Spirit, is called the *Ruakh Hakodesh* in Hebrew. It represents what Judaism calls the *Shekhinah*—the immanent, feminine Presence of God dwelling within the world. The second person of the Trinity, the Son, represents the intermediary force that links God's transcendence and imminence together. The Son is the intermediary aspect of God, the nexus between the Father who is Omni (omnipotent, omniscient, omnipresent), and our sense of God being personal.

University of Virginia professor Dr. Peter Ochs explains the comparison of Jesus as Son of God to the Jewish notion of God's speech. This seems to be a good analogy since elsewhere in the Younger Testament (John 1:1) Jesus is identified as the *Logos*, the divine word of God made flesh. Ochs writes:

> In Jewish tradition, God's speech brings God's word into the world, and through this word God creates the things of the world and teaches Israel and the nations to obey Him and imitate His actions. . . . The

Jewish concept of God's being author of the divine speech is therefore analogous in Trinitarian theology to the Father's begetting his divine Son.[51]

The people of Israel can also be likened to the Christian notion of the "Son of God," and the Torah is the oracle by whose commandments the people are brought closer to the Father. These are just some poetic possibilities for understanding the Trinity in Jewish terms. Obviously, we shouldn't force the Christian notion of Trinity into a Jewish framework, but it seems that Trinity did arise from the fertile soil of Judaism even though the theological terminology seems so different at first glance. It's fascinating to place the words from the Zohar which say, "The Holy One . . . Israel, and Torah are one," next to the words of John 10:30 where Jesus says, "The Father and I are one." Or consider those words of the Zohar in relation to John 1:1 where it says: "In the beginning was the Word, and the Word was with God, and the Word was God."

Son of God

Jewish and Christian doctrines are identical when it comes to the unity of God, ethical monotheism, and the metaphor of God as Father. Most of the time Jesus speaks about his relationship to God in a manner that religious Jews can understand. The only real difference is that Jews do not regard Father and Son as "persons," let alone separate "persons," of the Godhead. Jesus speaks of his heavenly Father as distinct from himself, such as "Very truly, I tell you, the Son can do nothing on his own, but only what he sees the Father doing; for whatever the Father does, the Son does likewise" (John 5:19). Jewish and Christian theologies are also mostly parallel regarding the Holy Spirit. The real challenge between the faiths comes in our differences concerning the notion of Jesus as the sole son and incarnation of God.

Both religions teach that all people are the children of God as in Deuteronomy 14:1 where it is written that "you are children of the LORD your God." This is affirmed in the Younger Testament where it is written in

Matthew 5:9, "Blessed are the peacemakers: for they will be called children of God." There is, of course, the metaphor of the entire people of Israel being called the son of God, as in Exodus 4:22 where God instructs Moses to tell Pharaoh, "Thus says the LORD: 'Israel is my firstborn son.'" King David as an individual also describes himself as the "son of God" in Psalm 2:7. In Acts 13:33, Paul then extends the Israel metaphor to Jesus. Paul says of God, "He has fulfilled for us, their children, by raising Jesus; as also it is written in the second psalm, 'You are my Son; today I have begotten you.'" This has been interpreted in some denominations to suggest that Jesus is now the exclusive son of God. However, the early Christian notion was that every person was a son or daughter of God since that was a continuity of Jewish belief. As it is written, "See what love the Father has given us, that we should be called children of God" (1 John 3:1).

Mediation

Do Jews believe in an intermediary between themselves and God? Absolutely not, and sometimes yes. Judaism does not believe that any intermediary (e.g., a priest, a rabbi, Torah, messiah, angel) is necessary to carry a person's prayers to God. But this does not mean that Jewish theology has no concept of mediation. In Hebrew, for instance, one of the words for "angel" literally means "messenger," and in the Bible these messengers might appear in either human or spiritual form. In most traditional Jewish prayer books, there is a nightly bedtime prayer calling to God to send down four archangels to protect the person during sleep. The words are, "In the Name of *Adonai*, God of Israel. At my right hand is Michael. At my left hand is Gabriel. Before me is Uriel. Behind me is Raphael. And above my head the *Shekhinah* of God." These angels are, for all practical purposes, mediators between people and God.

Although Jews do not pray "to" angels or ancestors, it might be said that we pray "through" them, and always in God's name. In Jewish prayers, we have the formulaic phrase "in the Name of *Adonai*" when we invoke angels to help us deliver our prayers to God. This whole idea will sound familiar to many mainstream Christians who also say that they do not pray "to" Jesus, but to the Father "in Jesus's name." Similarly, Jews do not pray to the Torah, yet each week when we read from it, the Torah becomes a kind of intermediary between the people and God. Torah is the most certain way that Jews can know the will of God for their lives. In a deep, poetic sense, we can even think of the words of prayer as "intermediaries" between our emotions and God. Judaism stresses, however, that no intermediary is necessary for God to hear our prayers.

The midrash quotes Moses as saying to God, "I am destined to become the intermediary between You and them when You give them the Torah and declare 'I am the Holy One, your God. The God of your fathers has sent me to you'" (Midrash: Exodus Rabbah 3:5). While he is described as an intermediary, the notion of mediation is not part of a doctrine within Judaism. Intercessory prayer is common in the Bible (see Genesis 20:17, Numbers 21:7, and Psalm 106:30). When a person prays on another's behalf, this too can be considered a form of mediation.

Vicarious or Substitutionary Atonement

Substitutionary atonement is a Christian term whose origin is rooted in traditional Judaism. Ironically, most Jews won't even recognize the concept until it is explained in Jewish terms. The prophet Isaiah wrote about the suffering of the Jewish people as a whole when he wrote, "But he was wounded for our transgressions, crushed for our iniquities; upon him was the punishment that made us whole, and by his bruises we are healed" (Isaiah 53:5). This verse has been interpreted by Christians to apply to the suffering of Jesus, but according to the rules of interpretation in Judaism, the extended meaning of a text does not replace the literal meaning. On a historical level, Isaiah is describing the Jewish people as God's servant.[52] This will be discussed later.

Jews have traditionally avoided the term *vicarious* or *substitutionary atonement* because of its specific connotation within Christianity. Yet the writings of our rabbis and sages repeatedly teach about the psychological transformation that can happen when a person empathizes with the suffering of others. Vicarious atonement, depending on how we define this idea, is a core teaching within both ancient and modern Judaism. From a more psychological perspective, it seems that all suffering brings about atonement through a process that combines sympathy, empathy, and identification with another person. The notion of only one person—even a very holy person—dying for our sins does not exist in Judaism.

There is, however, a notion that everyone's suffering brings others to feel empathy, and it is this empathy that leads to self-reflection and ultimately to some degree of atonement. Many of us have invoked the popular variation of John Bradford's expression, "There but for the grace of God, go I" when we've heard of something bad happening to someone. Sympathy for the suffering of others inspires the sensitive individual to atone for his or her own shortcomings. The notion that "Jesus died for your sins" is rooted in this ancient Jewish concept of a righteous, saintly person being taken by God on behalf of the community. The difference is that in Judaism, it is not exclusive to one person:

> **Talmud: Sotah 14a** God said about Moses, "Because he poured out his soul to death, and was numbered with the transgressors; 'Yet he bare the sins of many' because he secured atonement for the making of the Golden Calf. 'And made intercession for the transgressors'—because he begged for mercy on behalf of the sinners in Israel that they should turn in penitence."

The whole process of the remission of sin, forgiveness, and God's grace was well known to Jesus. We can be certain that he was quite familiar with the elegant mechanisms described in the oral tradition of his day concerning the remission of sin. Dr. David Flusser writes:

> Since the age of the Hasmoneans, Jews had believed that the saints who died to sanctify the name of God atoned for the sins of Israel.

It is reasonable to assume that during the Roman period this idea was applied not only to Jesus, but to all those who were executed by the authorities. Even Jews who did not accept Christianity evidently believed that Jesus, like the other martyrs of the Roman authorities, had atoned for the sins of Israel.[53]

On a transcendental level, the suffering of the Jewish people represents in the world what Jesus's crucifixion embodies in Christianity. One of the most powerful passages in the Younger Testament is based on the Isaiah 53 passage, "He himself bore our sins in his body on the cross, so that, free from sins, we might live for righteousness; by his wounds you have been healed" (1 Peter 2:24). Apply the spirit of this passage to the innocent victims of the Crusades, the Inquisitions, the Holocaust (or any other act of genocide against any people) and you get a sense of what substitutionary atonement means in Jewish terms. The psalmist expressed this powerfully when he chanted to God, "Because of you we are being killed all day long, and accounted as sheep for the slaughter" (Psalm 44:22).

Judaism teaches that human empathy for those who suffer brings about a certain amount of atonement within our own lives. This is parallel to the Christian idea of how atonement occurs through identification with Christ's suffering on the cross. In both Jewish and Christian theologies it is incorrect to conclude that vicarious atonement abrogates personal responsibility. The Torah clearly teaches that we're each accountable for our own sins. In Judaism, personal responsibility for sins cannot be taken on by someone else except in the case of a parent and child.

The Incarnation of God

Do Jews believe in God's incarnation? In ancient Egypt, Greece, and Rome, there was the widely accepted belief in the deification of the pharaohs and emperors—some of whom were seen as incarnations of the gods. Moses, the prophets, and the rabbis wanted to steer clear of this kind of heresy as Judaism was developing. I also suspect that by the fifth century, the rabbis wanted to unambiguously distinguish Judaism from Christianity, so they avoided the term *incarnation* which was so central to emerging Christian theology. On close analysis of the Hebrew Bible text, however, it seems that whenever God's infinite Self is revealed in the finite world, an incarnation, of sorts, takes place—something spiritual takes on some physical form to some limited degree. God's voice, God's Presence, and even God's angels are all forms of the Holy One's ongoing incarnation.

I am using the term *incarnation* to describe the physical manifestation of the Divine, and not the deification of anything in the physical world. The Christian doctrine of incarnation has to do with Jesus as the unique incarnation of God, whereas in Judaism we can say that 1) the spark of God exists in all of creation; 2) the Presence of God is imminent within creation; 3) the various attributes and manifestations of the Holy One are intelligible to sentient beings; and 4) angels, and any other being that God creates, serve to fulfill God's Will.

In fact, there is a Hebrew word for incarnation: *hitgashmut* means "taking on real, physical, or bodily form." When God speaks, his words can be thought of as incarnations since the preverbal essence of the words comes from the supernal world and enters the physical world as sounds. Whether the sounds are the audible words of God, or heard in the minds of the prophets, they can be thought of as incarnations. If God sends angels as messengers into the physical world, these angels are incarnations of a sort, regardless of whether the angels are physically embodied or mental apparitions. If God is described as having attributes (compassionate, loving, forgiving), then the attributes themselves are incarnations. Even if these attributes are simply mental, abstract ideas that our minds can grasp, they still can be considered incarnations.

In light of all of this, Professor Elliot Wolfson makes a startling parallel between the way Christians understand the incarnation of God in Jesus and the way Jews conceive of the Torah. He writes:

Just as early Christian exegetes saw in Christ, God made flesh, so the rabbis conceived of the Torah as the incarnation of the image of God. In the rabbinic imagination, moreover, the sage is a personification of the Torah. It follows, therefore, that insofar as the Torah is the embodiment of the divine image, the sage can be considered the incarnational representation of God. [54]

Similarly, Professor Jacob Neusner once offered a teaching that will likely surprise many Jewish readers: he said that the incarnation of God was "commonplace" within the various Jewish sects "from the formation of the Scriptures forward." He explained:

> The history of how diverse Judaisms imagined God contains more than a single, uniform chapter about God portrayed as a human being (ordinarily, a man). . . . In the Talmudic sage the word of God was made flesh. And out of the union of man and Torah, producing the rabbi as Torah incarnate, was born Judaism, the faith of Torah: the ever-present revelation. [55]

Despite these scholarly teachings, Jews avoid the term *incarnation* because of what it means within Christianity—that God is incarnate in Jesus. This is an age-old problem: Jews don't engage with Christian ideas simply because they are Christian ideas. The irony is that many so-called "Christian" ideas actually arose in the fertile soil of rabbinic Judaism. If religious Jews can't engage with certain ideas simply because they sound Christian, then we are going to be overlooking a magnificent part of our own history. Clearly within Judaism any notion of incarnation does not include the idea of deification. Jewish theology might say that God is incarnate within a sage or an angel, but it would not say that the sage or an angel is God. Certainly the prophets and rabbis never had in mind the apotheosis of the Torah, the sage, or the nation of Israel, but simply that God can be embodied for an indefinite period of time in the physical world. But the Jewish mystics everywhere have always had a teaching that can be summarized like this: God is unlimited in his power, and that means that he is not limited to being unlimited. The limitless God may elect to infuse a spark of his unlimited essence within each limited object in nature.

Now consider one other big theological word. Panentheism is the concept that God dwells within all of creation.[56] Unlike pantheism that says "everything is God," panentheism says that "God is in everything." Panentheism is closely associated to the idea of the *Logos* that came from Greek philosophy. During the eighteenth and nineteenth centuries, this concept (although not called panentheism) became highly developed within the Hasidic Jewish mystical sects. The view that "God is in everything" and the idea that God is immanent within creation are functionally identical. The notions of immanence and incarnation are parallel to one another. In Christianity, God is fully incarnate only in Jesus, but his spirit is said to dwell within all believers. In the Jewish view, God's essence dwells within all of creation.

This Jewish understanding of God's immanence can be found in the Bible most clearly in Exodus 25:8 when God says, "And have them make me a sanctuary, so that I may dwell among them." The correct grammar should state that if the people build a sanctuary God will dwell in "it." In the sixteenth century, Moses ben Hayim Alshich explained the word "them" is used in Hebrew to imply that God dwells within the people, not within the sanctuaries they make. The notion of God existing within the physical world is further refined in the Zohar, the classic work of Jewish mysticism, where it is taught that God surrounds all worlds and fills all worlds. This is affirmed in the midrash that says: "No spot on earth is devoid of God's Presence" (Numbers Rabbah 12:4). A nineteenth-century rabbinic writing states:

Mishnat R. Eliezer 11:44 It's normal for flesh and blood that when in his palace, he cannot be, at the same time, outside in the city, and vice versa. But with the Holy One, blessed be He, this is not so. He is always present both in the worlds above and in the worlds below, as is said, "The Lord is in His holy abode; let all the earth keep silent in His presence" (Habakkuk 2:20).

Not all denominations within Judaism accept this concept of panentheism because it appears to be perilously close to polytheism. In fact, in the nineteenth century, the Orthodox world tried to cut themselves off from the Jewish mystics over this theological idea. Today, the friction has decreased due to increased denominational dialogue, but the theological difference remains. Nevertheless, panentheism remains at the heart of several branches of Judaism, although that particular term is not usually used. The Christian notion of the indwelling spirit of Christ and the Jewish notion of God dwelling inside the people are functionally the same. Regarding Jesus himself, to say that he is the son of God in whom God dwells can be understood Jewishly if we put aside the concept of deification.

Judaism teaches that God dwells in the Jewish people. And Judaism does not elevate a belief in incarnation to the status of dogma. (It doesn't do this with any theological ideas, in fact—a major difference between our traditions.) This frees the Jew to accept, reject, study, or debate the notion of incarnation without any negative impact upon the spiritual state of his or her soul.

What, then, about the anthropomorphic images of God throughout the Tanakh? Were they understood figuratively or literally in biblical times? It seems from ancient commentary that what we call figures of speech were understood somewhat more literally to the Israelites. For example, when Moses wants to see God, he is told, "Then I will take away my hand, and you shall see my back; but my face shall not be seen" (Exodus 33:23). It's easy for some modern thinkers to be discomfited by such an anthropomorphic description of the Creator, but maybe we need to reexamine what we have lost by abandoning the Hebraic way of experiencing God and the natural world. We see similar images of God and language for God in how God is said to dwell within the tabernacle (Exodus 40:34–35), and then later in the Temple (1 Kings 8:13).

All of this speaks to God's incarnation. Consider the book of Proverbs, where God is personified as possessing three attributes: wisdom, understanding, and knowledge. Wisdom is the most vocal, and she repeatedly pleads with humanity to uphold the covenant. For example: "Does not wisdom call, and does not understanding raise her voice? On the heights, beside the way, at the crossroads she takes her stand; beside the gates in front of the town, at the entrance of the portals she cries out" (Proverbs 8:1–3). Early Christian Gnostics associated the incarnation of wisdom (Sophia) with Jesus. But Judaism associates wisdom with the Torah. She is personified in the book of Proverbs and incarnate as the Torah. Referring to Wisdom as the Torah, Solomon chanted, "She is a tree of life to those who lay hold of her" (Proverbs 3:18).

Original Sin and Exile

A core belief in Judaism is that humans are born with two natural but competing inclinations: a good inclination and an evil inclination. Jews learn that we are born with a pure soul and are given free will. Therefore, we are capable of making good or bad choices throughout our lives.

There is no sense of an original sin in Judaism in which the soul is innately stained and in need of salvation. However, Judaism acknowledges that humanity needs a process to return to God when we do sin—and we are always sinning. The process of *teshuvah* permits us to reconcile ourselves with God at any time. The evil inclination is even seen as having a potentially positive impact when its energy is transformed to the service of God. Not having a notion of the fall of humanity, Judaism developed an elegant and elaborate technology for reconciling with God when sins are committed. Colgate University's Steven Kepnes clarifies this distinction between the Jewish and Christian worldviews regarding an innate, original state of sin by writing:

Humans are not mired in a "state" of sin; they naturally can choose to do the good (Deuteronomy 30:14), which is not far off from them (Deuteronomy 30:11). . . . If humans suffered from a state of sin that limited their free will, the entire system of *mitzvot* would be compromised. . . . The simple Jewish view is that Christianity begins with a world plagued by sin and ends with Christ as savior; Judaism begins with a world as "very good" (Genesis 1:31) and ends with Torah as its complement and Shabbat as its completion (Genesis Rabbah on Genesis 2:12). Lacking a notion of original sin means that sin, atonement, and repentance are not the central concerns for Jews that they are for Christians. [57]

Of all the beliefs, concepts, and doctrines that separate Judaism from Christianity, probably the notions of Jesus's deification and original sin present the greatest challenges. Yet, if we can understand the incarnation of God in Jewish terms (i.e., a spark of God that resides in everyone), then the distance between the two faiths is lessened. So what about original sin?

Again, I turn to Dr. Steven Kepnes, who presents a remarkable argument by which original sin can be comprehended in Jewish terms. As he explains, original sin is parallel to the Jewish notion of *galut*, or exile. In both doctrines these are states we were born into—the Christian is born into original sin, and the Jew is born into a state of exile. In most Christian denominations, redemption is the process by which the believer is "saved from sin" as an individual. In the Bible, however, redemption usually describes the process whereby the nation of Israel is physically rescued from the various exiles (Egyptian, Babylonian, etc.) in which they dispersed from the land of Israel. Understanding this will shed light on Kepnes's contention that what original sin is for a Christian, exile is for a Jew. The Christian wants to be saved from sin. The Jew wants to be redeemed from exile. This explains why one of the many names for God in Hebrew is *Ga-al Yisrael*, the Redeemer of Israel. Kepnes explains:

If Jews do not want to use Augustine's phrase "original sin" to describe the conditions in which human life naturally transpires after Adam, they can be referred to the words of Genesis 4:7—"Sin crouches at the door"—or Genesis 8:21: "The devisings *(yetzer)* of man's heart are evil from his youth." Judaism also has a Hebrew term that, like "original sin," is suggestive of a state or condition that limits the human ability to be in free contact with God. This term is *galut*, exile. . . . The notion of *galut* marks all rabbinic Judaism, since the rabbis constructed Judaism after and out of the destruction of the Temple and the dispersion of the Jews from Jerusalem. . . . *Galut* thus means a deep sense of homelessness in a world that is not quite right. *Galut*, in its deeper spiritual meaning, is not only about longing for the physical return of the Jewish people to the land of Israel, it is about the longing for final redemption and for return to the Edenic state of harmony between human and human, between humans and the world, and between humans and God. . . . Like original sin, *galut* cannot be overcome by human will alone; exile will end only when God intervenes to make it end. [58]

Jewish theology teaches that it is the role of humanity to help perfect the world by sanctifying all that we do (eat, drink, smell, make love). The Jewish covenantal relationship with God is based on the fulfillment of mitzvot in order to uncover the sacred within physical existence. The attempt to overcome *galut* is a primary driving force within Judaism. Mitzvah by mitzvah, as a Jew helps perfect the world, the state of exile comes to an end, and the great redemption is one mitzvah nearer. In a complementary manner, original sin is the driving force that impels a Christian to be saved by Jesus's sacrifice. The Christians' covenantal relationship is an expression of praise, and glorification of their Messiah who died for the sins of the world. Regarding an innate state of sin versus a state of exile that we are born into, there does not need to be an argument over whose theology works better, or which system of atonement is better. God's bottom line seems to be that Christianity works best for Christians, and Judaism works best for Jews.

The Golden Rule

The Golden Rule did not originate with Jesus, nor was it a departure from Judaism. Many great sages (both secular and spiritual) such as Confucius, Plato, and Socrates either discovered the Golden Rule on their own, learned it from their contact with Jews, or learned it from each other. In the fourth century BCE Plato said, "May I do to others as I would that they should do unto me." A century earlier, Socrates said, "Do not do to others that which would anger you if others did it to you." In the Analects 12:2 of Confucianism, it is written, "Do not do to others what you would not like yourself."

It's likely that Jesus learned the principle of the Golden Rule from his elders, or he may have created a variation of the teachings of the great first-century teacher Rabbi Hillel, who is quoted in the Talmud as saying, "What is hateful to you, do not do to your neighbor: that is the whole Torah, the rest is the commentary. Go study it" (Shabbat 31a). Rabbi Hillel made his statement in the negative, and Jesus reframed it in the positive, but both ways of phrasing this incredible idea are based upon the Torah and rabbinic and universal wisdom.

It is important for both Christians and Jews to realize this, that Jesus's teaching of what we've come to call the Golden Rule was not a deviation from rabbinic Judaism, but central to it. As David Flusser writes:

> Both Jesus and Hillel before him saw the Golden Rule as a summary of the law of Moses. This becomes intelligible when we consider that the biblical saying, "love your neighbor as yourself," (Leviticus 19:18) was esteemed by Jesus and by the Jews in general as a chief commandment of the law. An old Aramaic translation of this biblical precept runs like this, "love your neighbor for whatever displeases you, do not to him." Jesus is saying about the double commandment of

love clearly was coined before his time. . . . The double commandment of love existed in ancient Judaism before, and alongside, Jesus.[59]

Salvation and Chosenness

Judaism has always upheld a universal vision for humankind—a vision of universal justice, universal morality, but not of a single, universal religion. In Malachi 2:10 the prophet asks, "Have we not all one father? Has not one God created us? Why then are we faithless to one another, profaning the covenant of our ancestors?" And in Isaiah 52:10 the prophet Isaiah reminds us that salvation is universal and available to all people, "The LORD has bared his holy arm before the eyes of all the nations; and all the ends of the earth shall see the salvation of our God."

The behavioral demands of ethical monotheism outlined in the Torah have been a gift from God to the whole world. For example, the book of Exodus tells of the enslavement and liberation of one particular people, and yet it has served as a model for many people who have sought political freedom and spiritual meaning in their lives. Its language and imagery inspired the Puritans as they "crossed the sea," the Mormons as they marched through the American wilderness, and most recently, the leaders of the civil rights movement.

Judaism has never taught that salvation, or eternal life, was dependent upon being Jewish, or even being a monotheist. An important rabbinic commentary teaches that "the righteous of all nations have a share in the world to come" (Tosefta-Sanhedrin 13:1). God did not create Judaism as *the* universal religion for all people. Rather, the Jewish people were to proclaim the "good news" that there is a single God who commands both love and justice. There is no "exclusivity contract" in Judaism. In the messianic era, Jewish theology teaches that Buddhists will continue to be Buddhists, Hindus will continue to be Hindus, and Native peoples will continue to practice their own tribal traditions. The difference will be that all people will celebrate the interconnectedness of the one Creator who is known by many names, in many languages, and within many cultures and religions. The prophet Micah expresses most eloquently the way that salvation of different peoples will be celebrated in the messianic era:

> **Micah 4:3–5** Nation shall not lift up sword against nation, neither shall they learn war any more; but they shall all sit under their own vines and under their own fig trees, and no one shall make them afraid; or the mouth of the Lord of hosts has spoken. For all the peoples walk, each in the name of its god, but we will walk in the name of the Lord our God forever and ever.

Vine and fig tree were well-known metaphors in the Middle East symbolizing fruitfulness and diversity. In Micah's prophesy they represented the various cultures and religions in the world. When he predicts that all peoples will walk "each in the name of its god," he seems to be referring to the multiplicity of names of God. Historically, Jews were chosen to teach, serve, and inspire the nations on their path toward adopting ethical monotheism within their own cultures and religions. There are those who say that the concept of Jews being the chosen people is arrogant, and there are many Jews who are uncomfortable with this title, too, as well as the responsibility it implies. This is why, in *Fiddler on the Roof,* Reb Tevya humorously says to God, "I know. We are Your chosen people. But, once in a while, can't You choose someone else?"

In reality, however, Jewish chosenness was never a claim to be above other people. Rather, it is the recognition by God of the obligation Jews accepted at Sinai. Along with this obligation, the Bible seems to imply that God expects the Jewish people to have an extra measure of accountability for their part in the covenant. In this sense, to be a "chosen people" means to be a "choosing people." Jews have shown that in their lowest moments of despair they continue to "choose" God, even amidst personal and national suffering. The honor of being chosen, however, comes with an extra measure of culpability. In Amos 3:2 ancient Israel was warned about the awesome responsibility of chosenness; "You only have I known of all the families of the earth; therefore I will punish you for all your iniquities." Thanks a lot, God!

Jewish chosenness is also a model for repentance. In the Bible, the Jews are not a paragon of perfection. To the contrary, they are an example of the imperfection of all humanity. The Torah describes the Israelites as "stiff-necked people" (Exodus 32:9) and they alternate between following and disobeying God's commands. Yet it is this very imperfection that has made Jews an accessible model for individuals and nations who are willing to honestly reflect upon their own mistakes. The power of Israel is not how well they do, but how well they do in owning up to their mistakes. King David is an excellent example of this on the individual level. When confronted with his sins by Nathan, David quickly repents (2 Samuel 12). The suffering of the Jews and, similarly, the crucifixion of Jesus are not examples of failure, but of irony and paradox. They are models for turning "mourning into dancing," and transforming failure into success.

The Holy One has given the Jewish people a unique role to play within history: to teach God's indivisible unity, and to be a model for doing *teshuvah* when they err. It's not the only role, certainly not the starring role, but it is unique. Let's put it this way—if I'm selected to be in an orchestra, I may feel proud to have been "chosen," but I also recognize that I am only chosen to play one instrument. Judaism sees its role as "chosen" in this sort of unique, but nonexclusive, manner. God has a special task for everyone. Regarding Christianity, I would ask—if Christians also see themselves as a chosen people, does their being chosen need to replace the election of the Jewish people? Or is there room for each of us to fulfill the unique roles that the Holy One has designated for each of us?

The Temple's Destruction and the Crucifixion

The great Mesopotamian, Egyptian, Babylonian, Greek and Roman Empires were founded on logic, reason, power, order, control, and success. The nation of Israel, whose citizens lived in the midst of these empires, was founded on something uniquely different: ethical monotheism. Judaism brought the world codified standards for universal morality, humane treatment of animals, hygienic practices, the sanctification of rest through Sabbath, and a vision of freedom from tyranny for all people. Israel has always been a model of a minority people who stumble, suffer, and yet cling to God. Even in the midst of adversity, Israel is the model of a people who work to fulfill its covenantal mission to help make the world a better place. It is a nation that is trampled upon, exiled, rebuilt, praised, reviled, exiled, and reborn once again—it's not a model of perfection, but of the perfection of imperfection.

Jesus is a microcosm of the nation of Israel. He is also the model of a man who suffers and clings to the covenantal mission that his heavenly Father sent him to fulfill—to bring a unified code of morality, monotheism, and sanctity to the Gentile world. Israel consistently seems to fail, and yet it's in the way Israel responds to failure that its light shines forth. Even in failure, Israel is able to say, "Thank you, God, for everything that is good in this world. May my suffering play a tiny part in the redemption of the world." Perhaps you can begin to see how Jesus fits within this worldview, how he is a model Jew. Judaism and Christianity have had the wisdom to understand what the mystery of low and high is really all about, and how God uses failure to redeem each of us. An extraordinary teaching by the great twentieth-century scholar Martin Buber makes the case for this understanding of what I call sacred failure:

> The Bible knows nothing of the intrinsic value of success. On the contrary, when it announces a successful deed, it is duty-bound to announce in complete detail the failure involved in the success. When we consider the history of Moses, we see how much failure is mingled in the one great successful action. . . . This glorification of failure culminates in the long line of prophets whose existence is failure through and through. They live in failure; it is for them

to fight and not to conquer. This is the fundamental experience of biblical leadership. [60]

On the surface it can seem that the Jewish people, by the fact of their exile, have failed in their mission to redeem the world. Jesus, too, by the fact of his crucifixion, can be seen as having failed. Yet it is precisely because of these two "failures" that so much of the world has come to believe in God. After all, the essence of the Jewish and Christian gospels is that there is a single God who helps each of us transform personal suffering and failure into something glorious. Adam and Eve failed in their mission to maintain an Edenic world. Noah's drunkenness shattered the relationship between his sons. Moses's anger disqualified him from entering the Promised Land. David committed murder and adultery, and was not worthy of building the Temple in Jerusalem. Yet each of these "failures" ultimately yielded great successes. Rabbi Irving Greenberg summarizes these failures as follows:

> Abraham was a "failure." He dreamt of converting the whole world to Judaism. He ended up barely having one child carrying on the tradition. . . . Moses was a "failure." He dreamt of taking the slaves, making them into a free people. . . . They died slaves in the desert, and neither they nor Moses ever reached the Promised Land. Jeremiah was a "failure." He tried to convince the Jewish people . . . to be ethically responsible and not fight Babylonia. No one listened. [61]

In Yiddish there is a word, *chutzpah,* that is difficult to translate. It means "guts" in the sense of courage, but it also implies "audacity." In Jewish tradition the rabbis often display *chutzpah* when challenging our biblical heroes. They even challenge God just as Abraham and Moses did. Rabbi Byron Sherwin takes the imperfections of the biblical leaders a step further by daring to implicate God in their failures. He writes:

Even God failed, for according to Jewish tradition the reign of God was supposed to begin with the revelation of the Torah at Sinai, but the people built the golden calf and God's expectation was not realized. Indeed, God failed so badly in creating the human race that He had to erase it with a flood and start again, like an artist who makes a mistake and must erase it, accept failure, and begin again. Indeed, the greatest individuals are always failures, because their goals are so exalted. [62]

Christianity is at its best when it is expressed from the cross—from the place of sacrifice, suffering, failure, and not from a position of power. Increasingly, many Christians seem to be coming to understand this anew, and there are Christian leaders emerging who are reclaiming this approach to sharing the Gospel of Jesus in their communities.

Jesus is a light unto the nations only from the cross, not by the sword of Constantine. Jesus is not a light to the nations when he is the handsome, Christian version of Prometheus, the powerful heir to the Roman Empire upheld by the "army of Christ." The message of Jesus, like the message of Israel, is that the transformation of mourning into joy is possible. Everyone in Jesus's inner circle thought he was going to become the Messiah-King and declare the Kingdom of God on earth. His Jewish mother thought so, his religiously observant disciples thought so, and the Roman government thought so. But they didn't understand his mission. He came not to succeed, but to fail. Describing the mission of Jesus, it is written: "He himself bore our sins in his body on the cross, so that, free from sins, we might live for righteousness; by his wounds you have been healed" (1 Peter 2:24).

Isaiah's suffering servant, be it Israel or Jesus or both, is not the message of the Greek and Roman empires because it is not a message of power and success. The gospel's message is that the worst suffering can be consoled and transformed; illness can be healed; the enslaved will be set free, and the low will be made high. This is why Rabbi Greenberg suggests that Jews ought to consider Jesus a failed messiah rather than a false messiah:

Jesus is no false Messiah. . . . Rather, when Christianity, in his name, claims absolute authority and denigrates the right of Judaism or of Jews to exist, then it makes him into a false Messiah. Short of such claims, however, Jews should recognize Jesus as a failed Messiah. This recognition would allow Jews to affirm that for hundreds of millions of people, Christianity has been and continues to be a religion of love and consolation. [63]

It may be time for Israel and the Church to fully own and appreciate the message of their respective "failures." Jesus offers a prophecy that did not come to pass: "So also, when you see these things taking place, you know that the kingdom of God is near. Truly I tell you, this generation will not pass away until all things have taken place" (Luke 21:31–32). Too many Church leaders mistakenly interpret away the real power of this verse. Jesus's strength is not that he succeeded. It's in the fact that he was crucified. Jesus's real power is not that his prophesy was fulfilled, but that it was not fulfilled. Jesus was a failed messiah as Israel was a failed nation. God says, "You shall be my treasured possession out of all the peoples. Indeed, the whole earth is mine, but you shall be for me a priestly kingdom and a holy nation" (Exodus 19:5–6). Israel's real power is in the paradox that it never became "a nation of priests," and yet through her example it has been a model for all those who've been persecuted and downtrodden. Israel's real power has always been in its failure, exile, destruction, suffering, and rebirth.

The prophet Isaiah of course wrote, "For a child has been born for us, a son given to us; authority rests upon his shoulders" (Isaiah 9:6). Christians interpret this verse as referring to Jesus, but in doing so they miss the opportunity to teach the deepest lessons about failure. The government was never upon Jesus's shoulder. He was crucified before the Romans would ever let him rule. A similar fate befell Simon bar Kokhba, a Jewish leader in the century after Jesus. The failure of Israel to be a nation of priests, and the failure of Jesus to fulfill the messianic expectations (for example, peace on earth) are where their respective powers lie; they each offer a gospel of hope to the hopeless, freedom to the enslaved, and healing to the wounded. According to Rabbi Greenberg we might want to look at this transformational theology, then, like this:

> The fact that Jesus did not even attain the minimal dignity of a final resting place—an undisturbed grave—should have been the final nail in the crucifixion of their faith. Instead, they increased hope and trust in God. . . . Once faith supplied the key of understanding, the empty tomb yielded the message of the resurrection. . . . The original people of God soon encountered their own crisis—the destruction of the Holy Temple in Jerusalem and the exile that soon followed. Was this catastrophe the end of the covenant . . . ? Instead of despairing, most Jews increased their hope and trust in God. The rabbis emerged to teach God's self-limitation, of God's "hiddenness," which was designed to call the people of Israel to participate more fully in the covenant. [64]

How do we make sense of the theological dilemmas that both Judaism and Christianity had to face in the light of their respective failures? The Jews were the chosen people, and the Church was claiming to be the wild olive branch grafted into the olive tree of Israel. Yet the Jews were forced out of Jerusalem after the failure of the Bar Kokhba revolt in 135 CE, and the Church was left with the legacy of a messiah who was crucified instead of being crowned king. Both religions dealt with the paradox, and Israel's failure was not a punishment from God. Instead, if you read Proverbs 3:11–12, Israel's suffering was not for its sins, but the rebuke of the father who disciplines the favored son. As Dr. Leora Batnitzky writes:

> The destruction of the Second Temple and the exile of the Jewish people from the land of Israel—is not the direct result of sinfulness of the people but of their favored status. The suffering of the Jewish

people is in fact a sign of their chosenness and future redemption, as well as God's love for the people. . . . The early Christians and early Jewish traditions inherited a similar problem: how to make sense of the connection between the reality of their suffering and their chosen status. Significantly, they responded to this problem in a similar way, which was to disconnect, though not to reject completely, a direct arithmetic of suffering and punishment for sin. [65]

Jesus may have failed as the Messiah son of David from a Jewish perspective, but he certainly succeeded as the suffering servant, Messiah son of Joseph, and as the Messiah for the Gentile world. Judaism may have failed to be a "light unto the nations," but the influence of this tiny people with a population today of 14 million cannot be underestimated. I think it's time for the Jewish people to take our understanding of the crucified Jesus from the first rung of acceptance to the second rung of acknowledgment, and maybe even to the third rung of celebration.

Somehow each religion has transformed catastrophe into compelling stories of hope and redemption. Taking "not one stroke of a letter" (Matthew 5:17–20) from the Torah's obligations, maybe it's time for the Jewish people to acknowledge the veracity of the Christ story for our Christian brothers and sisters. Two billion people on our planet are in a covenant with the God of Israel through their Messiah, Jesus. The triumph of Christianity no longer means the defeat of Judaism as it once did. Thanks to Christianity (and Islam), in an odd, mysterious, and roundabout way, the Jewish mission to bring ethical monotheism to the world has been a miraculous triumph.

Final Comparisons

There is no lack of writing on the differences between the Jewish and Christian conceptions of God, sonship, mediation, incarnation, atonement, and sin. Yet maybe it's time to remove the self-protective walls that have been built up within Judaism due to two millennia of persecution. Maybe it's time to take a look at these issues a bit more objectively. If we do, I believe that we'll see that most of the core Christian theological doctrines originated from within Judaism. If evangelical Christians can find a way to remove the imperative of the great commission to convert Jews to Christianity, then our perception of our differences will diminish even more. Once Jews are no longer seen as having to be converted or "completed" in order to be saved from eternal doom, a Christian may feel liberated from the one task that the church has failed at over the last two thousand years—taking the gospel and trying to impose it upon the Jewish people from whom the gospel originated.

Jews and Christians face a mystery that I suggest no longer needs an either/or kind of response. If Jews worship God directly, and Christians worship God through Jesus, do we really think that is a significant difference to God? Since Christians believe that Jesus is the son of God, does this belief have to replace the metaphor that everyone is a son or daughter of God? As Jacob Neusner writes, "The struggle . . . originated in the simple fact that, to begin with, both religions agreed on pretty much everything that mattered. They differed on little, so they made much of that little."[66] We all wait for the Messiah—or the messianic age—to come.

IV
Theological Misunderstandings

=====
Lost in Translation

A S A FAN OF THE TWENTIETH-CENTURY POET PABLO NERUDA, and as a non-Spanish speaker, I like to compare three or more translations of the same poem in order to understand what Neruda was trying to express. It never ceases to surprise me how one Spanish word can have so many possible translations. This is, of course, just as true when translating a word from any modern language into English. If translating from a modern tongue is such a challenge, imagine how difficult it is to translate a word from biblical Hebrew into any contemporary vernacular. Add to this the fact that since ancient Judea was on the western edge of Asia, it reflected an entirely Middle Eastern worldview opposed to the European view of the world that all Western languages reflect.

The bottom line is that when trying to understand first-century Judaism and the genius of Rabbi Jesus, a lot gets lost in translation. We are translating not only one language to another, but also from one continent to another, and from one era to another. It is an exciting challenge for students of the Bible, but frustrating for the religious people who already have fixed beliefs. Healthy interfaith dialogue begins by seeking to clear up unintentional misunderstandings, many of which are based on faulty translations of sacred texts.

The characterization of "the God of the Old Testament" as a vengeful and jealous God that has been superseded by the "God of love and mercy" in the New Testament is simply incorrect. There was no changing of the guard, or replacement of one god for another. The Jewish Scriptures brought the world a description of a totally unified God whose attribute of love is balanced by justice, and whose frustration with the Jewish people has always been tempered by mercy.

Even before the canonization of the Younger Testament, the rabbis described the human response to God as being motivated by some combination of love and fear. In the Torah, God is revered for the divine attributes of both love and justice (Exodus 34:6–7). In the Scriptures, God is gracious and slow to anger (Psalm 145:8) and "reproves the one he loves, as a father the son in whom he delights" (Proverbs 3:12). As noted earlier, within first-century Judaism the double commandments of loving God and our neighbors were considered among the greatest of all mitzvot.

Historically, this has too often been ignored in order to "prove" that Judaism is a religion based on law imposed by a wrathful deity, whereas Christianity is a religion based on grace, forgiveness, and the God of love. It's as if some early Church fathers thought that acknowledging the covenantal validity of Judaism would somehow diminish the message of the emergent Christianity. Ironically, the opposite is true—both faiths will be stronger when they acknowledge and celebrate their interdependence with each other.

Love is not an option for either Jews or Christians. It's a response to two commandments in the Torah that Jesus, and other rabbis of his day, spoke of as the two great commandments: "You shall love the LORD your God with all your heart" (Deuteronomy 6:5), and "You shall love your neighbor as yourself" (Leviticus 19:18). The faithful in both religions do not believe that these two central commandments to love can be carried out perfectly, but that we must strive to love God and our neighbors to the best of our ability. And when we fail? With God's help, we try again.

Judaism teaches that having been created in the image of God (Genesis 1:27), we should strive to make all our actions in imitation of God, *imitatio dei*—taking care of the most wounded and vulnerable among us. This notion was adopted by Christianity, and is evident throughout the Younger Testament. Jews and Christians have each been given extraordinary models for transforming "mourning into dancing." Jews may have suffered under the hand of tyrants throughout the ages, but they've always bounced back and transformed their suffering into an even greater sense of purpose. For its part, Christianity established the model of a messiah who suffered on the cross, but was resurrected so each believer might come to live in hope and gratitude.

I Am the Way

The Ten Commandments begin with the declaration that God alone is *Anokhi*, the Hebrew word meaning *I AM*. Missionaries who have witnessed to me over the decades have quoted the following verses to demonstrate why I must accept Jesus as my Savior. Jesus said, "I am the way, and the truth, and the life. No one comes to the Father except through me" (John 14:6). Yet I've always read this verse with Hebrew eyes and never felt it called me to become a Christian, nor that it implied that my Judaism was "incomplete" without Jesus. In fact, this verse confirms for me my own covenant with God. Why?

Try reading the verse in a more literal manner. Since *I AM* is God in Judaism, it's possible Jesus was referring to God in this passage. Since ancient Greek, like ancient Hebrew, did not use punctuation marks, then "I am the way" could just as easily be read with the insertion of a comma: "*I AM*, the way. . . ." In other words, "God is the way, and the truth, and the life." Jesus might have been teaching that each of us has within us a spark of *Anokhi*, the godly *I AM*.

Of course, Jesus would have said these words in Hebrew or Aramaic, so here we have the classic problem that arises when any language is translated. The phrase *except through me* in most Christian translations is rendered "but by me." However, the Greek word *dia* has the multiple meanings of "through, by, with" and "for the sake of." Another interpretation is that as a Jew I too go to God "by" the same way that Jesus went—through mitzvot, and adhering to the covenant of my fathers, the covenant of Moses. In that sense, I can say that because I practice Judaism I go to God by Jesus; by the same way he goes—through fulfilling the commandments of the Torah.

Similarly, Christians sometimes interpret John 8:58 as Jesus saying that he existed before Abraham. Jesus says "'Very truly, I tell you, before Abraham was, I am.'" However, another possible interpretation of this verse is that Jesus was simply stating that before Abraham, there was *I AM*, God. This kind of examination of language brings a Hebraic sensibility to the New Testament. Multiple meanings can open up new possibilities to strengthen and enliven a Christian's faith, just as they have done for Jews for thousands of years. In the Hebraic way of thinking, one interpretation being "right" doesn't necessarily mean another interpretation has to be wrong.

Jesus's identification as being one with God, as in "the Father and I are one" (John 10:30), is consistent with the mystical stream within Judaism. Oneness with God is not the same as saying, "I am the same as God." As we have seen, Judaism has a long, rich, and sometimes controversial tradition of panentheism, which comes from the Greek and means that *Theos* (God) resides *en* (in) *pan* (everything). This seems to be comparable to the Christian notion of the "indwelling spirit of Christ" as it is taught in 1 Corinthians 3:16, "Do you not know that you are God's temple and that God's Spirit dwells in you?"

Hallowed Be Thy Name

Jews, Christians, and Muslims all share the belief that there is only one God. In Judaism this oneness is understood as a kind of paradox. Harry Nilsson's pop song declared that "one is the loneliest number you'll ever do." And certainly in our world, one is the smallest number. Yet when we say God is one, we don't mean the smallest or loneliest—we are paradoxically describing a oneness that encompasses everyone and everything. My individual oneness is limited, but God's oneness is unlimited. We face a conundrum when trying to describe the infinite and eternal God with words that are limited. Jewish mystics give us the mind-boggling notion that God cannot be limited even by being unlimited. God is truly unlimited, but purposely self-limits in order to be able to interact with creation.

In the Hebrew language that Jesus was raised with, each of God's many names describes some unique aspect of divinity. The Hebrew name *El Shaddai*, for example, is usually translated as "Almighty." But it actually means something like "Nurturing God," and comes from the Hebrew word *shad*, meaning "breast." The name *Eloheem* is translated as "God," but it literally means "gods." It is interpreted through the lens of monotheism as the Unity of All Plurality. Theologically, *Eloheem* is associated with nature and our sense of God's transcendence. Then there is a name of God that represents the most intimate kind of relationship between the Creator and the creation. Known as the Tetragrammaton, this Hebrew name of God likely holds the secret to Jesus's powerful prayer that opens with the words "Our Father, Hallowed be thy Name."

Of all the names of God in the *Tanakh*, none is so central to understanding the Hebraic way of thinking as the Tetragrammaton, transliterated as YHVH[67] in English, but never pronounced in Jewish worship. It is also known as the "Four-Letter Name." It is ironic that the early seventeenth-century King James Bible scholars chose the masculine, hierarchical word "Lord" to represent the Tetragrammaton, which in Hebrew expresses an intimate, nonhierarchical sensibility. This one translational choice has had a huge impact on the way English readers conceive of the Creator. The Four-Letter Name is unique in Hebrew. First, it has a feminine ending. Second, although it is a noun, it behaves like a verb. It is quite similar to the word *being* in English, which can be used as either a noun or a verb. One possible translation of the Tetragrammaton is "Existing One," or simply "Being." But Lord?

The masculine and royal connotations of "Lord" do not accurately render the meaning of the awe-inspiring Four-Letter Name. In Jewish spiritual practice this name is never pronounced. By not uttering this name, a silent admission is made that, as finite beings, we can never fully grasp the infinite God—we can never contain the limitless in a name that, by its very nature, is limited. Instead, Jews most often call God Adonai, meaning

"My Lord." By saying Adonai while reading YHVH, the supplicant has the opportunity to actually experience a paradox—attempting to name the unnamable, while knowing that this is impossible. We thereby may know, for just an instant, God as both transcendent and immanent.

Theologically, the Father and Son of the Christian Trinity represent God's transcendence in the Father and immanence in the Son. The Holy Spirit seems to be the unifying force that ties the transcendent and immanent aspects of God together. Whenever you read the word LORD in the Bible, it is usually a translation of the Four-Letter Name. When King David chanted "The LORD is my shepherd" (Psalm 23), he uses the Tetragrammaton. When Jesus said "Hallowed be thy Name," he very likely was referring to YHVH, the Tetragrammaton. It is, indeed, a hallowed name.

When the story of creation is recounted in Genesis 2:4, the Tetragrammaton is used for the first time together with the name *Eloheem*. In English we get "Lord God," but the Hebrew sense of these two words together is far more profound. The reader is given the impression that the union of two seemingly opposite ideas about divinity is taking place: God is personal (*YHVH*) and impersonal (*Eloheem*), close and far, energetic (verb) and tangible (noun), singular and plural, feminine and masculine, within this world and beyond this world. Today in Jewish prayer books the formula for any blessing brings these two distinct names of God next to representing our very diverse perceptions of the Divine. The blessing formula begins "Blessed are You, Lord our God, Sovereign of the Universe." Sadly, it loses its multi-layered meanings in translation. But just knowing about the differences between "Lord" and "God" in the Hebrew that Jesus spoke can only enhance the way a Christian reads the Bible.

Messiah: The Anointed One

In biblical and modern Judaism, the title of messiah ("Christ" if we use the Greek translation, *moshiakh* in Hebrew) was given to "anointed" human beings. Jews believe that God alone is the Savior, and that a messiah is an individual anointed by God for a specific task. Christianity has merged the two (Savior and messiah) into the person of Jesus, whereas a literal reading of the Hebrew Bible shows that "messiah" and "Savior" are never used synonymously. In the Tanakh, God the Savior is not messiah. Further, a person can be anointed *by* God, but cannot *be* God. Humans are made in God's image, and each of us contains a spark of God within ourselves, but in the Jewish Scriptures, Savior is a name reserved for God, and not for a son or daughter of God. In ancient as well as modern Judaism, the title of messiah always means an anointed human, and is distinct from God who is the Savior. This doesn't mean Christian theology cannot merge the two, as it has, but this merger is based on Christian doctrine, not on the biblical Hebrew. As the prophets say:

> **Isaiah 45:21–25** There is no other god besides me, a righteous God and a Savior; there is no one besides me. Turn to me and be saved, all the ends of the earth! For I am God, and there is no other.

> **Hosea 13:4** Yet I have been the LORD your God ever since the land of Egypt; you know no God but me, and besides me there is no savior.

Then, in the two Younger Testament passages below, we see a continuity in the Jewish notion of the oneness of God being the Savior:

> **Luke 1:47** And my spirit rejoices in God my Savior.

> **1 Timothy 1:1** Paul, an apostle of Christ Jesus by the command of God our Savior and of Christ Jesus our hope.

However, in citations from the book of John and Acts we see an innovation that never existed before in Judaism—that of a messiah ("Christ" in Greek) being identified with the Savior (God).

John 4:42 It is no longer because of what you said that we believe, for we have heard for ourselves, and we know that this [Jesus] is truly the Savior of the world.

Acts 5:31 God exalted him [Jesus] at his right hand as Leader and Savior, so that he might give repentance to Israel and forgiveness of sins.

There's one view within Judaism that the Messiah will come only when the nations of the world are already at peace—in other words, when humanity has already done its part to usher in the messianic age. An opposing view is that the Messiah will come when the world is so devastated with war, crime, and injustice that God will have to send the Messiah. Judaism permits the question to stand as a mystery with no definitive answer, but the rabbis implore us to behave as if the coming of the Messiah is in our hands. In *Fiddler on the Roof,* as the Jews are being exiled from their village, Motel the tailor says to the rabbi, "Rabbi, we've been waiting for the Messiah all our lives. Wouldn't now be a good time for him to come?" The rabbi cleverly replies, "I guess we'll have to wait someplace else." Within both Judaism and Christianity, there is the belief that praying, waiting, and hoping for the Messiah does not lessen our responsibility to help make this a better world in the meantime. When will the Messiah come? Only God knows.

Several people are mentioned in the Elder Testament with the title of messiah (or christ—which is the Greek word for the Hebrew messiah): every king in the Bible, every priest, and even the non-Jewish king of Persia named Cyrus who was anointed to overthrow the despotic Babylonian empire and help the exiled Jews return to Judea. The words *messiah, anointed one,* or *christ* were used as descriptions rather than as proper nouns in the Elder Testament. All the messiahs named in the Tanakh had specific missions ordained by God. Jews believe that the future Messiah will be fully human as well.

Because the word *christ* has a special meaning in Christianity, Jews do not use this term when translating the Hebrew word for messiah into English. In the Tanakh *messiah* is an honorific term, and not exclusive to just a few indi-viduals. It implied a special anointing coming directly from God. Saul was a messiah (1 Samuel 15:1), and when David became king, the anointing left Saul and was transferred to David. Solomon was a messiah (1 Kings 1:39); the priests were messiahs (Leviticus 4:3); Aaron was a messiah (Exodus 28:41); the prophet Isaiah was a messiah (Isaiah 61:1); Cyrus was a messiah (Isaiah 45:1). In Psalm 105:15, God instructs us, "Do not touch my anointed ones; do my prophets no harm," which could also be correctly translated as "Do not touch my messiahs, and do my prophets no harm," or even "Do not touch not my christs, and do my prophets no harm."

Aaron and his sons were the first people to be anointed:

Exodus 28:41 You shall put them on your brother Aaron, and on his sons with him, and shall anoint them and ordain them and consecrate them, so that they may serve me as priests.

Leviticus 8:12 He poured some of the anointing oil on Aaron's head and anointed him, to consecrate him.

Isaiah was a messiah:

Isaiah 61:1 The spirit of the Lord God is upon me, because the LORD has anointed me; he has sent me to bring good news to the oppressed, to bind up the brokenhearted, to proclaim liberty to the captives, and release to the prisoners.

King David was a messiah:

Psalm 2:2 The kings of the earth set themselves, and the rulers take counsel together, against the LORD and his anointed [David]. . . .

Psalm 18:50 Great triumphs he gives to his king, and shows steadfast love to his anointed, to David and his descendants forever.

All the priests in the lineage of Aaron were messiahs:

Leviticus 6:22 And so the priest, anointed from among Aaron's descendants as a successor, shall prepare it; it is the LORD's—a perpetual due—to be turned entirely into smoke.

All the priests were known as anointed as messiahs:

1 Samuel 2:35 I will raise up for myself a faithful priest, who shall do according to what is in my heart and in my mind. I will build him a sure house, and he shall go in and out before my anointed one forever.

All the kings of Israel were messiahs:

1 Samuel 2:10 The LORD will judge the ends of the earth; he will give strength to his king, and exalt the power of his anointed.

In fact, you don't have to be Jewish to be a messiah:

Isaiah 45:1 Thus says the LORD to his anointed, to Cyrus, whose right hand I have grasped to subdue nations before him and strip kings of their robes, to open doors before him—and the gates shall not be closed.

A future prince will be a messiah:

Daniel 9:25 Know therefore and understand: from the time that the word went out to restore and rebuild Jerusalem until the time of an anointed prince, there shall be seven weeks.

Christian theology, and inadequate translations of the Bible, give the impression that there is only one Christ, so it sounds odd to our ears to say that Isaiah was "christed" or that King David was a "christ," but that would be the more literal translation of the Hebrew word in Greek. Both Christians and Jews often don't realize that the same word *christos* that describes Jesus in the New Testament is used in Greek translations of the Jewish Scriptures to describe King David and the other Jewish "anointed" people.

Since the expulsion of the Jews from Jerusalem, the capital of the ancient Jewish homeland, two thousand years ago, the Jewish people have yearned for a messiah to come and aid God in the process of redeeming the people. Keep in mind that the notion of redemption in Judaism is not only a redemption of individual souls, but the redemption and physical rescue of the Jewish people from oppression—bringing them again to the Promised Land from wherever they are in exile. Although Jews today do indeed dwell once again in their ancient homeland, the role of the coming messiah has yet to be fulfilled to help redeem humanity.

Judaism teaches that the future messiah will not just be a king for the Jewish people, but will help bring the entire world into the messianic era when "the wolf shall live with the lamb" (Isaiah 11:6), and when people "shall beat their swords into plowshares" (Isaiah 2:4). He will be of the Davidic line on his father's side since all the anointed kings of Israel were of the Davidic lineage following patrilineal descent. The future messiah will be a son or daughter of God, since Judaism believes that every individual is a son or daughter of God. The future messiah will not be seen, however, as the incarnation of God, according to the Christian understanding of Jesus's incarnation.

The Jewish expectation of the messiah is simple: the whole world will be at peace, and the "government will be upon his shoulders"; he or she will be a political leader as well as a spiritual leader. This did not happen during or after Jesus's lifetime, or during the lifetimes of several other candidates for the title of messiah such as Bar Kokhba in the early part of the second century. Another expectation of the messiah is that the universal wisdom of the Torah will flow forth to the entire world. Interestingly, this in part happened with the spread of Christianity and Islam over the past two millennia. A third expectation is that the Temple will be rebuilt in Jerusalem, and offerings of some kind will be reinstated.

In the Younger Testament, Luke (Luke 4:14–30) recounts how Jesus proclaims himself to be anointed, and he seems to speak of this in the same sense as Isaiah, since he is quoting the prophet's words. Obviously, there was nothing strange in his proclamation, since Luke informs us that the Jewish people at the Sabbath service that morning "marveled at the gracious words" which he spoke. Jesus was not some revolutionary out to replace Judaism. He taught from within the prophetic and emerging rabbinic tradition. Like the prophets before him, and many of his fellow rabbis, he taught that Jewish ethics were aimed at helping the helpless and bringing hope to the hopeless.

Luke 4:14–30 Then Jesus . . . went to the synagogue on the sabbath day, as was his custom. He stood up to read, and the scroll of the prophet Isaiah was given to him. He unrolled the scroll and found the place where it was written: "The Spirit of the Lord is upon me, because he has anointed me to bring good news to the poor. He has sent me to proclaim release to the captives and recovery of sight to the blind, to let the oppressed go free, to proclaim the year of the Lord's favor. . . ." Then he began to say to them, "Today this scripture has been fulfilled in your hearing."

Some Christian translations capitalize the pronouns *He* and *Him* when referring to Jesus in order to demonstrate the theological position that Jesus is God incarnate. This translational choice (the ancient Greek does not use upper and lowercases as we do) has to do with the "theological Jesus" and not the "historical Jesus." I read the above passage in the plain and simple sense of its being about a Jewish rabbi named Joshua being a guest teacher and reader in his local synagogue and being deeply admired by the congregation. In Judaism, being a messiah is the greatest honor that God can bestow on a person, but the title of "messiah" was never understood as a divine term in biblical Judaism.

Finally, as important as the messianic expectation is within Judaism, it does not hold the same central position that it does in Christianity. The messianic era will mark the fulfillment of our mutually shared vision for world peace and justice, but the coming of the messiah must be kept in perspective to the day-to-day obligations of our covenantal responsibilities. There is a lovely teaching attributed to one of the most important rabbis of the first century, Rabbi Yokhanan Ben Zakkai. He said, "If you have a sapling in your hand and are told, 'Look, the Messiah is here,' you should first plant the sapling and then go out to welcome the Messiah" (Avot de-Rabbi Natan 3). In other words, keep your priorities in proper order.

The Notion of Two Messiahs

A study of Elder Testament prophesies and rabbinic writings about the messiah will inspire the student to wonder: will the future messiah suffer or be honored? Will the messiah be killed or be crowned king? Will the messiah be a warrior or a spiritual leader? Will the messianic kingdom come peacefully or after a catastrophic event? Jewish tradition is vague, and honors several opposing views concerning the messiah.

After the Bar Kokhba revolt against the Roman Empire in 135 CE, an idea was debated within Judaism that there might be two messiahs. The first messiah would hold the title of Messiah son of Joseph (sometimes called Messiah son of Efraim). He'd be a "suffering servant" who would be killed. The second messiah would be Messiah son of David, and he would fulfill the prophecies for peace on earth, an end to war, and the other messianic prophesies. The idea of two messiahs is based on one possible interpretation of the prophet Zechariah's words:

Zechariah 4:12–14 And a second time I said to him, "What are these two branches of the olive trees, which pour out the oil through the two golden pipes?" He said to me, "Do you not know what these are?" I said, "No, my lord." Then he said, "These are the two anointed ones who stand by the Lord of the whole earth."

This is also somewhat parallel to the Christian concept of the Second Coming. The first time Jesus came and was killed—he is the suffering messiah within Christianity. Most Christians believe that he will fulfill the remaining biblical prophecies when he returns. What will be the circumstances that bring about the Second Coming? There is much discussion, debate, and disagreement within the diverse denominations and movements within Christianity concerning the Second Coming. But Catholics and many Protestants certainly pray that Christ will return again.

Over the centuries, Jews have suggested that a number of people might be the next messiah: Bar Kokhba in the second century; Isaac Luria and

Hayyim Vital in the sixteenth century; the Stoliner Rebbe in the eighteenth century; and Lubavitcher Rebbe in the twentieth century. The majority of Jews accepted none as Messiah son of David because none fulfilled the basic messianic prophesies. Yet all of them are still seen as saintly, great Jewish leaders, and all of them worked valiantly on behalf of the Jewish people. The occidental mind wants a neat black-and-white answer, not an ambiguous mystery concerning our understanding of Jesus and the messiah. After two thousand years we still do not have a clear answer. Maybe it's time to acknowledge that God may have something else in mind. The Messiah son of David, according to Zechariah, will take his throne in a humble manner:

> **Zechariah 9:9–10** Lo, your king comes to you; triumphant and victorious is he, humble and riding on a donkey . . . and he shall command peace to the nations; his dominion shall be from sea to sea, and from the [Euphrates] River to the ends of the earth.

Is there room within our traditions for a fresh approach to the Jewish/Christian messianic dilemma? Rabbi Yechiel Eckstein asks, "Can Jews and Judaism be stretched to the point where they can affirm that Jesus, a Jew and mortal human being, was in some way 'sent' by God to bring salvation to the Gentiles through Christianity?" [68] The possibility that Jesus was Messiah son of Joseph has been discussed by Rabbi Zalman Schachter-Shalomi and Rabbi Irving Greenberg, among others. [69] It's an idea worthy of consideration since it frees us from having to force any proofs of his Davidic lineage. Remember that in Matthew and Luke, Jesus's Davidic lineage can only be traced through his adoptive father, Joseph.

The idea of Jesus being Messiah son of Joseph, from a Jewish perspective, might also free theologians from having to force their interpretations of the prophecies. To the Jewish reader of the Bible, Jesus did not fulfill prophecies expected of the Messiah son of David, which would include freeing Israel from the yoke of foreign oppression. The spiritual components of the messianic expectation within Judaism includes the resurrection of the dead, the ingathering of the exiles, and a world at peace. So, can Jesus be the Messiah for Christians and at the same time be honored as a rabbi by Jews? Can Jesus be accepted as Messiah son of Joseph to Jews while being seen as Messiah son of David to Christians? Can he be the incarnation of God to many Christians and a great human being to Jews? Thus far in history, neither Jews nor Christians have been able to deal with contradictions very well. We want our black-and-white answers. Mystery and paradox require a certain kind of mindset that has to be cultivated over time.

To conclude, there is a charming story told by Rabbi Nancy Fuchs-Kreimer, a story that she heard from Rabbi Zalman Schachter-Shalomi:

> The Messiah finally arrives. Jews and Christians, after waiting for so many centuries, rush to meet him. The Jews cry out, "This is the first time you have come, is it not?" The Christians, raising their voices above the Jews, insist, "This must be Your second coming that we have been waiting for!" The Messiah smiles wearily and waits for the noise to subside. Then, in a quiet and gentle voice, long suffering, he says, "My dear, foolish children. I have come not once, not twice. I have been here hundreds of times. But you have all been so busy fighting with one another you have never even noticed."[70]

Salvation, Grace & Redemption

When Jews and Christians use the word *salvation*, they often mean two very different things. The Hebrew word for "salvation" generally means the "physical rescue and victory over one's enemies, often through the intervention of God." The notion of salvation in the Tanakh doesn't have the same sense of salvation of the soul as most Christians assume it does. In the mystical streams of Judaism, Christianity, Islam, and Hinduism the soul of a person has been metaphorically described as a "spark of God." In this sense, it does not need to be saved from anything. As a person I might need to be "rescued" from an enemy, or I may need to be "saved" from my own negative inclinations, but this is quite different from wondering if I am spiritually "saved," and whether I'll go to heaven or hell after I die. Although salvation of the soul might have been a concern in the first century (see Matthew 19:25), it has not been a primary concern for most of Jewish history.

Pinchas Lapide said, "The rabbinate has never considered the Torah as a way of salvation to God. . . . We regard salvation as something entirely within God's exclusive domain, so we Jews are advocates of 'pure grace.'"[71] The Jewish idea that all people have a place in God's kingdom regardless of their religion is summed up best in the Oral Torah: "The righteous of all nations have a share in the world to come" (Tosefta–Sanhedrin 13:1). Simon Peter may have been thinking of that when he said, "I truly understand that God shows no partiality, but in every nation anyone who fears him and does what is right is acceptable to him" (Acts 10:34–35).

God's grace is simply that, *grace*. No dogma to profess. No prescribed ritual. No formula to recite. One doesn't have to be any particular religion. Judaism doesn't contain any notion of an exclusive means of salvation. To "call upon the name of the LORD" is the key that opens up the door that both King David and Paul were teaching about. In Judaism, it's taught that the decision about who gets eternal life is in God's hands, and should not be a topic for flawed human or denominational speculation.

It's easy for Jews and Christians to misunderstand each other when the same Hebrew words and concepts for "salvation" and "grace" are translated (or interpreted) into English and understood differently. Whereas a Christian declares himself saved (in the spiritual sense) by grace, the Jew is hoping to be saved (in the sense of physical rescue) by that same grace. Judaism teaches that salvation is one element in a worldwide redemption for all people, and part of our planetary, collective future. Salvation in its literal biblical sense is a yearned-for goal that encompasses the individual, collective humanity and all of creation. It's the healing "salve" evidenced by physical rescue from danger, as well as each individual's renewed connection to God. In Judaism, salvation is not a goal achieved by conversion to any one religion or by the profession of a creed or dogma.

When Jews pray for the salvation of all humanity, the prayer is tied to a biblical understanding of redemption—it's not based on an expectation that anyone will convert to Judaism. Grace is understood as the underlying state of all existence. It's experienced as we, individually or collectively, express gratitude and thanksgiving. Salvation is the result of grace, and grace is a result of salvation; the two are interconnected. By grace we come into a relationship with God, and the result is rescue (salvation) from that which oppresses us (internally or externally), regardless of our religion or belief systems.

Salvation in the Younger Testament

The notion of salvation expressed in many parts of the New Testament is basically an extension of Jewish theology. To first-century followers of Jesus, salvation was Jewish in both form and explanation—primarily physical in nature, nonexclusive to Jews, tied to the general redemption of all people, and entirely in God's hands. It was not for people to speculate about whose soul would or would not go to heaven. This way of understanding salvation has not changed in Judaism to this day—we are entitled to judge each other's behavior, but we leave it to God to judge the intentions of our hearts and the fate of our souls. I sense that this is what Jesus tried to teach when asked, "Who then can be saved?" He answers, "For mortals it is impossible, but for God all things are possible" (Matthew 19:25–26).

Then things began to change. The notion of the spiritual salvation of the individual, distinct from the notion of rescue from oppression, most likely developed as the early church began to distinguish itself more and more from its Jewish roots. As Christianity began to take shape, we see the Hebrew notion of salvation as "rescue" being transformed into something spiritual. In the Bible, *salvation* usually describes the rescue of a person from a dangerous situation, or describes the liberation of Israel as a nation.

Within the early Church its meaning shifted to describe the rescue of an individual's soul from eternal damnation. We see this subtle shift in passages like Ephesians 1:13 where Paul personalizes and spiritualizes salvation when he writes, "In him you also, when you had heard the word of truth, the gospel of your salvation, and had believed in him, were marked with the seal of the promised Holy Spirit." Early Christianity slowly began to focus more and more on the afterlife, with salvation being a means for each person to achieve his or her place in the world to come.

Aside from the differing meanings attached to the word, the Church began to develop this idea that accepting Jesus as Lord and Savior was the only way to achieve salvation and eternal life. In our modern age, the Catholic Church, most mainstream Protestant denominations, and a handful of evangelical groups no longer accept the doctrine of *extra ecclesiam nulla salus*, which means, "outside the church there is no salvation." Regrettably though, there remain millions of Christians who continue to be taught that every person who does not accept Jesus as his or her Lord is going to hell and has no eternal life. To many fundamentalists, it appears that no matter how good, kind, innocent, or loving a person is, that counts for nothing compared to the single requisite of accepting Jesus as the exclusive savior of souls. Some fundamentalists also teach that Jews will be given a second chance to accept Jesus in the future.

Under the inspired and courageous leadership of Pope John XXIII and the Vatican II Council in the 1960s, the Catholic Church led the way for the rest of the Christian world to eliminate the nonbiblical doctrine of exclusive salvation. In the past fifty years, many denominations have scaled back their belief that outside of Jesus, God-fearing people are not saved. The danger of the idea of exclusive salvation is that even within the Church, some denominations claim that members of other denominations are not saved. One group requires baptism by dunking, while another group expects baptism by sprinkling. Religion begins to resemble politics, with each faction stubbornly proclaiming, "We have the truth, and others are wrong!" Is God's grace operating here? I don't think so, and more and more Christians agree.

As many fundamentalists have discovered, asking a Jew whether he or she is saved is responded to with a puzzled look. In the Jewish mindset, the question "Are you saved?" is a non sequitur, since Judaism was never a faith with a focus on the salvation of the soul. Rather, Jews have understood their mission is to help God bring redemption to the world when everyone will have a chance to know God under his or her own "vine and fig tree"—that is, within each unique culture and religion. Judaism teaches that we don't obtain spiritual salvation by works, or by the profession of a creed. From a Jewish perspective, the question of who is and is not saved spiritually is not a matter for human speculation. Our job is to try to make the world a better place just as Moses, the prophets, and Rabbi Jesus did.

So for a moment, try putting yourself in the position of a Jewish man or woman any time during the past two thousand years, hearing the gospel message tied to the notion of exclusive salvation. It meant then, and continues to mean today, a complete betrayal of the everlasting covenant God made with the Jewish people. Throughout history Jews were given the choice of converting to Christianity or spending eternity in hell—the very idea of which is antithetical to everything taught by God in the Bible. Paul teaches the original Jewish concept of salvation when he quotes the prophet Joel, stating that "everyone who calls on the name of the Lord shall be saved" (Romans 10:13).

Is it really "good news" for a Jew to be told that all of his ancestors for two thousand years didn't make it into heaven? It's a cruel thought, and unsound theology as well. I appreciate that the desire to "save Jews" sometimes comes out of sincere concern, but such efforts (and funding) would be better spent trying to save people from hunger and hatred. To most Jews (and other non-Christians as well), it's insulting to be told that our souls are "incomplete." Clearly, there are certain Younger Testament verses that have been interpreted as referring to Jesus at the exclusion of other pathways to God. For example,

"Then Peter, filled with the Holy Spirit, said to them, 'Rulers of the people, and elders. . . . There is salvation in no one else, for there is no other name under heaven given among mortals by which we must be saved'" (Acts 4:8 and 12). The same doctrine of exclusive salvation is justified by the verse "So that everyone who believes in him [Jesus, the only Son] may not perish but may have eternal life" (John 3:16).

Is the idea that Jews and other non-Christians cannot have salvation really what either Jesus or the apostles were teaching? Or is it a matter of faulty interpretation, mistranslation, or later adulterations and additions to the text that we cannot prove? John's gospel certainly seems clear that Jesus and the Father are an inseparable unity, and "anyone who does not honor the Son does not honor the Father who sent him. . . . Anyone who hears my word and believes him who sent me has eternal life, and does not come under judgment, but has passed from death to life" (John 5:23–24). Reading Paul in Romans 9–11, it does not seem as if he was excluding Jews from their relationship with God if they were not followers of Jesus. The gospel that Jesus was preaching can certainly be interpreted as inclusive: "For I am not ashamed of the gospel; it is the power of God for salvation to everyone who has faith, to the Jew first and also to the Greek" (Romans 1:16). In other words, the spiritual mechanism for salvation historically came to the Jews first through the unfolding biblical covenants, and then to the rest of the world.

At times, Paul does not seem to be saying that God's covenant intended for the Gentiles should be preached to Jewish people who already had a covenantal, grace-based relationship with the Creator. Rather, the covenant promising God's forgiveness and salvation was made available to the Gentiles through the Noahic covenant (referred to in Acts 15:29), and then reshaped by Paul into the "new" covenant referred to by Jeremiah. Paul's genius was in his teaching that a personal relationship to God, through Jesus, was available to everyone without having to become Jewish. I want to believe that Paul's message was *from* the Jews, and not *to* the Jews, and that he understood the role of the Jewish people as a "light unto the nations."

Jewish tradition holds that King Solomon wrote the book of Ecclesiastes late in his life when he proclaimed, "Whatever God does endures forever; nothing can be added to it, nor anything taken from it" (Ecclesiastes 3:14). If God makes a covenant and says that it's everlasting, eternal, and will "stand firm forever," what gives humans the authority to ignore the plain meaning of these words? A century after Solomon's reign the prophet Isaiah said "the word of our God will stand forever" (Isaiah 40:8). The survival of the Jewish people against all odds, and the rebirth of the nation of Israel after two thousand years, is evidence of God's ongoing, covenantal relationship with the Jewish people. Too many well-meaning fundamentalists have been taught that God has a plan for the Jewish people in the future, and yet permitted six million Jewish souls to go to hell during the Holocaust because they weren't Christian. Obviously, this kind of defective theology is not acceptable to Jews and a majority of Christians.

ELEVEN

Grace, Redemption, and Suffering

REGARDING OUR UNDERSTANDING OF GOD'S GRACE, THE JEWISH and Christian understanding has far more in common than is generally acknowledged. The Apostle Paul argues on behalf of his fellow Jews against those who were advocating for grace being exclusive to the followers of Jesus. He teaches, "So too at the present time there is a remnant, chosen by grace" (Romans 11:5). With perfect Socratic reasoning he goes on to say, "But if it is by grace, it is no longer on the basis of works, otherwise grace would no longer be grace" (Romans 11:6). The translation of "chosen by grace" is "election by grace" in the King James Version. It seems as if Paul recognizes that God is sovereign to elect, select, choose, save, or rescue whomever, whether we understand it or not. This election is not based on good deeds, worthiness, merit, being Jewish, being Christian, keeping kosher, professing Jesus as Lord, avowing a certain creed, or being a member of a particular denomination. It certainly isn't bound or limited by the rules of logic and human discernment. Following Paul's line of reasoning, if the election of grace were dependent on any human action or belief, then it would "no longer be grace."

Judaism takes this mechanism of election by grace to the extreme. God chooses whomever God chooses, whenever God chooses, for whatever reason God uses. We can give God our opinions about people, but we don't even get a vote, and we rarely get to know the verdict about what will ultimately happen to their souls.

There are countless stories in the vast Jewish storytelling tradition that tell of thieves, fools, beggars, drunkards, prostitutes, robbers, prisoners, wanderers, and Elijah in disguise—either mysteriously fulfilling God's will, or testing our religious sincerity. Our hearts are warmed when we hear these stories, but there are two profound and simple truths within them: God's ways are not our ways, and God is sovereign. Humans simply do not have the wisdom to judge another person's spiritual salvation—that's God's job. We are certainly obliged to judge another's actions according to the Torah's demand for moral behavior, but rarely do we fully know another's true intent; we simply have faith that God knows.

Some more conservative Christians familiar with the "election of grace" believe that this election is limited to a small group of extraordinary individuals from the Elder Testament (e.g., Abraham, Jacob, Saul, David, Solomon). This concept is often used to describe how Jewish people were able to get into heaven before Jesus's lifetime. The tradition (in art, story, and legend) of the "Harrowing of Hell," as seen in Dante and elsewhere, sometimes depicts Jesus doing this on the eve of the first Easter, literally pulling the most righteous Jews from limbo. The concept is also sometimes used to explain how a tiny number of non-Christians might be able to have salvation today without becoming Christian. The Younger Testament, however, does not indicate that Paul believed this special election was limited to a handful of biblical heroes.

Although the "election of grace" is a Christian concept, its underlying validity can be understood through a Jewish lens as long as it is not restricted to a handful of people. To be a Hebraic idea, the "election of grace" must apply to everyone, in all ages, in all cultures, in all social classes, and in all religions. In Judaism we believe that God's grace is limitless. It certainly is not bound to any single sort of belief.

The notion of "election of grace" presents Christians with the opportunity to adjust their beliefs to the Hebraic intent of Scripture and to what Jesus actually taught. For the first time in two thousand years, Christians are taking the opportunity to welcome their Jewish brothers and sisters as "those who have received a faith as precious as ours" (2 Peter 1:1) rather than trying to convert them or dissuade them from fulfilling their covenantal obligations as commanded by God in the Torah. A more generous definition of the "election of grace" seems to be the theological key needed to open the gate of understanding that remains locked in much of Christendom concerning the salvation of the Jews and people of other faiths as well.

I remember asking a kind, well-meaning missionary pastor who I knew if he really believed that the five million Jewish adults and one million Jewish children who were murdered in the Holocaust could really be in hell. He sincerely started crying as he told me that he had no choice but to believe that the adults, as good as they might have been, could not have made it to heaven without Christ. I wept with him, but for a different reason. I couldn't believe that he really believed what he was saying. I said, "My God is not so small as yours. God's mercy is not so merciless." Then I asked him, "Who said you have 'no choice' anyway? God's grace is not restricted in the Jewish Scriptures, and I don't believe it's restricted in your Scriptures either. Our human understanding is restricted, but God's grace is not."

Two Views of Redemption

Judaism and Christianity define the word *redemption* with slightly different emphases. The goal of redemption in Christianity tends to start with each individual being saved from sin. The goal of redemption in the Tanakh, on the other hand, tends to start with redeeming the nation from exile, and redeeming individuals from prison or some other terrible situation. In the Pentateuch, the word for redemption is *g'ulah*, which is not used in relation to the spiritual state of one's soul. Yet Jewish and Christian goals of redemption seem to be two sides of a single coin—a national focus for Judaism and a personal, spiritual focus for Christianity, salvation from sin for Christianity and rescue from exile for Judaism. As different as these two views of redemption seem to be, I believe that on a spiritual level, they are consonant with one another.

Ever since the Roman occupation of Judea, there was a deep faith that someday the Jewish people would be fully restored to their land, which is what happened in 1948. The verb *redeem* in Hebrew has many meanings: avenge, revenge, ransom, redeem from slavery, redeem land, redeem oneself. The biblical idea of redemption is a difficult concept for the modern mind to grasp. It's based on the sense that everything has a cost, either in physical terms (like redeeming a captive with money, in Leviticus 25:25); in social justice terms (redeeming a nation from bondage, in Exodus 6:6); and in familial terms (redeeming the firstborn son, in Exodus 13:15). The idea of spiritual redemption is Christian (see Hebrews 9:12 15).

The theological concept of redemption can be compared to the principle of balance in physics. One of Newton's great laws of motion states, "For every action there is an opposite and equal reaction." The Torah view of the world is optimistic and views history in an upward spiral with the world getting better through every commandment we fulfill. If I do a good deed, it might inspire you to do a good deed. And when I do something bad, there is, so to speak, a price to pay. It's a spiritual price, but the payback mechanism has an impact in the physical world as well.

The Hebrew concept for this balancing mechanism in the world is called "measure-for-measure." Whatever I do has a measure-for-measure consequence. If I do something good, then more good can come from it. If I do something foolish, how can I make it up? I feel regret. I confess. I repent. I make restitution. Finally, I figure out a way to avoid making that mistake again. But in reality, can I ever fully make up for the damage that was done in the physical world (to friends, family, community, environment) by my gossip, my abuse, or my sin? No, not completely. I can never repair all the damage that has been done as a consequence of my wrong actions. There is always a small amount of residual damage remaining from my sins. This can be compared to the scar that is formed after an injury. The scar is an ongoing reminder of the injury and the tiny bit of residual damage that remains.

This is what redemption is all about. Whatever remains of my sins must be made up for somehow. Just as Newton's laws of motion are true in our world, so "measure for measure" is true in the realm of spiritual physics. Something has to make up for what I cannot repair. Redemption is a process inherent in nature itself. Redemption makes up for the energy lost by our committing sins. Each time an innocent child suffers, or a saintly person suffers, or when we suffer, God permits that suffering to make up for each of our personal sins that we have not been able to repair. Catholics call this "redemptive suffering." Along with suffering, when any person repents, it also helps bring about a degree of redemption. Why? Because there is, so to speak, some leftover energy from the courage it took for the person to repent. Jews believe that God applies this leftover energy to the "account" of the sins of the whole world.

How does redemption work? Permit me to explain it with a trite example. Let's say that before I sin, God gives me five brownie points just for not sinning. Then I sin and God takes away two brownie points. Now I only have three brownie points left, so I sincerely repent. Somehow it moves the mercy of God to such a degree that I receive three brownie points back—two for the points I lost, and one extra as a bonus for my courage to repent. Now I have six brownie points, but I only needed five to keep things balanced. In the Talmud this is expressed with the idea that a person who repents is actually on a higher spiritual level than even the righteous who rarely sin. How can this be? It's part of the mystery of the physics of repentance. In Judaism the ethical actions, moments of repentance, and acts of reparation create a collective force that eventually leads to the redemption and liberation (physical and spiritual) of all people.

This is also what is meant by the "merit of the ancestors." Our ancestors have accumulated a certain number of brownie points, and the Holy One permits this "merit" to be deposited in our own accounts if such a need arises. What we call the redemption in Judaism is the accumulated good deeds of all people reaching such a critical mass that it evokes a direct response from God. This process will eventually bring about an "anointed" appointee of the Creator who will usher in the "Kingdom of God," which is an era of unimaginable peace and justice in the world. So who is this spiritual redeemer in Judaism? Each of us contributes to the redemption through the good that we bring into our world. Within Judaism, the term *redeemer* is usually reserved for God. We participate in the redemptive process by being redeemers to one another during times of bondage and crisis. With each of our good actions, we add to the general redemption of the world. Everything we do counts and adds up, so to speak.

Etymologically, it's probable that there is a direct connection among three words central to Jewish theology: exile (*galut*), redemption (*g'ulah*), and revelation (*galui*). As spiritual concepts, they form the triad upon which the Jewish story is told, so it's an exquisite idea that these words are actually etymological cognates of each other. In classical Jewish theology, Egypt represents the "exile" of the Hebrews when they were enslaved. The Exodus represents "redemption" when the slaves were liberated from bondage. Sinai represents the culmination of the exile and the redemption—the "revelation" of Torah and the birth of the Jewish people. On another level, when we bring these three words together we get a perfect picture of the psychological link between exile, liberation, and revelation—understanding what good could possibly come out of the bondage. My friend, colleague, and Episcopal priest, Rev. Anne Bartlett, says that the Christian analog to this Jewish concept would be Good Friday (exile), Easter Sunday (redemption), and Pentecost (revelation).

The Purpose of Suffering

Those who interpret the suffering of the Jewish people as a result of their sins, and then contradictorily describe the suffering of Jesus as the true sign of his election, are playing by an unfair and cruelly biased set of interpretive rules. Robert Gibbs of the University of Toronto expresses it well:

Jewish suffering through the ages has been subject to various interpretations. . . . The conflict with Christian theology arises when these same interpretations become justifications for "your sufferings." When the prophet's words are turned against the Jews by those who stand opposed to the Jews, they function in a remarkably different way than when they arise as explanations of our suffering. The "dialogue" of judgment upon the other is a violence. [72]

So why do the Jews suffer? Why did Jesus die suffering? I would answer both questions with this: Israel suffered for the same reason Jesus suffered. After all, he's a son of Israel, and a mirror of his people for the world to see and be redeemed by. In this light, describing Jewish suffering in the shadow of the Holocaust, Martin Buber wrote, "We [Jews] demonstrate with the bloody body of our people, the unredeemedness of the world." [73]

To the prophets and rabbis, injustice is something the Jews are to help all people overcome. By doing so, the Jew finds himself or herself up against empires, rulers, despots, and bigots who make the Jewish people suffer. To the rabbis, Israel's suffering was seen as a consequence of standing up for the Torah. Suffering isn't glorified or romanticized in Judaism—it's simply accepted as a reality. In their liturgical and personal spiritual lives, Christians look for ways that each believer may participate in Jesus's suffering, and then hallow that suffering as an expiation for all sinners. In the face of suffering, Jews look to God for meaning, all the while fulfilling their part of the covenant.

This attitude is shaped by a long history of martyrdom among the Jewish people who acknowledge both the reality of suffering and the end of needless suffering when the messiah comes. What we might call the Passion of Israel is sanctified in the form of the stories many of our holidays are about; Passover, Tisha B'Av, Yom Kippur, Hanukkah, and Purim all have the theme of transforming suffering into joy. To the Jew, there's no need to ennoble suffering through any special doctrine—it's ennobled the moment it occurs. In the Talmud it is taught, "A person should always try to be among the persecuted rather than the persecutors" (Talmud: Baba Kamma 93a). Jesus echoed this idea when he preached, "Blessed are those who are persecuted for righteousness' sake, for theirs is the kingdom of heaven" (Matthew 5:10).

A search of the word *suffer* in the Hebrew Scriptures reveals something interesting. One of several Hebrew words that is sometimes translated as *suffer* (*nasa*) is not generally used to mean "to experience pain." The word has the connotation of "bearing" or "putting up with something," giving it a value-neutral meaning. Words coming from the Hebrew root mean to "lift up, exalt." Interestingly, the King James translators report Jesus saying, "Suffer the little children to come unto me" (Mark 10:14). The word *suffer* means to "allow," and this might shed some light on the suffering of Israel or Jesus or anyone else. Another person's suffering "allows" us the opportunity to be more fully human through our empathy and compassionate responses. Could it be that when the righteous suffer, God is suffering too? This certainly seems to be part of the message from the cross that Christians have brought to the world. Rabbi Irving Greenberg asks a question many have considered: "Where was God during the Holocaust?" He then answers:

> I suddenly understood that God was with people ("I will be with him in distress" Psalm 91:15)—being tortured, degraded, humiliated, murdered. Where else would God be when God's loved ones were being hounded and destroyed? So, how were the rabbis able to justify the suffering of the innocent and the righteous . . . ? There is the sense within Judaism that having a covenantal relationship with God does not make life easier, but actually even more challenging. [74]

It's always difficult to understand the suffering of the innocent, and historically there have been terrible abuses based on the idea that suffering is punishment for sin. Certainly Christianity knows this well in its understanding of the sacrificial suffering of their Messiah. And in the image of the prophet Isaiah's famous "suffering servant" passage, the prophet makes a clear distinction between those who suffer because of their own sins, and those who suffer on behalf of the sins of others (see Isaiah 52:13–53:12). In conclusion, consider the words of Thomas Merton, the great Catholic mystic and writer, when he warns us of the dangers of judging others based on a doctrine of retributive suffering. Merton startles the reader with his understanding of anti-Semitism, which he calls theological suicide:

> The theology of suffering is strongly tinged with ideas of punishment, and morality becomes a morality of obedience rather than love. In this aggressive, solemn, dark and feudal Christianity . . . there grows up the hatred and contempt of the Jew, whose role is more and more that of the theological Christ-killer on whom the curse has fallen. But perhaps there was in this a deep unconscious guilt for Christians who did not truly understand Christ.[74]

To Merton, knowing Christ is to comprehend the irony that Jesus seems to have failed when he was taken to the cross, but that it was out of failure that he was a light to the nations. Christians see themselves in Jesus precisely because he suffered, just as they do. This theology is also deeply rooted in the vicarious suffering of the nation Israel. We are thus able to see how Jesus is a precise microcosm, a fractal if you will, of the nation in which he was born.

Each of us is interconnected in the web of existence, and we are deeply affected by each other's suffering. If Christ's suffering brings a Christian to see the cross in everyone's suffering, then the Christian will do all he or she can to help relieve that suffering. It's then that the gospel has done its job. If Israel's suffering brings a Jew to see his or her suffering in the suffering of everyone else, it's then that the Torah has done its job. Without taking action to relieve suffering there can be no Jew; there can be no Christian.

TWELVE

Faith Without Works
Is Dead

THERE SHOULD BE NO EITHER/OR ABOUT THE RELATIONSHIP between
faith and works in any religion. The book of James in the Younger
Testament expresses the authentic Jewish idea about the essential
interconnection between faith and works. "Faith without works is dead,"
James famously says.

Judaism believes that God may judge us through the attribute of mercy,
but it's still in our covenantal job description to make the world a better
place. It is not a coincidence that a disproportionate number of Jews are
involved in law to bring justice, in medicine to bring healing, in physics to
deepen our understanding of the cosmos, and in the arts to bring the world
more beauty. From a Jewish viewpoint, faith and works are two parts of a
whole. One leads to the other. Neither is better, nor can one be judged apart
from the other. Do good and you will be led to greater faith. Have faith and
you will be led to doing good works. Religion and what we do in the world
are completely intertwined. You could say that what we do in the world is
evidence of the depth of our spiritual practice.

It is an inaccurate stereotype to describe Judaism as a religion of works
in the same way that it would be inaccurate to describe Christianity as an
otherworldly faith lacking works. True, Christian theology tends to stress
faith in the world to come, just as Jewish culture tends to stress works and
sanctifying this world. But both Christianity and Judaism share a common vision and hope for world redemption and for perfecting this world
through good deeds. As Dr. Steven Kepnes writes, "The sense that there is a

flaw within humanity and the world, and that humans and the world are in need of healing, salvation, and redemption runs deep through Judaism and Christianity."[76]

It's not a coincidence that so many of our great hospitals in America have the words Sinai, Lutheran, Methodist, Presbyterian, Adventist, and Providence in their names—Jews, Catholics, and Protestants have emphasized the good associated with healing as an outward expression of faith. Look at these powerful verses that teach us about the importance of both our faith and our works:

> **Jeremiah 17:10** I the LORD test the mind and search the heart, to give to all according to their ways, according to the fruit of their doings.

> **Talmud: Makkot 23b–24a** Six hundred and thirteen commandments were spoken to Moses. When Habakkuk came, he summed them up in one principle, saying, "The righteous shall live by his faith" (Habakkuk 2:4).

> **James 2:26** For just as the body without the spirit is dead, so faith without works is also dead.

We may want an absolute, black or white answer to the question of whether God justifies us solely by the attribute of divine grace, or as a response to our good deeds. We don't have one. But in the first century, Rabbi Akiva gave us a paradox to ponder when he said, "The world is judged by Divine grace, yet all is in accord with the number of a person's deeds" (Mishnah: Avot 3:19).

If you ask a Jewish person if he or she is justified by faith or works, you will usually get a quizzical look. Jewish theology tends to avoid this kind of dualistic, cut and dried either/or question. The concept of God's grace is so infused within Jewish theology that most Jews aren't even familiar with the concept of justification by faith. As mentioned elsewhere, "salvation" in the Hebrew Scriptures was almost always about rescue from physical danger. In Christianity, salvation became spiritual in nature rather than physical—tied to how an individual attains eternal life. In Judaism, the attainment of eternal life is seen as entirely in God's hands. Our job is to "worship the LORD with gladness" (Psalm 100:2) and, while we're at it, help make the world a better place. Jewish theology does not have a major focus on heaven, eternal life, or the salvation of the soul; life is short and there's just too much good to do in the world.

My teacher, Rabbi Zalman Schachter-Shalomi, once answered someone who wondered if Jews were saved by faith or works. I heard him respond something like this: "In the autumn, we're saved by works. By stocking up on supplies and preparing for winter, it's our works that gets us saved. On the other hand, from spring through summer, we're saved by grace. We see that God's bounty abounds in the nature, and survival does not so much depend on our actions. So, that's when we're saved by grace." A proper Jewish response to the question, "Are you saved by faith or works?" might be "Yes. Both. There is no either/or." In the Younger Testament, James answered in a way not unlike Rabbi Zalman:

> **James 2:21–24 and 26:** Was not our ancestor Abraham justified by works when he offered his son Isaac on the altar? You see that faith was active along with his works, and faith was brought to completion by the works. Thus the scripture was fulfilled that says, "Abraham believed God, and it was reckoned to him as righteousness," and he was called the friend of God. You see that a person is justified by works and not by faith alone. For just as the body without the spirit is dead, so faith without works is also dead.

Rabbi David Novak tries to dispel the myth that Judaism is legalistic and that Christianity somehow lacks a legal framework. His argument lessens the divide between Judaism and Christianity concerning the doctrine of justification by faith:

> When Christians stop seeing Judaism as legalism, they will be in a much better position to realize the importance of law in Christianity. And when Jews stop seeing Christianity as antinomian, as against the law, they will be in a much better position to realize the importance of

grace in Judaism. Indeed, such understanding of each side by the other might lead each tradition not only to a better understanding of the other but to a better understanding of itself. Jewish-Christian dialogue is more than just externally directed apologetics. . . . Antinomianism is as much a distortion of Christianity as legalism is a distortion of Judaism.[77]

I believe that the book of James is the most Jewishly grounded book in Christian Scripture. Much of this is due to James's refusal to enter into an either/or dialectic when he taught about faith and works. The whole idea of justification by faith is actually derived from the prophet Habakkuk who taught, "Look at the proud! Their spirit is not right in them, but the righteous live by their faith" (Habakkuk 2:4). This was quoted by Paul who taught, "For in it the righteousness of God is revealed through faith for faith; as it is written, 'The one who is righteous will live by faith'" (Romans 1:17).

Judaism recognizes the interrelationship between religious belief and behavior, and between our actions and God's grace. To the Israelites, earth and heaven, the body and the soul, this world and the world to come, belief and behavior, are all parts of a singularity. The Jewish notion of faith and works in the time of Jesus is expressed beautifully by James. Keep in mind that James is not a Christian writer, but a religious Jew expressing a Jewish theological viewpoint.

James 1:22–27 But be doers of the word, and not merely hearers who deceive themselves. For if any are hearers of the word and not doers, they are like those who look at themselves in a mirror; . . . If any think they are religious, and do not bridle their tongues but deceive their hearts, their religion is worthless. Religion that is pure and undefiled before God, the Father, is this: to care for orphans and widows in their distress, and to keep oneself unstained by the world.

Late in his life, Martin Luther ruthlessly turned against the Jewish people, and he also proposed that the book of James be removed from the New

Testament because it linked grace to works. James taught, "Faith by itself, if it has no works, is dead. But someone will say, 'You have faith and I have works.' Show me your faith without works, and I by my works will show you my faith" (James 2:17–18). As to legalism in ancient Judaism, every government, religion, church, synagogue, and institution develops an internal culture where the rituals, customs, creeds, and beliefs become confused with the ethical principles they represent. Judaism was and is no exception, and I imagine the same is true at some point for every denomination within Christianity as well. There are dozens of instances in the Bible where God rebukes Israel for confusing ritual behavior with internal change (read the prophets). Legalism is a form of idolatry, and is found wherever mechanistic behavior replaces spontaneous and joy-filled service directed to God.

Healing on the Sabbath

Twenty-two hundred years ago, our enemies would attack us on a Saturday knowing that religious Jews wouldn't defend themselves because of their literal interpretation of not working on the Sabbath. Part of the Hanukkah story is about how the Maccabees united the Jewish people by showing them that it was part of their covenant with God to defend themselves, even if it meant desecrating the Sabbath. In the Talmud we read how the principle of "saving a life" became a primary criterion in determining what acts could and could not be performed on the Sabbath.

One hundred and fifty years after the Maccabees rededicated the Temple in Jerusalem, opinions varied concerning healing on the Sabbath. There was a strict opinion that came from the School of Shammai that prohibited healing on the Sabbath unless it absolutely could not be postponed. There was also a more lenient, widely accepted opinion from the School of Hillel that permitted Sabbath healing. In most areas of Jewish law, from the first century CE to the present, the rulings of Rabbi Hillel have taken precedence. Lamentably, almost all of the rabbis, scribes, and Pharisees that are written about in the Younger Testament seem to be followers of Shammai, or

Sadducees, or just unkind people. It is such a loss that most of my Christian colleagues have never even heard of the amazing, enlightened sages and rabbis who lived just before, during, and after the first century.

It is in this context that we read the account in Luke 13:14, where it is reported: "The leader of the synagogue, indignant because Jesus had cured on the sabbath, kept saying to the crowd, 'There are six days on which work ought to be done; come on those days and be cured, and not on the sabbath day.'" The fact is that many of the rabbis in the first and second centuries, especially those who followed the more lenient rulings of Hillel, would have agreed with Jesus, and would have permitted healing on the Sabbath. "If a man receives circumcision on the sabbath in order that the law of Moses may not be broken, are you angry with me because I healed a man's whole body on the sabbath? Do not judge by appearances, but judge with right judgment" (John 7:23–24). Clearly, Jesus was responding to people who didn't agree with the rulings of Hillel that Sabbath healing was permissible. And in every case where life was in danger, healing was not only permissible; it was obligatory, just as it is today. Dr. David Flusser wrote:

> Jesus's assertion that it is lawful to save a person and not let him perish was surely not foreign to many of his hearers. Jesus alluded to a well-known classical expression of the Jewish humane approach to the other, as it is contained in the important rabbinical saying: "Therefore, humans were created singly, to teach that if any man has caused a single soul to perish Scripture accounts it as if he had caused the whole world to perish; and if any man saves the life of a single soul, Scripture accounts it as though he had saved the whole world." (Talmud-Sanhedren 4:5)[78]

For the past two millennia, simplistic readings of the Gospel accounts have given too many well-meaning Christians the false impression that Judaism in the first century was rigid, legalistic, and inhumane for not permitting Sabbath healing. After Jesus supposedly performed an illegal healing on the Sabbath, Matthew 12:14 reports, "But the Pharisees went out and conspired against him, how to destroy him." For this reason, Dr. Flusser once explained, "It is most unlikely that the Pharisees would've acted that way. The most wicked among them would never have resolved to kill Jesus because he performed a work of healing on the Sabbath—a permissible deed anyway. For this reason Luke's version (Luke 6:11) is preferable here."[79]

Judaism has a built-in self-improvement mechanism that is rare in the history of religions. This mechanism is comprised of the sanctification of reproof (Leviticus 19:17), debate "for the sake of heaven," and constructive self-criticism. To the rabbis, reproof must be done with respect and compassion, something akin to what we call "tough love" today. For this very reason, the Talmud does not just record majority opinions and final rulings. It documents both sides of the arguments that the sages made concerning the day-to-day issues that were important to the people. It was ruled, "Every case where life is in danger supersedes the Sabbath" (Talmud: Yoma 86). From a historical standpoint, it seems implausible for "the Jews" to have persecuted Jesus for advocating beliefs and practices that were already agreed upon by a large segment of Jewish leadership.

The Catholic feminist scholar Dr. Rosemary Radford Reuther made an astute observation when she wrote: "By applying prophetic judgment to 'the Jews' and messianic hope to 'the Church,' Christianity deprived the Jews of their future. They also denied to Jews the record of their greatest moral accomplishment, the breakthrough from ideological religion to self-critical faith. By the same token, the Church deprived itself of the tradition of prophetic self-criticism."[80]

====

THIRTEEN

What's Troubling Paul?

J ESUS'S WORDS REFLECT A LOVE OF TORAH AND HIS COMMITMENT
to the performance of both ritual and moral mitzvot. His methods of
teaching read, sound, and feel authentically Jewish. Paul, on the other
hand, often presents a special challenge, and it's difficult to know what to
make of him.

Paul says he was a Pharisee. Yet in his early years when he persecuted
the followers of Jesus (Acts 8:1–4) he behaved like a man who was in
collaboration with the Roman Empire—not like an ordinary Pharisee. His
comments about Judaism in the letters to the Corinthians and the Galatians
have supersessionist underpinnings compared to his statements in Romans
and Acts. Did Paul really love his own Jewish faith, or was he just pretending
to practice Judaism in order to win people over to the new gospel?

> **1 Corinthians 9:20–22** To the Jews I became as a Jew, in order to win Jews.
> To those under the law I became as one under the law (though I myself am
> not under the law) so that I might win those under the law. To those outside
> the law I became as one outside the law (though I am not free from God's
> law but am under Christ's law) so that I might win those outside the law. . .
> . I have become all things to all people, so that I might by any means save
> some.

If he's really a practicing Jew, how could he say, "Though I myself am
not under the law?" I'd like to believe that there was a deeper message in
Paul's words, and that he did not abandon his Jewish covenantal obligations. But some of his writings, especially the book of Galatians, betray any
positive assessment I might have about his loyalty to his native Judaism.

On the other hand, why would Paul have taken Timothy to be circumcised (Acts 16:3) unless he believed in the ritual mitzvot? After all, adult circumcision is no light matter today, let alone two thousand years ago. Why did Paul offer a sacrifice in the Temple long after Jesus had been crucified (Acts 21:26) when such sacrifices were supposedly superseded by Jesus's resurrection? These actions lead the reader to believe that it is possible that Paul expected his Jewish brethren to uphold the ritual commandments, even while he taught a different set of imperatives to his Gentile audiences.

Sometimes Paul seems to uphold the validity of the mitzvot. At other times it seems he believes there was a shift from the Mosaic covenant to a Christ covenant. Peter and James had the same difficulties with Paul that many Jews subsequently have (see Galatians 2). Paul asks important questions and makes brilliant observations, but it's difficult to be certain where he stands, since he makes seemingly opposite statements at different times. Below, does Paul believe that Jewish people need to keep the ritual commandments of the Torah, such as circumcision, or not?

Romans 2:25–29 Circumcision indeed is of value if you obey the law; but if you break the law, your circumcision has become uncircumcision. So, if those who are uncircumcised keep the requirements of the law, will not their uncircumcision be regarded as circumcision. . . . For a person is not a Jew who is one outwardly, nor is true circumcision something external and physical. Rather, a person is a Jew who is one inwardly, and real circumcision is a matter of the heart—it is spiritual and not literal. Such a person receives praise not from others but from God.

It's hard to justify Paul's seemingly blatant antipathy to Judaism in his more controversial teaching. The following allegory by Paul describes Judaism, and the earthly Jerusalem, as a slave woman, whereas the followers of Christ are free. What is Paul's remedy for the slave woman (Judaism) but "Cast out the slave and her son!" In light of Jewish history this passage is very troubling.

Galatians 4:21–31 Tell me, you who desire to be subject to the law, will you not listen to the law? For it is written that Abraham had two sons, one by a slave woman and the other by a free woman. One, the child of the slave, was born according to the flesh; the other, the child of the free woman, was born through the promise. Now this is an allegory: these women are two covenants. One woman, in fact, is Hagar, from Mount Sinai, bearing children for slavery. Now Hagar is Mount Sinai in Arabia and corresponds to the present Jerusalem, for she is in slavery with her children. But the other woman corresponds to the Jerusalem above; she is free, and she is our mother. For it is written,

> "Rejoice, you childless one, you who bear no children,
> 　　burst into song and shout, you who endure no birth pangs;
> for the children of the desolate woman are more numerous
> 　　than the children of the one who is married."

Now you, my friends, are children of the promise, like Isaac. But just as at that time the child who was born according to the flesh persecuted the child who was born according to the Spirit, so it is now also. But what does the scripture say? "Drive out the slave and her child; for the child of the slave will not share the inheritance with the child of the free woman." So then, friends, we are children, not of the slave but of the free woman.

I have searched the Tanakh and other rabbinical writings to see if I could find some kind of parallel to Paul's more controversial writings. I have not even found minority support for his antinomian opinions. His attitude toward the role of women in the church (1 Timothy 2:12–15) is disturbing in itself, but sadly, I can find parallels to Paul's male chauvinism within ancient and modern Judaism. However, unless I am interpreting his letters incorrectly, his more radical statements about the Torah are outside the wide spectrum of Jewish beliefs. The Jewish reader of Paul is left with more questions than answers. On the other hand, it needs to be noted that most contemporary scholars do not think that Paul was the author of 1 and 2 Timothy, but that it was written in his name.

Paul wrote, "There is no longer Jew or Greek, there is no longer slave or free, there is no longer male and female; for all of you are one in Christ Jesus" (Galatians 3:28). Historically, a few commentators have interpreted this verse as a noble call in support of egalitarianism, or as a rallying cry to end racism, ethnocentrism, sexism, and elitism. But more often than not, Paul's words have been interpreted as the Church superseding minority religions (Judaism) and this verse has been used to justify the elimination of ethnic identity and differences that actually enhance a healthy, pluralistic civilization. At times, anything that was construed as being un-Christian was seen as being anti-Christian and perceived as a threat. When Jews hear the words "There is no longer Jew or Greek," an alarm bell rings loud and clear, which is why Dr. Amy-Jill Levine perceptively points out that "Paul's vision that 'there is no longer Jew or Greek . . . in Christ Jesus' is not good news for Jews, whose identity is then erased." Dr. Levine sees a positive outcome in the preservation of the particularism of the Jewish people in relation to the universal goals of the Church. She writes, "Had the church remained a Jewish sect, it would not have achieved its universal mission. Had Judaism given up its particularistic practices, it would have vanished from history. That the two movements eventually separated made possible the preservation of each."[81]

When Jesus and other first- and second-century rabbis are critical of particular attitudes and practices within Judaism, they are doing so as insiders whose goal is to improve the religion they practice, not to replace it. As we know, Jesus, his family, and disciples lived thoroughly Jewish lives, and his teachings and admonitions were made as a Jew speaking to his fellow Jews. Yet Dr. Amy-Jill Levine cautions us to recognize that "once Jesus' words became placed in the gospel narratives and addressed to Christian churches, comments spoken *to* Jews became perceived, by the church as well as the synagogue, as comments spoken *against* Jews."[82] I hope that Paul's often harsh criticism of Judaism was in the tradition of the constructive, self-criticism that has always been at the heart of Judaism. I hope to discover with more conviction that Paul's criticism of Judaism was that of an insider, and as one who loved his Judaism. It is, of course, intellectually unfair for Christians to take self-criticism of Jews made by Jews on behalf of Judaism and then use it against them. Paul's model of rebuke may be best put to use by the church as it looks within itself for correction and improvement, and not to apply such criticism solely to Judaism.

V
Troubled Past and Hopeful Future

FOURTEEN

Anti-Semitism

MANY EARLY CHURCH LEADERS AND SCHOLARS JUSTIFIED their emerging religion by comparing, contrasting, and self-proclaiming itself as the fulfillment of the religion upon which it was founded. One might be tempted to call it the greatest of theological ironies. In order to bolster up the newly developing religion, early Church leaders and scholars disseminated inaccurate, and too often derogatory, descriptions of its parent faith to the non-Jewish world. Christianity was frequently defined in contrast to Judaism rather than as a separate religion. Dr. Amy-Jill Levine writes, "A substantial number of my Christian students view Jesus as opposed to Judaism rather than as a Jew himself. . . . They suggest that Jews rejected Jesus because he proclaimed peace and love instead of violence against the Roman occupiers of Jerusalem."[83]

Sadly, even today too many Christian teachers unconsciously continue to disseminate this same inaccurate information about the Judaism that Jesus and the disciples followed. This is the root of the idea still heard in some churches that "what the Old Testament conceals the New Testament reveals." Dr. Levine suggests that the "proclamation of the church can, and should, stand on its own; it does not require an artificial foil, an anti-Jewish basis, or an overstated distinction." She further observes that in some parts of the New Testament, the "worse Judaism can be made to look, the better Jesus will look in comparison." Using Judaism as the foil against which the Church proclaims itself the fulfillment, completion, and perfection of Judaism actually does a great harm to both Judaism and Christianity. Dr. Levine insightfully argues:

In the popular Christian imagination, Jesus still remains defined, incorrectly and unfortunately, as "against" the Law, or at least against how it was understood at the time; as "against" the Temple as an institution and not simply against its first-century leadership; as "against" the people Israel but in favor of the Gentiles. Jesus becomes the rebel who, unlike every other Jew, practices social justice. He is the only one to speak with women; he is the only one who teaches nonviolent responses to oppression; he is the only one who cares about the "poor and the marginalized" (that phrase has become a litany in some Christian circles). Judaism becomes in such discourse a negative foil: whatever Jesus stands for, Judaism isn't it; whatever Jesus is against, Judaism epitomizes the category. No wonder even today Jesus somehow looks "different" from "the Jews." Jesus and his followers such as Peter and Mary Magdalene become identified as (proto-) Christian; only those who chose not to follow him remain "Jews." This divorcing of Jesus from Judaism does a disservice to each texturally, theologically, historically, and ethically. [84]

Throughout the Younger Testament we can see what the science of optics calls a figure/ground relationship; an ongoing contrast is made between Judaism and the emerging Christian faith. Judaism is used as the blurry background in which the in-focus, foreground figure of Christianity took shape. There's an old joke that says, "The Jews brought ethical monotheism to the world, and they still haven't forgiven them for it." Dennis Prager and Rabbi Joseph Telushkin elaborate on this theme:

In the ancient world, every nation but the Jews worshiped its own gods and acknowledged the legitimacy of others' gods. The Jews declared that the gods of the non-Jews were nonsense: "They have mouths but cannot speak, eyes but cannot see, ears but cannot hear. . . ." (Psalm 115:5–6). There is but one God and He had revealed himself to mankind through the Jews. One need not be a theologian or historian to understand why these doctrines bred massive anti-Jewish resentment. The Jews' belief in God threatened more than their neighbor's gods. It challenged their values.[85]

To the ruling authorities Jews were seen as enemies of the state. Dennis Prager and Rabbi Telushkin proposed an utterly simple but profound idea: "[The] ultimate cause of anti-Semitism is that which has made Jews Jewish—Judaism." In explaining their thesis that Judaism's very existence is the cause of anti-Semitism, they point out the following:

> Jews have always seen anti-Semitism as the somewhat inevitable and often quite rational, though of course immoral, response to Judaism. . . . Once we perceive that it is Judaism which is the root cause of anti-Semitism, otherwise irrational and inexplicable aspects of anti-Semitism become rationally explicable. . . . Anti-Semites persecuted Jews for the same reasons Romans persecuted Christians, Nazis tortured members of the Resistance, and Soviets imprison dissidents. In each instance the group is persecuted because its different beliefs represent a threat to the persecuting group.[86]

There's an inside joke that Jewish people tell: "What's the definition of a Jewish holiday? Answer: They tried to kill us. We prayed. We fought. We won. Let's eat!" Well, not all Jewish holidays are based on defending ourselves against a hostile world, but enough of them are to make this joke funny. Passover celebrates our liberation from slavery in Egypt, Purim celebrates Queen Esther's courage, and Hanukkah celebrates victory over the Syrio-Greeks. Add in modern memorial days like Yom HaShoah that commemorates the Holocaust, and you get the idea that Jews are realistic, not paranoid, about anti-Semitism. Historically, Judaism's mission as defined by the Torah often challenges the status quo of kings, rulers, and religious authorities. Just as Jesus, a first-century rabbi, was seen as a threat to the Roman Empire, so thousands of other Jewish religious leaders have been seen as threatening to despotic regimes throughout history.

Unconscious Theological Anti-Semitism

In his monumental work on the history of the Church and the Jews, *Constantine's Sword*, former Catholic priest James Carroll recounts the evolution of his own thinking about how anti-Semitism crept into Christianity. Carroll writes, "I learned that in the earliest Gospel, Mark, it is 'the crowd' that sets itself against Jesus; then, in Matthew, the antagonist is identified as 'all the people'; but those categories I saw through the lens of John, who identified the enemy of Jesus as 'the Jews.' In John (John 19:6–7 and 15) the record is crystal clear, and his account of the crucial events shapes the Christian imagination still."[87]

> **John 19:6–7, 15** When the chief priests and the police saw him, they shouted, "Crucify him! Crucify him!" Pilate said to them, "Take him yourselves and crucify him; I find no case against him." The Jews answered him, "We have a law, and according to that law he ought to die because he has claimed to be the Son of God. . . ." They cried out, "Away with him! Away with him! Crucify him!" Pilate asked them, "Shall I crucify your King?" The chief priests answered, "We have no king but the emperor."

Imagine how disturbing this contextual distortion of Jewish history has sounded to Jews for the past two thousand years. Imagine the violent consequences to these verses when they were heard by impoverished and illiterate masses throughout Europe, especially in the Easter Passion plays. To a Jew, the ultimate irony is that the passage is describing the horrific death of a great rabbi who died because Rome thought that the people might make him their king. He died as a Jew loyal to the Torah and the land of Judea.

These verses downplay the barbarous Roman war against the Jews, and have been utilized throughout Church history to prove that Jews are "perfidious." We can see the seeds of anti-Semitism that were planted by most of the church fathers, and we see it coming to fruition in the Easter sermons and Passion plays of churches throughout history. We see anti-Semitism in the "blood libels" of the Middle Ages, which almost always led to beatings, pogroms, and massacres of local Jewish populations. We see the hatred of Jews carried to horrific proportions during the Crusades and the Inquisition.

The blood curse upon the Jews:

Matthew 27:25 Then the people as a whole answered, "His blood be on us and on our children!"

Jews are associated with the devil:

John 8:44 You are from your father the devil, and you choose to do your father's desires.

Jews killed God—deicide:

Thessalonians 2:14–15 The Jews, who killed both the Lord Jesus and the prophets, and drove us out; they displease God and oppose everyone.

Jews are negatively associated with money:

John 2:15–17 He drove all of them out of the temple, both the sheep and the cattle. He also poured out the coins of the money changers and overturned their tables. He told those who were selling the doves, "Take these things out of here! Stop making my Father's house a marketplace!"

Judas betrays Jesus for money:

Matthew 26:14–15 Then one of the twelve, who was called Judas Iscariot, went to the chief priests. "What will you give me if I betray him to you?" They paid him thirty pieces of silver.

In the United States today, Jews and Christians are experiencing the highest level of mutual respect and ecumenical exchange in our two-thousand-year history. Interfaith conferences are common; more and more books about the Jewish roots of Christianity can be found; more and more Jews are interested in Jesus's Jewish heritage. A little over four decades ago, the *Nostra Aetate,* meaning "In Our Time," was published, gallantly demonstrating the Catholic Church's courage to repent for its historical participation in anti-Semitism. The words *perfidis judaeis* (perfidious Jews) were removed from the liturgy read on Good Friday, and liturgical changes continue to be made by Protestant denominations and individual pastors.

Incorrect Interpretations Today

Incorrect and usually unconscious interpretations of Gospels that portray Jesus as being "against" the Torah while somehow offering a new theological alternative to Judaism are rapidly being discarded. When we hear Jesus expounding on some aspect of Torah in the famous Sermon on the Mount with the words *You have heard it said*, it's then contrasted with *But I tell you*. It's easy to get the sense that what he's proposing was an alternative to traditional Judaism. In fact, his innovative interpretations about the way to fulfill the mitzvot were in line with many of the rabbis in the first century. Dr. David Flusser notes:

> The famous "but I tell you" is not an expression of Jesus' opposition to Moses. In reality, Jesus' personal opinion, which follows after this phrase, is mostly attested also in the other Jewish sources. He has chosen one of two contrasting Jewish opinions, which benefit his ethics. Even Matthew 5:44 "love your enemies" is within the framework of Judaism. . . . Nothing of what Jesus says in the sermon particularly conflicts with the content of the Mosaic legislation.[88]

Within Christianity, a normative interpretation of Matthew 5:17 says that Jesus shows his respect for the Torah, but that he has now come to "fulfill" the law in the sense of completing, or putting an end to, the necessity for the law. Jesus says, "Do not think that I have come to abolish the law or the prophets; I have come not to abolish but to fulfill." A closer look at the Greek meaning of the words "law" and "fulfill" yields other interpretations.

Christian scholars David Bivin and Roy Blizzard Jr. point out that the words *abolish* and *fulfill* are technical terms used in rabbinic argumentation. What was "abolishing the Law" for one rabbi was "fulfilling the Law" (i.e., correctly interpreting Scripture) for another.[89] Take a closer look at some of the Greek and Hebrew words themselves.

The word *law* has a legal connotation. However, "teaching" is the primary meaning of the Hebrew word *Torah*. Would you rather listen to a teaching or follow a law? The Hebrew contains both meanings in the same word. To a Jew, the Torah unifies experience (a personal relationship with God) and obligation (our moral duty to the Creator). This is what Jesus was trying to "fulfill." The word in Greek, *pleroo,* is translated as "fulfill" in the Matthew verse. The *New American Standard Lexicon* offers this interpretation of *pleroo*: "to fulfill, i.e., to cause God's will (as made known in the law) to be obeyed as it should be. . . ." It seems probable that Jesus came to support the Torah's commandments, which he hoped would be obeyed with correct intention.

Jesus, along with the rabbis in his lifetime, had the task of teaching, ratifying, and "fulfilling" God's commandments. Today religious Jews speak of "fulfilling" a mitzvah in the sense of "performing one's duty" rather than completing or doing away with the obligation. Dr. Young takes this argument a step further:

> The Hebrew equivalent of *pleroo* is *kiyem*. The root of *kiyem* means "cause to stand" and has the sense of "uphold," "observe," "fulfill," or 'place on a firmer footing." It too is used in contexts that deal with interpreting Scripture. . . . The theological polemics within Christianity during its struggle for self–definition caused the church to sever itself almost completely from Judaism. [90]

In Matthew 5:19 Jesus teaches, "Therefore, whoever breaks one of the least of these commandments, and teaches others to do the same, will be called least in the kingdom of heaven; but whoever does them and teaches them will be called great in the kingdom of heaven." Jesus appears to be saying that he wants his Jewish followers to "ratify" and "perform" the 613 mitzvot of the Torah. He doesn't teach that the commandments are to be replaced. He explicitly implores the Jewish people to "do" and "teach" even the least important commandment.

Incorrect Interpretations of the Crucifixion Story

Regarding anti-Jewish bias arising from inaccurate interpretations of the Younger Testament, it's instructive to examine Jesus's triumphal entry into Jerusalem, where a large Jewish population was excited to welcome him, hoping that he'd be the one to liberate them from the Roman occupation of Judea. It's written in Matthew 21:9 that the crowd was shouting to Jesus, "Hosanna to the Son of David! Blessed is the one who comes in the name of the Lord!" This was on Sunday. It seems highly improbable that by Thursday of that same week, a large urban population, swollen by the upcoming holiday of Passover, would, for no apparent reason, turn on Jesus and suddenly cry out "crucify him." The New Testament in most translations does not make an adequate distinction between the phrase *the Jews* (implying "all the Jews") or simply *a few Jews* who were likely in cahoots with Roman authorities, and who were distrusted by the vast majority of the Jewish religious leaders and general population.

The notion of a few Jewish leaders saying, "We have no king but Caesar" has to be understood in historical context. It might be comparable to the handful of Jews during the Holocaust who tried to gain favor with the Nazi regime. These passages in the Younger Testament should never be translated as "the Jews" without clear annotation. The historical reality was that there were some "elders, chief priests, and scribes" who were considered traitors by the Jewish people because they were supporting the Roman Empire, and in many cases they were on the empire's payroll. This minority of corrupted leaders certainly would have felt threatened by Jesus, just as they felt threatened by hundreds of other rabbis who struggled on behalf of the people while under Roman rule. The Younger Testament story tells that Jesus had to be taken away at night for his trial. Why? Legitimate Jewish trials were not ordinarily convened at night. Could it be that the general population might have rioted if one of their beloved rabbis was arrested during the day?

Pontius Pilate was Roman governor of occupied Judea. He was a barbaric, vicious character who was described by Jewish philosopher Philo of Alexandria as having "vindictiveness and furious temper" and who "was a man of an inflexible, stubborn, and cool disposition...."[91] Dr. David Flusser writes, "This negative assessment of the governor does not differ much from what Josephus reported about him . . . [but] the Pilate of the Gospels . . . appears as a sensitive and just man, as a pawn in the hands of the Jewish leaders."[92]

Inaccurate historical context and prejudiced interpretations have all contributed to a general sense of "blaming the Jews" for the death of Jesus within Christianity. Many scholars agree that the brutality of Pilate and the Romans was played down in the Gospels for reasons of political expediency. An objective study of the New Testament shows hundreds of negative comments about "the Jews" and very few comments about the Romans, and when the Romans are spoken about, the language seems hushed and neutral. Many modern pastors and preachers in America teach that it wasn't just the Jews, but that "all mankind" was responsible for the death of Jesus. Universal blame, however, was not what was preached to the illiterate masses in Europe, Latin America, Africa, and Asia over the past two thousand years. In almost all teachings of the church fathers, and in the European Passion plays, it was "the Jews," not just a tiny group of corrupt leaders, and certainly not "all mankind," who were calling for Jesus's crucifixion.

Deicide, the "murder of God," was what most Christians were taught about the Jews since the third century, and it's not uncommon for older Jews today to recall being called "Christ killers" when they were growing up. The scriptural basis for the charge of deicide can be found throughout the Younger Testament. In Acts 2:36 it is written, "Therefore let the entire house of Israel know with certainty that God has made him both Lord and Messiah, this Jesus whom you crucified." Here we have a direct statement saying that "the house of Israel" crucified the Lord.

In 1 Thessalonians 2:14–15 it is written: "The Jews, who killed both the Lord Jesus and the prophets, and drove us out; they displease God and oppose everyone." It's distressing that the libel of "the Jews" being responsible for deicide was not officially rescinded and repented for until the second half of the twentieth century. Even today, anti-Semitism remains at an unacceptably high level, even in the United States. The interpretation that "all mankind" is responsible for the death of Jesus may be enlightened, but such an interpretation wasn't the norm during most of the Church's history.

Anti-Semitism Among the Church Fathers

In his second-century text, *Dialogue with Typho*, Justin Martyr haughtily tells his fictitious Jewish antagonist, "The Scriptures are not yours, but ours." In 177 CE the Bishop of Lyon, named Irenaeus, claimed, "Jews are disinherited from the grace of God." Tertullian (160–230 CE) wrote a treatise entitled *Against the Jews* in which he declared that God had rejected the Jews in favor of the Christians. These otherwise intelligent founding fathers created a theology based on a hatred of Judaism that is still influential today. Even after the era of the Church founders, anti-Semitism was preached by some of Christianity's greatest theologians. For example, Thomas Aquinas (1225–1274) taught that the Jews had killed Jesus and were therefore damned. He taught the only way Jews could be saved would be for them to renounce Judaism and be baptized.

Notre Dame Professor Michael A. Signer places their prejudice in the context of the theological debate and competition that took place from the second through the fifth centuries of the Common Era. He writes:

In their search to distinguish their teachings from the Jewish communities, early Christian writings such as the Epistle of Barnabas (ca. 130–135) and the Didache (ca. 90–100) emphasize those elements in the New Testament that describe the superiority of the way of Jesus. These documents speak about Christianity as the way of light and Judaism as the way of darkness. They indicate that narratives in the Hebrew Bible already demonstrate the diminished status of the Jewish people. For example, when Moses shatters the tablets of the Ten Commandments, God replaces the first tablets with a "law of punishment." This "law of punishment" is replaced only with the coming of Jesus (Barnabas 14:1). By contrast, some of the actions by Moses in the Torah are explained as foreshadowings of Jesus. For example, Barnabas interprets the posture of Moses with his arms outstretched and supported by Aaron and Joshua during the battle against the Amalekites (Exodus 27:8–13) as anticipating Jesus on the cross (Barnabas 12:2–3).[93]

The church fathers misused the typological method of biblical interpretation that described "old" Testament stories as foreshadowing "new" Testament fulfillment. It took acts of intellectual deception to transfer the blessings to the Jews in the Bible over to the Church. Only the biblical curses are left for the Jews, along with other "heathen infidels" who "reject" the gospel. The words that the church fathers used regarding Jews were a recipe for catastrophe in later centuries. Following are highly abridged selections of the anti-Semitic teachings from a few of the church fathers.

Justin Martyr (100–165): "Those who slandered Him should be miserable. . . . Jews suffer because they are guilty of not having recognized the One with whom they had to do in their own history. When he appeared, they killed him. Not knowing this One, the Logos, Jews fail to know God."

Origen (185–254): "The Jews suffer here and will suffer in the hereafter 'on account of their unbelief' and other insults which they heaped upon Jesus. These calamities they have suffered because they were a most wicked nation, which, although guilty of many other sins, yet has been punished so severely for none as for those that were committed against our Jesus.

Cyprian: Bishop of Carthage (200–258): "That by this alone the Jews could obtain pardon of their sins, if they wash away the blood of Christ slain in His baptism, and, passing over into the Church, should obey His precepts."

Eusebius of Caesarea (260–339): "Seditions, wars, and mischievous plots followed each other in quick succession, and never ceased in the city and in all Judea until finally the siege of Vespasian overwhelmed them [the Jews]. Thus the divine vengeance overtook the Jews for the crimes which they dared to commit against Christ."

Gregory of Nyssa (331–396): "Slayers of the Lord, murderers of the prophets, adversaries of God, men who show contempt for the law, foes of grace, enemies of their fathers' faith, advocates of the Devil, brood of vipers, slanderers, scoffers, men whose minds are in darkness, leaven of the Pharisees, assembly of demons, sinners, wicked men, stoners and haters of righteousness."

St. Ambrose of Milan (340–395): "The Jews are the most worthless of all men. They are lecherous, greedy, and rapacious. They are perfidious murderers of Christ. The Jews are the odious assassins of Christ and for killing God there is no expiation possible, no indulgence or pardon. Christians may never cease vengeance and the Jews must live in servitude forever. God always hated the Jews. It is incumbent upon all Christians to hate the Jews."

John Chrysostom (344–407): "Many, I know, respect the Jews and think that their present way of life is a venerable one. This is why I hasten to uproot and tear out this deadly opinion. . . . The synagogue is not only a brothel and a theatre, it also is a den of robbers and a lodging for wild beasts. . . . No Jew worships God, certainly not in the synagogue, a temple of idolatry."

St. Jerome (345–420): "I only wish to cast down the arrogance of the Jews who prefer the narrowness of the synagogue to the breadth of the Church. If they would follow the letter that kills and not the spirit that makes alive, let them show us a Promised Land flowing with milk and honey. . . . You have committed many crimes, O Jew, you have been the slave of all the surrounding nations. For what reason? Surely because of your idolatry!"

St. Augustine (354–430): "God regards not the sacrifice of Cain, but he regards the sacrifice of Abel. Abel, the younger brother, is killed by the elder brother;

Christ, the head of the younger people, is killed by the elder people of the Jews. Abel dies in the field; Christ dies on Calvary. . . . So the unbelieving people of the Jews is cursed from the earth, that is, from the Church, which in the confession of sins has opened its mouth to receive the blood shed for the remission of sins by the hand of the people that would not be under grace, but under the law. And this murderer is cursed by the Church; that is, the Church admits and avows the curse pronounced by the apostle: 'Whoever are of the works of the law are under the curse of the law' (Galatians 3:10)."

In a tragic irony, the great reformer of the Church, Martin Luther, also became obsessed with his hatred of Jews in his later years. His shameful treatises, *Shem Hamphoras* and *Concerning the Jews and Their Lies,* are readily available in libraries and on various websites. Following are excerpts from the latter essay first published in 1543. They were used in the Nazi era as a framework for the way Jews were to be dealt with in Germany:

What then shall we Christians do with this damned, rejected race of Jews . . . ? First, their synagogues or churches should be set on fire, and whatever does not burn up should be covered or spread over with dirt so that no one may ever be able to see a cinder or stone of it.

Secondly, their homes should likewise be broken down and destroyed. For they perpetrate the same things there that they do in their synagogues. . . . Thirdly, they should be deprived of their prayer-books and Talmuds in which such idolatry, lies, cursing, and blasphemy are taught. Fourthly, their rabbis must be forbidden under threat of death to teach any more.

Fifthly, passport and traveling privileges should be absolutely forbidden to the Jews. For they have no business in the rural districts since they are not nobles, nor officials, nor merchants, nor the like. . . . Sixthly, they ought to be stopped from usury. All their cash and valuables of silver and gold ought to be taken from them and put aside for safe keeping. . . .

Seventhly, let the young and strong Jews and Jewesses be given the flail, the ax, the hoe, the spade, the distaff, and spindle, and let them earn their bread by the sweat of their noses. . . . To sum up, dear princes and nobles who have Jews in your domains, if this advice of mine does not suit you, then find a better one so that you and we may all be free of this insufferable devilish burden the Jews.[94]

Thankfully, in the past thirty years some Lutheran synods in America and Europe have officially condemned the bigotry and hatred that came out later in Luther's life. As much as the Jews have been hurt physically, the church has been damaged spiritually when it failed to denounce defamatory statements against the Jews. Referring to his own followers, Jesus said, "Truly I tell you, just as you did it to one of the least of these who are members of my family, you did it to me" (Matthew 25:40). Today, many Christians and Jews believe it's time to end two thousand years of mutual defamation, and to begin the next two thousand years with a sense of mutual respect, admiration, and partnership.

===

FIFTEEN

Triumphalism and Replacement Theology

OST RELIGIONS HAVE DENOMINATIONS THAT ASSERT SOME degree of triumphalism—the belief that its doctrines are superior to all others, and that someday its theology will triumph over all others. It's not hard to find denominations within Judaism today that are triumphalist. They teach that their theology is better than that of the other Abrahamic religions, and to the other Jewish denominations as well. In both fundamentalist Christianity and Islam, however, triumphalism is taken to the next level in the belief that all people actually must become Christian or Muslim or accept the consequence of spiritual damnation. During the Crusades, for example, the armies of Christendom carried the message of Christian triumphalism throughout Europe into Asia.

I grew up in New York City surrounded by my own community's ethnocentrism, a result of a thousand years of European anti-Semitism. Growing up immediately after the Holocaust and pogroms of the twentieth century, I understood the conditions that fueled these ethnocentric attitudes. After all, many minorities take on defensive postures in order to bolster their own self-worth when the outside world is prejudiced against them. But I never understood the need for triumphalism—Jewish, Christian, or Muslim. After all, isn't diversity integral to the creation itself? Doesn't the Creator have a special purpose for every religion, like the various instruments in an orchestra or the organs in the body?

The first time I consciously came into contact with Christian triumphalism as a young graduate student in the early 1970s, I was startled.

It was not like the street-level ethnocentrism and prejudice I grew up with between Jews, Italians, Irish, Blacks, and Puerto Ricans. Rather, the triumphalism I faced as a young adult was intellectually based. It was not expressed through derogatory terms one ethnic group might use against another. Rather, it was rooted in the soil of well-argued ideas that seemed rational on the surface.

I was really in for a shock in 1981 to read in the pages of *Christianity Today*, the magazine bible of evangelicalism, these words from Vernon Grounds, president emeritus of Denver Seminary. He elevated his belief in Christian triumphalism to a new height of jarring candor:

> We Evangelicals maintain that by the whole Christ-event, Judaism *qua* religion has been superseded, its propaedeutic purpose accomplished. Since Messiah has come and offered his culminating sacrifice, there is no temple, no priesthood, no altar, no atonement, no forgiveness, no salvation and no eternal hope in Judaism as a religion. Harsh and grating expressions as to its salvific discontinuity are called for—abrogation, displacement, and negation. And those expressions are set down here, I assure you, with some realization of how harsh and grating they must indeed sound to Jewish ears.[95]

I doubt that Dr. Grounds, one of the most important leaders of Christian evangelicalism in the twentieth century, realized just how distorted such a proclamation would have sounded to the Jewish ears of Jesus, Mary, and Joseph. Also, to be fair, Grounds unconditionally condemned the violent and anti-Semitic acts committed in the name of the Church throughout history. He finished his discourse with a question to his evangelical colleagues that I believe was naive but sincere: "Can an evangelicalism that intolerantly opposes any least anti-Semitic innuendo, carry on its evangelistic mission while cooperating ecumenically with its Jewish friends and neighbors? My hope, my prayer, is that it can."

Christian triumphalism can best be understood through a doctrine called replacement theology (also known as supersessionism). Dr. Grounds's statement is a prime example of the intellectual foundation used to uphold and justify replacement theology. We have already seen instances of it throughout the pages of this book. Let's now pause to consider the ideas one more time.

Propositions of Replacement Theology

- God's promises to Abraham regarding the Jewish people have been transferred to the Church under the "new" covenant as foretold by the prophet Jeremiah.
- God's covenant to the Jewish people (particularly the Mosaic covenant) has been abrogated and nullified and replaced by the "new" covenant.
- Since the Pentecost, the term "Israel" refers to the Church, and all the covenantal blessings given to Israel by God have now been conveyed to the Church.
- The Church is the historic continuation of the Synagogue to the exclusion of Israel and the Jewish people in the Kingdom of God unless they repent and accept Jesus as their Savior.
- The Jews, like any other non-Christians, have no eternal life or place in heaven unless they repent, profess Jesus as Lord and Savior, and are baptized.

Only a small percentage of Christians are prejudiced against Jews, but too many Christians have prejudicial beliefs about Judaism. This is due to the influence of ideas that come out of replacement theology, which is insidious and has affected the way Christians have characterized Jews, Judaism, and Israel. To use perhaps the prime example, there's nothing inherently negative intended when Christians use the terms Old and New Testament, but these terms actually arise out of replacement theology, which tries to prove that the old covenant has been superseded by the new covenant.

The heresy of replacement theology is that it teaches ideas and concepts about Judaism that are false. Almost all opinions about the Mosaic covenant are quotes from flawed interpretations of Younger Testament, and not from real Jewish beliefs. The references in the Younger Testament that seem to speak against Judaism are based on characterizations, misinterpretations, and mistranslations that are not from Jewish theology, not from the Tanakh, and not based on an understanding of biblical Hebrew.

A Historical Perspective

There was a clear theological split between the Synagogue and Church at the Council of Nicaea in 325 CE, which resulted in the nonbiblical doctrine that the "new" covenant had replaced the "old" covenant, and justification by faith had replaced justification by works. Today, those who target Jewish people for conversion are given misinformation that "proves" how Christianity "completes" or "perfects" Judaism. The Torah and the Mosaic covenant are described with terms like bondage, flesh, death, shadow, imperfect, unprofitable, weak, and earthly. Imagine how painful it is for a Jew who loves God to hear his or her Torah being misrepresented. It's equally painful for many Christians to realize how their religion has been used against Jesus's own religion. Unfortunately, some early followers of Jesus made inaccurate characterizations about Jews that remain embedded in Church teachings. Knowing the historical and cultural context in which these early Christians were writing is crucial for getting an accurate picture of the Judaism during the Roman occupation.

According to the historian Josephus, 1.1 million Jews were killed, enslaved, or died of starvation during the First Jewish-Roman War between 66–73 CE.[96] Jewish theologian Rabbi Joseph Telushkin writes, "Some 50,000 to 100,000 Jews were themselves crucified by the Romans in the first century."[97] You would hardly know this from reading the Younger Testament. Soon after Jesus's death, it seems as though some of his followers tried to curry favor with the Roman Empire (see 1 Peter 2:13–14)—not because they agreed with the Romans, but because they believed that the Kingdom of God was at hand. This position separated them from those Jews who were involved in active opposition (through both insurgency and political means) to the occupation. Just as there were informers working with the Romans in the first century, there were both Jewish and Jewish-Christian informers during the second century. These informants did much to injure the future of Jewish/Christian relations over the next few hundred years—an injury that remains to the present day.

Replacing of the Servant of Isaiah 53

In the Jewish method of Bible interpretation, an allegorical or applied meaning of a word or story cannot replace its literal one. The suffering servant described in magnificent, poetic detail from Isaiah 52:13–53:9 is an allegory describing the Jewish people. In many passages over thirteen consecutive chapters, Isaiah explicitly describes the people of Israel as God's "servant"[98] such as "But you, Israel, my servant, Jacob, whom I have chosen" (Isaiah 41:8–9). Israel is metaphorically described as "despised and rejected by others; a man of suffering and acquainted with infirmity; and as one from whom others hide their faces he was despised, and we held him of no account" (Isaiah 53:3). Regrettably, these prophetic verses are confirmed by much of Jewish history.

However, in Matthew 12:15–18, Jesus is described as the suffering servant—an allegorical extension of the plain meaning of the biblical text. This isn't a problem until theologians discard the intended meaning of the allegory and replace it with the new interpretation. The description of Jesus as the servant is an important image in Christian theology, and is valid in a Christological context. An extended meaning can be creative to help make the Bible relevant to all people in all times, but it can't supersede the original meaning of the biblical text.

Following is a good example of how translation and the manipulation of grammar can be used in replacement theology. The pronouns describing the servant are capitalized in the Revised King James translation below: "him" becomes "Him," "servant" becomes "Servant" in order to identify the servant as Jesus. The Hebrew, however, contains no upper and lowercases. It is not a problem when Christian theologians apply the Isaiah verses to Jesus's suffering, just as Dr. Martin Luther King, Jr. extended the Exodus story to the civil rights movement. But Matthew does not imply that seeing Jesus in Isaiah's words replaces the role of Israel as God's servant.

> **Matthew 12:15–18** Jesus . . . ordered them not to make him known. This was to fulfill what had been spoken through the prophet Isaiah: "Here is my servant, whom I have chosen, my beloved, with whom my soul is well pleased. I will put my Spirit upon him, and he will proclaim justice to the Gentiles."

Replacement of Torah by Faith in Christ

The Jew comes to God by Torah, and the Christian comes by Jesus, but the God they worship is the same, and the ethical imperatives they follow are identical. There is no separate "God of the Old Testament." Replacement theology, however, is based on interpretations of verses like Acts 13:39 where Paul says, "By this Jesus everyone who believes is set free from all those sins from which you could not be freed by the law of Moses." This verse comes across like a one-sided ad for a competing product and mistakenly teaches that it isn't necessary for a Jew to fulfill the Torah's commandments if he or she accepts Jesus. The psalmist expressed best how Jewish people experience the mitzvot when he chanted, "If your law had not been my delight, I would have perished in my misery" (Psalm 119:92).

In chapter three of the book of Galatians, Paul implies that the commandments might be set aside to make room for the "promise of the Spirit through faith." In Galatians 3:24–26, Paul says, "Therefore the law was our disciplinarian until Christ came, so that we might be justified by faith. But now that faith has come, we are no longer subject to a disciplinarian, for in Christ Jesus you are all children of God through faith." Does this mean that Jews have "graduated" from the school of Torah, and no longer need to follow its commandments if they accept Christ? Or can it be interpreted to mean that Jews are to fulfill the commandments, but that with Jesus there was an opening created for the polytheistic world to have a covenantal relationship with God without becoming Jewish?

Replacement of the Law by Grace

Replacement theology also, of course, characterizes Judaism and Torah's laws as outmoded, legalistic, rigid, and lacking grace. The King James Version thus translates John 1:17 as "For the law was given by Moses, *but* grace and truth came through Jesus Christ." The word *but* is placed in italics by the translators to indicate that this particular word is not present in the Greek New Testament manuscripts. With the insertion of the word *but*, the passage denotes a comparison between the Torah and Christ. Take out the bracketed word *but* and suddenly both passages are no longer compared, but simply placed next to each other. Placement of two equal and parallel images was a common literary technique in the Hebrew Scriptures known as parallelism. It is a device that usually aimed at showing the linkage, rather than the difference, between diverse concepts.

In Romans 6:14, Paul says, "For sin will have no dominion over you, since you are not under law but under grace." Here the word *but* is in the Greek, and may be Paul's attempt to tell his non-Jewish listeners that they are not bound by the ritual commandments of Mosaic covenant. If this interpretation is correct, then Paul is not making a comparison between Torah and Christ, but the observation that Jews and Gentiles come to God with different covenantal obligations. Contrary to lacking grace, the Jewish Bible is filled with examples of God's amazing grace. The psalmist chants, "Let your steadfast love come to me, O LORD, your salvation according to your promise" (Psalm 119:41). In Exodus 34:5–6 humanity is given the divine template to understand God's thirteen attributes of mercy, which includes grace. For this reason, Dr. Lawrence Hoffman reminds us of both the similarity and the unique difference between Judaism and Christianity: "In its pre-covenantal state, Israel did not merit Torah. God gave it as an act of grace, in the same way that (for Christians) God sent Jesus. But once the Torah has been given, Jews enter into a covenant with God."[99]

Replacement of Judaism by a "Better Covenant"

The idea of replacement of an "old" covenant for a "new" covenant seems to be restated by the author of Hebrews. He writes, "But Jesus has now obtained a more excellent ministry, and to that degree he is the mediator of a better covenant, which has been enacted through better promises" (Hebrews 8:6). New Testament scholar Dr. Pamela Eisenbaum writes that this verse represents a "Supersessionist theology. Not only is Jesus the mediator of a better covenant, but the first covenant was faulty because it failed to create the perfect relationship between humans and God."[100] In the rabbinical writings, covenants were not rated as better or worse than each other. They are more like a tapestry—some universal for all people, some particular for the Jewish people.

King Solomon taught us to keep the mitzvot in order to invoke God's "good promise." Why? As Solomon put it, "so that all the peoples of the earth may know that the LORD is God; there is no other" (1 Kings 8:60). Not just Jews, Christians, and Muslims. Members of the Abrahamic faiths are too often reluctant to acknowledge that they serve a common interest—to bring the message of redemption, hope, renewal, and forgiveness to the world.

Mutual Misrepresentation

Too many Christian and Jewish theologians continue to describe each other's faith systems in patronizing terms. Too many Christian denominations continue to cling to the supersessionist myth that "we have the truth, you had the truth—and one day you will have the truth again when you accept Christ as your Lord." Jewish theology, for its part in this ancient dysfunctional communication, defensively responds, "We have the truth, you almost have the truth, and one day you will have the whole truth when you recognize that Jesus is not really the incarnation of God." Christian denominations sometimes talk about other Christian denominations in similarly patronizing terms, and Jewish denominations do the same within Judaism.

Dr. Robert Gibbs reminds us that our mutual history of misrepresentation has not been an equal yoke. Jewish misrepresentation of Christianity throughout the centuries has caused unnecessary division and lost opportunities to help bring about God's kingdom. Christian misrepresentation of Judaism has caused massive upheaval in Jewish culture and the repeated loss of homeland and life for millions of Jews. Professor Gibbs writes, "Since Constantine, Christians have rarely been martyrs, particularly not at the hands of non-Christians, and almost never at the hands of Jews. Jews, alas, have been martyred at a disturbing rate throughout the centuries, most often at the hands of others, and especially at the hands of Christians."[101]

Christians have typically read back into the Bible, interpreting Jewish history as prefiguring and foreshadowing the story of Christ. Jewish biblical heroes are sometimes even described as proto-Christians. Naturally, these typological descriptions are never well received in the Jewish community since everything good in the Jewish Scriptures is interpreted as foreshadowing Christianity. To a supersessionist, for example, both the Akedah and the Sinai event foreshadowed Calvary and were "fulfilled" on the cross. There's little recognition that Jewish heroes in the Bible might actually be archetypes for later Jewish heroes that many Christians have never even heard of. Typology, and interpreting a biblical text as foreshadowing a future event, is fine as long as the basic rules of interpretation and intellectual integrity are not violated. For example, to say that Isaac's suffering at the Akedah foreshadowed Christ is a powerful statement, and it may be true for some Christians. But to deny that the interpretation of Isaac's suffering can also be understood as foreshadowing the Crusades, or the Holocaust, is intellectually dishonest.

How have Jews responded to replacement theology? Not so well. The Hebrew word *goy* literally means "nation," whether the nation is a Gentile nation or the Jewish nation. Yet it's sometimes used in a pejorative sense, just as the term *Jew* is sometimes used derogatorily. The pejorative use of these terms by Jews or Christians is offensive and unacceptable. Even without prejudice, Jewish theologians in the Middle Ages were, at best, only able to see Christian history as a preparation for the coming of the "real" messiah. Rabbi Abraham Joshua Heschel taught it's as if the Synagogue recognized "Christianity to be *preparatio messianica*, while the Church regarded ancient Judaism to have been a *preparatio evangelica*."[102] Yet it must be noted again that historic efforts have been made since Vatican II to heal the rift between Church and Synagogue. Since the Holocaust and Israel's rebirth as a nation, many Christians truly comprehend that Judaism has flowered, evolved, and transformed in the past two thousand years almost as much as it did in its first two thousand years.

Today, the concept of Jesus being the incarnation of God is so far from the way mainstream Jewish theology is taught that many Jews struggle to understand how this can even be a belief, let alone a belief held sacred by almost two billion people today. Just as there are some Christians foolishly waiting for Jews to accept Jesus, there are Jews foolish enough to think that Christians will grow out of their faith in Christ's divinity. After two millennia, can we not see that both groups are waiting in vain and wasting their prayers? Stubbornness, dogmatism, ethnocentrism, narrow-mindedness, parochial theology, and denial of reality are equal opportunity transgressions!

Regarding Jewish ignorance about Christianity, too often I encounter my own Jewish friends who associate the Church with many of the wrongs of the Western world. Certainly the Crusades and Inquisitions arose from within the Church. But the abuses of colonialism, imperialism, Manifest Destiny, slavery, and cults like Nazism were, in reality, just as anti-Christian as they were anti-Semitic. Regarding Nazism, for example, Rabbi Heschel boldly challenges both Jews and Christians to realize the following:

Nazism in its very roots was a rebellion against the Bible, against the God of Abraham. Realizing that it was Christianity that implanted attachment to the God of Abraham and involvement with the Hebrew Bible in the hearts of Western man, Nazism resolved that it must both exterminate the Jews and eliminate Christianity, and bring about instead a revival of Teutonic paganism. Nazism has suffered a defeat, but the process of eliminating the Bible from the consciousness of the Western world goes on. It is on the issue of saving the radiance of the Hebrew Bible in the minds of man that Jews and Christians are called upon to work together. None of us can do it alone. Both of us must realize that in our age, anti-Semitism is anti-Christianity and that anti-Christianity is anti-Semitism.[103]

In searching for a solution to the problem of replacement theology, Yale University Professor Emeritus Dr. George Lindbeck asks, "Can we bring back a non-supersessionist understanding of the church as Israel?"[104] Calling for changes within the way the Church sees Judaism, Dr. Lindbeck acknowledges the unequal amount of change that each faith will likely make as new theological solutions are found in the future. Judaism must transform its defensive, sometimes prejudicial, attitude about the extraordinary contribution that Christianity has brought to the world. Though Jews can never accept the idea of Jesus as God, Judaism certainly can reclaim Jesus as native son, *rebbe*, teacher, storyteller, and miracle worker who lived as a Jew and died as a Jew. Indeed, his blessed memory continues to do its part in fulfilling Isaiah's injunction for the Jewish people to be a "light unto the nations." In addition, while Jews cannot accept Jesus as God, this doesn't mean there cannot be acceptance, and even celebration of Jesus's gospel.

SIXTEEN

The End of Days

MANY RELIGIOUS PEOPLE, BOTH CONSERVATIVE AND LIBERAL, are describing a new era that appears to be emerging in our world today. Some of these descriptions are apocalyptic, while others are beatific. Jewish tradition holds that the messiah will come as a result of either apocalypse (see Deuteronomy 31:29, Isaiah 2:4, Daniel 12:1), or as a result of people having realized the dream of achieving worldwide harmony and peace. In other words, the messiah comes to either rescue the world or to affirm what humanity has achieved. Let us hope for the latter!

Traditionally, Jews and Christians have used the term *end of days* or *end times* to describe the period of time that will begin a major shift in global consciousness (see Isaiah 2:2, Micah 4:1). This period will then be followed by the "messianic era" which is marked by world peace. Today we hear the term *paradigm shift* used by both religious and nonreligious people to describe what seems to be happening in our world. People agree that some kind of major planetary transformation is occurring, for better or for worse. Spiritually minded people in all the religions are struggling to define these global changes.

In the period when Jesus was teaching, an earlier paradigm shift was occurring within Judaism. The religion was being reshaped from Temple-based to synagogue-based, and from being centered on bringing tangible offerings (fruit, grain, animals) to bringing prayers as acceptable offerings. The first and second centuries could also be described as an "end of days." Jesus and thousands of other creative Jewish teachers were tortured, exiled, and crucified by the Roman Empire. The beloved Temple in Jerusalem lay in ruin. Yet, at the same time, biblical instructions and precepts were being reinterpreted and applied by the rabbis in new and innovative ways. Jesus, the first-century rabbi, was at the center of this monumental transformation.

As we know, messianic expectations ran high in the early part of the first century. Jews enthusiastically awaited the coming of the messiah and the end of days spoken about in the Tanakh. The idea in the Younger Testament that Jesus might be the messiah would have been perceived as dangerous by the Romans, but not as radical to the Jews of Jesus's day. Just as we see today in Judaism, two thousand years ago Jews had diverse messianic views. However, many Jews in the first century fervently believed that the Kingdom of God was at hand, and that a messiah would be anointed by God to be the earthly liberator and King of Judea. Both "messiah" and "Kingdom of God" had political connotations, and in the early centuries of the common era, the term *end of days* was used to describe the ingathering of the Jewish people back to their homeland, as well as the fulfillment of other messianic prophesies.

Jews may not have agreed with Jesus's messianic claim, but such an assertion would not have been blasphemy in and of itself. His words in Luke are exactly what the Jews were hoping for: a messiah who would usher in the era of liberty and world peace. In that Gospel account, it's written, "The Spirit of the Lord is upon me, because he has anointed me to bring good news to the poor. He has sent me to proclaim release to the captives and recovery of sight to the blind, to let the oppressed go free" (Luke 4:18). If the messiah was also to be a healer, all the better.

Jews had, and still have, many diverse opinions and questions about the character of the future messiah. Will the messiah suffer or triumph as king? Will he or she come when the world is at peace or in devastating crisis? The normative Jewish view is that the messiah will usher in an era of peace and harmony for the whole world. But within Judaism there's room for many opinions concerning eschatology, the theology regarding the world's destiny. Here are some traditional messianic prophesies from the Tanakh, along with some more contemporary, psychological interpretations:

- The messiah will be a great leader, bringing peace to the entire world (Micah 4:3, Isaiah 2:4, and Isaiah 11:6–8). It's only natural that Jews imagine that the messiah will be Jewish, Christians imagine that the messiah will be Christian, and Muslims await the Mahdi, who will follow Islam. But maybe we're all in for a surprise. I remember in the mid-1990s one of my teachers, Rabbi Shlomo Carlebach, told his students that he was awaiting the arrival of Mr. and Mrs. Messiah since "in our day and age a male messiah would not be able to serve the whole population." We all laughed, but it opened us to the possibility of a non-gender specific messiah. There are also many Jews who don't espouse any kind of belief in the coming of a messiah. Rather, they look forward to a messianic age where the prophesies of world peace will be achieved.

- There will be a universal knowledge of God (Jeremiah 31:33, Isaiah 11:9, Zechariah 14:9, and Isaiah 56:7). There is no expectation within Judaism that when the messiah comes, humanity will, en masse, convert to Judaism. Maybe in the messianic era the universal knowledge of God means that people see the interconnectedness of all the religions, like different singers who are part of a single choir.

- The messiah will oversee the building of the third Temple in Jerusalem (Ezekiel 37:26–28). Obviously, this messianic condition was established after Jesus's crucifixion. Within traditional Judaism this expectation is taken literally, but with the advent of Jungian psychology, as well as both Jewish and Christian mysticism, we can imagine each of us building the new temple within ourselves.

- The messiah will oversee the return of the Jewish people to their homeland (Isaiah 43:5–6). This was a messianic expectation conceived of after the Romans exiled large parts of the Jewish population from their capital city of Jerusalem. Many contemporary Jews believe that this prophecy began to be fulfilled with the birth of modern Zionism in the early twentieth century. Again, from a more mystical perspective, we can ask ourselves, "What is the Promised Land that each of us needs to return to right now?"

- There will be some kind of miraculous resurrection of all those who once lived (Isaiah 26:19), a belief that is shared by many Christians as well. Here, too, many modern Jews and Christians do not necessarily take this prophecy literally, but interpret it as the opportunity for each person to look inward in order to resurrect the dead places in each of our lives.

There is no end to speculation and anticipation of the end of days for both Christians and Jews. It seems like the time for followers in each religion, and in each denomination, to express their hopes, dreams, and messianic beliefs with a great deal of humility. It is, after all, uncertainty that feeds human creativity. This may be the time when new messianic poetry, music, dance, and art can transform prophetic expectations from a sense of triumphalism to a sense of mutual celebration.

And of course, central to our views of the end of days are our views as to what happened two thousand years ago. Simply put, it's historically inaccurate to say that "the Jews rejected Jesus" during his lifetime. Jews comprised about 10 percent of the population of the Roman Empire, and were spread throughout the Middle East and along the Mediterranean. It's probably fair to say that 98 percent of the Jewish population never even heard of Jesus while he was alive, thus precluding any chance of a general acceptance or rejection. The small percentage of Judeans who were aware of him, or who followed him, were mostly Jews. In the century after Jesus's crucifixion it became clear that, from a Jewish perspective, he had not fulfilled any of the key prophecies that were the generally accepted conditions Jews expected from the messiah.

Without those fulfillments, is it really fair to blame religious Jews for not being convinced the messiah had come? Clearly, Jewish expectations for the messiah necessitate a somewhat literal fulfillment of the prophecies outlined by Isaiah, Zechariah, Jeremiah, Micah, and the other prophets. Having said this, it's clear that Christians experience Jesus as their Messiah. Can Jews accept the fact that for Christians Jesus has fulfilled messianic prophesies? Can Christians live with the fact that Jesus can be the Messiah for Christians and not for Jews? And if we all can do this, what might it mean for our anticipation of the future?

Messianic Prophecies

The following are Jewish interpretations to just a few popular biblical passages.

A Child is Born Isaiah 9:6–7 is literally about the great reformer-king of Israel named Hezekiah. At the same time, the rabbis believed these verses could be extended to also apply to a future messiah. This messiah will be an actual ruler, as it's written, "a son given to us; authority rests upon his shoulders." Christianity interprets these passages as referring to Jesus. Christian Bibles translate the words *Wonderful Counselor, Mighty God, Everlasting Father, Prince of Peace* as titles referring to the messiah. In Hebrew, however, the only title given to Hezekiah, or a future messiah, is "Prince of Peace." The prefatory terms refer only to God. Here, too, it's certainly the privilege of Christians to interpret these titles as referring to Jesus, but an interpretative translation ought not replace the plain meaning.

The Root of Jesse Isaiah 11:9 speaks of a time when "the earth shall be full of the knowledge of the LORD." On a simple level, this prophecy was not fulfilled in the historical period two thousand years ago. After a hundred years of struggle to defeat the Roman occupation of Judea, a large part of the Jewish population was exiled from Jerusalem. This prophecy is about a time when the Jewish people are to be gathered from "the four corners of the earth" to their ancient homeland. But it can also be understood as a time when all the nations, cultures, and religions in the world recognize their interdependence upon one another, and upon the planet itself. This too may be a part of the "knowledge of the LORD."

A Prophet like Me In the citation from Acts 3:22, Jesus is compared to Moses, and the passage is understood as a fulfillment of Deuteronomy 18:15 where it is written that "The LORD your God will raise up for you a prophet like me [Moses] from among your own people; you shall heed such a prophet." The term *prophet* is a human title within Judaism. On the tombstone of Moses Maimonides, the great twelfth-century physician and thinker, the engraving reads: "From Moses to Moses there was none like Moses." Some religious Jews believe that Maimonides is a good candidate for having fulfilled the prophesy of being a teacher like Moses. In the Jewish interpretative tradition, prophetic texts may have multiple meanings, and there is no single, correct interpretation.

The LORD Your God Will Gather You Many Jews and Christians believe that the prophecies of Deuteronomy 30:2–5 describe the history of the Jewish people in several different eras. After the destruction of the Temple in Jerusalem in 586 BCE, the Jews were scattered from Judea and then regathered fifty years later. Again, after the destruction of the second Temple in 70 CE, many Jews were exiled from their homeland. In recent history, the Jewish people have been returning to Israel from every corner of the earth in fulfillment of this prophecy.

The Wolf Shall Lie Down with the Lamb Religious Jews interpret the metaphor of the wolf and the lamb dwelling together from Isaiah 11:6 as an indication of the peace and justice that is expected during the messianic era. In both Jewish and Christian thought, this prophesy is yet to be fulfilled.

Daniel's Seventy Weeks Daniel 9:25–26 speaks of "an anointed prince." These verses literally refer to Cyrus, King of Persia:

> Know therefore and understand: from the time that the word went out to restore and rebuild Jerusalem until the time of an anointed prince, there shall be seven weeks; and for sixty-two weeks it shall be built again with streets and moat, but in a troubled time. After the sixty-two weeks, an anointed one shall be cut off and shall have nothing, and the troops of the prince who is to come shall destroy the city and the sanctuary. Its end shall come with a flood, and to the end there shall be war. Desolations are decreed.

The interpretation that Daniel's prophesy refers to Cyrus can be demonstrated three verses later in Daniel 10:1. Remember that earlier prophets had already called Cyrus a "messiah" or "christ" in Isaiah 45:1: "In the third year of King Cyrus of Persia a word was revealed to Daniel. . . . The word was true, and it concerned a great conflict. He understood the word, having received understanding in the vision" (Daniel 10:1). In 2 Chronicles 36:20–23 we read that Cyrus is the fulfillment of Jeremiah's messianic prophecy, and possibly relates to Daniel's prophesy as well. It was seventy years from the destruction of the first temple in Jerusalem by the Babylonians to its rebuilding by the non-Jewish messiah Cyrus. Daniel refers to this metaphorically as "seventy weeks," a week metaphorically representing a year. On the simplest level of interpretation, this text has to do with the rebuilding of the city of Jerusalem, not its destruction by the Romans in 70 CE. Its meaning can even be extended to refer to the future messiah:

2 Chronicles 36:20–23 He took into exile in Babylon those who had escaped from the sword. . . . All the days that it lay desolate it kept sabbath, to fulfill seventy years. In the first year of King Cyrus of Persia, in fulfillment of the word of the LORD spoken by Jeremiah, the LORD stirred up the spirit of King Cyrus of Persia.

Thus says King Cyrus of Persia: The LORD, the God of heaven, has given me all the kingdoms of the earth, and he has charged me to build him a house at Jerusalem, which is in Judah. Whoever is among you of all his people, may the LORD his God be with him! Let him go up.

Mutual Affirmation

As already noted, *Nostra Aetate,* issued on October 28, 1965, under Pope Paul IV, was the historic declaration on the relationship between the Catholic Church, Protestants, Judaism, and other non-Christian religions. For the first time in history, the Church courageously affirmed the ongoing covenantal relationship that the Jews and Protestants have with God. Why did it take two thousand years for the Church to make this affirmation? Answering a question with a question, why did it take until the Middle Ages for Judaism to affirm that Christianity was a monotheistic religion?

Dr. David Ellenson, professor at Hebrew Union College, writes: "A tendency toward Jewish religious tolerance—one might even say appreciation—of Christianity as a form of monotheism began to appear among Jews of Christian Europe in the twelfth century." Dr. Ellenson cites Rabbi Isaac, a medieval authority, who understood that when a Christian worships Jesus, he or she is involved in a spiritual process called *shituf* in Hebrew—making an association between Jesus and the Father. Even though Jesus isn't an appropriate name of God for Jews, Rabbi Isaac found enough intellectual wiggle room to affirm that Christianity was monotheistic based on this concept of association. Dr. David Ellenson goes on to share the importance of another important theologian who understood the importance of Christianity:

At the same time, the central European rabbi Jacob Emden (1697–1776) carried this posture to new heights. In a commentary upon Mishna Avot 4:11—"Every assembly that is for the sake of Heaven will in the end be established"—he stated, speaking of both Islam and Christianity, "Their assembly is also for the sake of Heaven, to make Godliness known among the nations, to speak of Him in distant places." Elsewhere, he declared that Jesus "the Nazarene, brought a double kindness in the world. On the one hand, he strengthened the Torah of Moses majestically. . . . On the other hand, he did much good for the gentiles . . . by doing away with idolatry and removing the images from their midst.[105]

Nevertheless, until the twentieth century, rabbis almost never extolled Jesus as a great rabbi whose ministry was able to bring light to the Gentile nations. Due to the endemic state of anti-Judaism in Christian nations, it was uncommon for religious Jewish intellectuals to have an objective understanding of the historical Jesus. One senses a similar hesitancy in some of the statements made by some Catholic and Protestant leaders, even after *Nostra Aetate,* about salvation outside of Jesus. It was a brave, giant step for the Catholic Church to acknowledge that non-Catholics could have an authentic relationship with God. Change is always slow and difficult. For both Jews and Christians, the rewards of change will be great, commensurate to the sacred struggle the faithful are willing to undertake.

Paul tells the followers of Jesus that they see in a "mirror dimly" (1 Corinthians 13:12). Regarding his Jewish brothers and sisters he comments, "I want you to understand this mystery: a hardening has come upon part of Israel, until the full number of the Gentiles has come in" (Romans 11:25). Many Christians simply do not understand how the Jews can follow the commandments after the time of Christ. Conversely, most Jews simply don't understand how a covenant for the Gentiles could have been created through Jesus's death and resurrection. There seems to be a mystery here. If Paul is correct, then Christians perceive the covenant of Judaism in a mirror dimly, and a hardening has come upon part of Israel. The remedy? Patience. Trust in God!

What Torah is for Jews, the gospel is for Christians. The gospel, as taught in the Younger Testament, presents that same moral imperative that it adopted from the Elder Testament. Paul's genius can be seen in the creative way he maintained the Jewish view that non-Jews did not have to become Jewish in order to be justified. Jews and non-Jews who already walked with God under the Mosaic or the Noahic covenant never needed a portal to God through Christ. Jesus, like the prophets before him, was simply trying to get his own people, the Jews, to fulfill the covenant to which they had already agreed. In Judaism, mitzvot may be reinterpreted to conform to new circumstances but they are not replaced. Jesus was one of hundreds of rabbis struggling to reinterpret the Torah in an age of desperation and turmoil. Today, it's in the best interest of Jews for Christians to be the best Christians they can be. And it is in the best interest of Christians for Jews to be the best Jews we can be. This applies to people in every other religion as well.

So what took Jewish theologians so long simply to acknowledge Christianity in God's redemptive plan? What took Christianity even longer to recognize the ongoing covenantal relationship that Jews had with God? Why does it remain so difficult for some fundamentalists to affirm that the souls of Jews have the same chance of going to heaven as anyone else? Why does it remain so difficult for Jews to celebrate the historical Jesus without age-old fears rising to the surface from the Crusades, the Inquisition, pogroms, expulsions, and the Holocaust? Looking back, it is easy to be cynical and say, "It's terrible that it took so long for Jews and Christians to recognize the efficacy of each other's faith." But seeing God's redemptive plan unfolding before our eyes at this moment in history, maybe it's time that we simply say, "Thank You God that this moment of mutual recognition is happening! Help us fulfill Your will from now on." It's time simply to breathe a sigh of relief that so many Jews and Christians have finally arrived and are prepared to do the sacred work of reconciliation.

The Mystery of the Nexus

In an increasingly smaller and more transparent world, how will our two faiths that have so much in common relate to each other? Our religions are in the midst of momentous internal transformations that are being caused by the same external forces (egalitarianism, the information age, common ecological concerns, responding to religious extremism, and the rise of secularism).

How will Judaism and Christianity each change in the next century? I believe that the church will slowly reclaim its Jewish roots, and some aspects of Christian theology will see a radical revamping. I also believe that efforts to convert Jews will be seen more and more as repugnant from within the church itself.

As for Judaism, a defensive posture and an allergic reaction to Christianity keeps the cycle of misunderstanding going. The first step in healing this two-thousand-year-old enmity between Ecclesia and Synagogue will be for the faithful in each religion to acknowledge the "presence of a divine plan" in each other's roles, a step being taken at the present time by unprecedented numbers of Jews and Christians. This acknowledgment, of course, does not mean agreement on all the theological issues that seem to separate us—just the simple acknowledgment that we are all part of the bigger plan. With God's help we may someday be able to celebrate our differences—like the string section celebrates the woodwind section in an orchestra.

Rabbi Abraham Joshua Heschel (whose writings, I know, are already treasured by many Christians) asks us:

> Is Judaism, is Christianity, ready to face the challenge? When I speak about the radiance of the Bible in the minds of man, I do not mean its being a theme for "Information, please" but rather an openness to God's presence in the Bible, the continuous ongoing effort for a breakthrough in the soul of man, the guarding of the precarious position of being human, even a little higher than human, despite defiance and in the face of despair.[106]

Do we want to maintain the stereotypes and the polarities between our faiths, or are we willing to search further? Certainly we can discuss, debate, and learn from each other concerning crucial doctrines like repentance and grace. Maybe we'll learn that the separation between Church and Synagogue has never been as great as we have been led to believe. I hope so.

Hans Küng, the visionary Roman Catholic theologian, examines the history of Jewish-Christian relations and makes a courageous call for an act of communal *teshuvah* toward the Jewish people by the church. He writes, "Only one thing is of any use now: a radical metanoia, repentance and re-thinking; we must start on a new road, no longer leading away from the Jews, but toward them."[107] It is true that, in a tragic way, both Jews and Christians have often been captives in their own theological prisons. Inaccurate biblical interpretations and nonbiblical dogmas have contributed to two thousand years of anxious relations between Synagogue and Church. Maybe today the Holy One is calling upon each of us now to help bring a full healing to Jews and Christians. Maybe the Holy One is calling upon us to help liberate each other through humble speech, acts of contrition, reconciliation, and finally to mutual celebration.

Many historians, religious and secular alike, have noted that the survival of the Jewish people in the midst of extreme prejudice is an anomaly of history. God has always had a plan for the Jews; it's all laid out in the Bible. For two thousand years most Jews have not felt safe enough to formally acknowledge that Jesus too is part of a divine plan in bringing the polytheistic clans, tribes, and kingdoms within the Roman and Greek empires into a covenantal relationship with the Creator. For much of the past two thousand years, many Christians in positions of political and military authority have not been able to acknowledge that Judaism continues to be part of God's plan.

From the beginning of the second century I believe that Christianity and Judaism needed each other to be strong and independent faiths. Can we understand that covenant does not compete against covenant? That suffering does not compete against suffering? To most Christians, Jesus can never just be a good man and wise rabbi. And to a Jew, the Savior can never be a man. Can we now begin to celebrate the mystery of these two views of Jesus? Can we now begin to hold this paradox with a sense of wonder rather than competition?

The Composer has written a magnificent hymn for the choir to sing. The melody is exalted, and the rhythm is the pulse of creation itself. The musicians are taking their seats, tuning instruments of every kind. Heavenly angels have fanned out their wings around us all, ready to join us with glorious harmonies. Having waited for the last two thousand years, the conductor has lifted the baton and is ready to lead us. We are members of a single choir, a single orchestra—each in our own section, each with our own special part. Are we finally ready to sing?

ACKNOWLEDGMENTS

ALL OF US WHO DO INTERFAITH WORK ARE STANDING ON THE shoulders of courageous twentieth-century pioneers in Jewish/ Christian dialogue. I am indebted to my mentor, Rabbi Aryeh Hirschfield, who first showed me the connection between Elijah, Jesus, and the Baal Shem Tov. Special thanks to Rabbi Shlomo Carlebach, Neshama Carlebach, and to my colleagues in the Jewish Renewal movement and the OHALAH rabbinical association who are engaged in cutting-edge interfaith work. Thanks to my own partners in interfaith dialogue: Rev. Anne Bartlett, Rev. Dr. Barbara Campbell, Rev. Leslie Becknell-Marx, Rev. Pam Shepherd, Rev. Dr. Anthony Hutchinson, Pastor Ron Timen, Rev. Adam Walker Cleaveland, Lama Yeshe Parke, Lama Pema Clark, Agnes Baker-Pilgrim, Dr. Jean Houston, and Dr. Krishna Gokani.

I want to express my deepest appreciation to Dr. Amy-Jill Levine for her invaluable scholarly critique and suggestions; to Jon Sweeney, my editor at Paraclete Press, for his guidance and exceptional editing; to my wife, Debra Gordon-Zaslow, for her personal support and editorial feedback; and to my writing partner, Joe Lieberman, for his superb contribution to this book. Finally, I ask for God's continued blessings for my rebbe, Rabbi Zalman Schachter-Shalomi, whose pioneering efforts in interfaith work have brought people of many faiths together to study, discover, and celebrate with one another.

ABOUT THE AUTHORS

RABBI DAVID ZASLOW has been the spiritual leader of Havurah Shir Hadash, a synagogue in Ashland, Oregon, since 1996. Ordained in the Jewish Renewal movement, he travels the country leading Sabbath services for synagogues, as well as workshops co-sponsored by churches and synagogues on the Jewish roots of Christianity. He is the editor of a Hebrew/English prayer book for spiritual renewal entitled *Ivdu et Hashem B'simcha: A Siddur for Spiritual Renewal.* In 1988 he was awarded an American Book Award for educational materials.

JOSEPH A. LIEBERMAN is a photojournalist, investigative reporter, and author of travel and textbooks. His most recent work is *School Shootings: What Every Parent and Educator Needs to Know to Protect Our Children* (New York: Citadel Press 2008). He is currently freelancing for a number of magazines, including *Oregon Jewish Life.*

NOTES

1   Martin Buber, *Two Types of Faith* (New York: Collier Books, 1986), 12.

2   The title *rabbi* wasn't formally conferred upon teachers until after 70 CE. However, Jesus is referred to as rabbi in three Gospels (Matthew, Mark, and John) that were written after his lifetime. The title was likely used informally before 70 CE to mean "teacher."

3   Brad H. Young, *Jesus, the Jewish Theologian* (Peabody, MA: Hendrickson Publishers, 1995), xxxiv.

4   Clark Williamson, "A Christian View of Redemption," in *Christianity in Jewish Terms*, ed. Tikva Frymer-Kensky, David Novak, Michael A. Signer, David Fox Sandmel, and Peter Ochs (Boulder, CO: Westview Press, 2000), 287.

5   Nancy Fuchs-Kreimer, "Redemption: What I Have Learned from Christians," in *Christianity in Jewish Terms*, 276.

6   Young, *Jesus, the Jewish Theologian*, xxii and xxxiv.

7   David Flusser, *Jewish Sources in Early Christianity* (Tel Aviv: Mod Books, 1989), 24–25.

8   David Flusser, *Jesus* (Jerusalem: The Hebrew University Magnes Press, 1997), 58.

9   Amy Jill Levine, *The Misunderstood Jew* (San Francisco: HarperCollins, 2006), 8.

10 M. Friedman, *Encounter on the Narrow Ridge: A Life of Martin Buber* (St. Paul, MN: Paragon House, 1998), 293.

11 Levine, *Misunderstood Jew*, 197.

12 Young, *Jesus, the Jewish Theologian*, foreword by David Wolpe, xiii.

13 A first-century Jewish philosopher who lived in Alexandria, Egypt, who proceeded the era of rabbinic Judaism. He tried to unite certain aspects of Greek philosophy to Jewish philosophy.

14 Brad Young, *The Jewish Background to the Lord's Prayer* (Dayton, OH: Center for Judaic-Christian Studies, 1984), 11.

15 Lawrence A. Hoffman, "Jewish and Christian Liturgy," in *Christianity in Jewish Terms*, 179.

16 Ibid., 24.

17 Michael A. Signer, "Searching the Scriptures," in *Christianity in Jewish Terms*, 89.

18 Hayyim Nahman Bialik, Yehoshua Hana Ravnitzky, William G. Braude, and David Stern, *The Book of Legends/Sefer HaAgada* (New York: Schocken Books, 1992), 39.

19 Maurice Harris, *Moses: A Stranger Among Us* (Eugene, OR: Cascade Books, 2012), 38.

20 Augustine of Hippo, *Contra Faustum* [Reply to Faustus the Manichaean], ca. 398 CE.

21 Jacob Neusner, *Self-Fulfilling Prophecy* (Boston: Beacon Press, 1987), 106.

22 Ibid., 118.

23 Flusser, *Jesus*, 105.

24 Ibid., 71, 92.

25 Young, *Jesus, the Jewish Theologian*, 228.

26   Macy Nulman, *The Encyclopedia of the Sayings of the Jewish People* (New York: Jason Aronson, 1997), 41.

27   Lawrence A. Hoffman, "Jewish and Christian Liturgy," in *Christianity in Jewish Terms*, 180 and 181.

28   Robert Wilken, "Christian Worship," in *Christianity in Jewish Terms*, 198, 200.

29   Ibid.

30   Jacob Milgrom, *Leviticus 1–16* (New York: Doubleday, 1991), 228.

31   Shalom Spiegel, *The Last Trial—The Akedah* (Woodstock, VT: Jewish Lights, 1993). From the *New Preface* by Judah Golden, vii.

32   Steven Kepnes, "Original Sin, Atonement, and Redemption in Jewish Terms," in *Christianity in Jewish Terms*, 300.

33   W. Gunther Plaut, ed., *The Torah* (New York: URJ Press), 1981, 154

34   Immanuel Kant, *Streit der Fakultaten*, in *Encounters Between Judaism and Modern Philosophy: A Preface to Future Jewish Thought*, trans. Emil Fackenheim, (New York: Schocken, 1973), 34.

35   Leora Batnitzsky, "On the Suffering of God's Chosen," in *Christianity in Jewish Terms*, 209.

36   Spiegel, *The Last Trial-The Akedah*, 84–85.

37   Ibid., xvi–xvii.

38   This is final benediction line in the third prayer of the Amidah.

39   The term *scapegoat* means either (1) someone punished for the errors of others, or (2) someone falsely blamed for the sins of another.

40   See http://m.chabad.org/library/article_cdo/aid/91458/jewish/The-Test.htm (accessed August 15, 2013).

41   Tzvi Freeman, "The Test," http://www.chabad.org/library/article_cdo/aid/91458/jewish/The-Test.htm (accessed July 9, 2013).

42   From the song *Highway 61 Revisited* by Bob Dylan.

43   Mary Ellen Chase, *Life and Language in the Old Testament* (New York: Norton, 1955), 35.

44   Ibid., 34.

45   Hoffman, "Jewish and Christian Liturgy," in *Christianity in Jewish Terms*, 182.

46   Ibid., 182–183.

47   Here are three contemporary translations of the Torah:
      The Chumash, The Stone Edition (New York: Mesorah Publications, 1993).
      The Torah: A Modern Commentary, by W. Gunther Plaut (New York: UAHC Press, 1981).
      The Pentateuch (Torah and Commentary), by Samson Raphael Hirsch (Jerusalem, Israel: Feldheim Publishers, 2005).

48   Chase, *Life and Language in the Old Testament*, 36.

49   Williamson, "A Christian View of Redemption," in *Christianity in Jewish Terms*, 287.

50   Levine, *Misunderstood Jew*, 17.

51   Peter Ochs, "The God of Jews and Christians," in *Christianity in Jewish Terms*, 65.

52   Isaiah 41:8–9, Isaiah 42:1, Isaiah 43:8, Isaiah 44:1, Isaiah 44:21, Isaiah 45:4, Isaiah 48:20, Isaiah 49:3, Isaiah 49:6.

53   Flusser, *Jewish Sources in Early Christianity*, 59.

54 Elliot R. Wolfson, "Judaism and Incarnation: The Imaginal Body of God," in *Christianity in Jewish Terms*, 247.

55 Jacob Neusner, *Incarnation of God: The Character of Divinity in Formative Judaism* (Philadelphia: Fortress Press, 1988), 4.

56 See http://en.wikipedia.org/wiki/Panentheism (accessed July 9, 2013).

57 Kepnes, "Original Sin, Atonement, and Redemption in Jewish Terms," in *Christianity in Jewish Terms*, 294.

58 Ibid., 295–98.

59 Flusser, *Jesus*, quoting Targum Pseudo Jonathan on Leviticus 19:18.

60 Martin Buber, "Biblical Leadership," in *Israel and the World: Essays in a Time of Crisis*, (New York: Schocken Books, 1987), 125–26.

61 Rabbi Irving Greenberg, "Toward An Organic Model of the Relationship," in *For the Sake of Heaven and Earth* (Philadelphia: Jewish Publication Society, 2004), 153.

62 Byron L. Sherwin, "Who Do You Say That I Am?" in *Jesus Through Jewish Eyes*, ed. Beatrice Bruteau (Maryknoll, NY: Orbis Books, 2011), 37.

63 Rabbi Irving Greenberg, "Judaism and Christianity: Covenants of Redemption," in *Christianity in Jewish Terms*, 156.

64 Ibid., 151.

65 Leora Batnitzky, "On the Suffering of God's Chosen," in *Christianity in Jewish Terms*, 208.

66 From *Scriptures of the Oral Torah* translated with commentary by Dr. Jacob Neusner (New York: Harper and Row, 1987), 21.

67 Sometimes rendered as Jehovah or Yaweh. The name *Yah*, used in the suffix of "halleluyah," is an abbreviated form of the Tetragrammaton.

68 Yechiel Eckstein, *What Christians Should Know About Jews and Judaism* (Plano, TX: W Pub Group, 1984), 268.

69 Discussed by Rabbi Zalman Schachter-Shalomi, *Paradigm Shift* (New York: Jason Aaronson, 1993), 34; and by Rabbi Irving Greenberg in *For the Sake of Heaven and Earth* (Philadelphia: Jewish Publication Society, 2004), 153.

70 Fuchs-Kreimer, "Redemption," in *Christianity in Jewish Terms*, 275.

71 Pinchas Lapide was an Orthodox rabbi and scholar born in Germany in 1922. The citation is from Marvin R. Wilson, *Our Father Abraham* (Grand Rapids, MI: Eerdmans, 1987), 21.

72 Robert Gibbs, "Suspicions of Suffering," in *Christianity in Jewish Terms*, 226.

73 Friedman, *Encounter on the Narrow Ridge*, 293.

74 Rabbi Irving Greenberg, "Confronting the Holocaust Again," in *For the Sake of Heaven and Earth*, 25.

75 Thomas Merton, *Conjectures of a Guilty Bystander* (New York: Doubleday, 1965), 130.

76 Kepnes, "Original Sin, Atonement, and Redemption in Jewish Terms," in *Christianity in Jewish Terms*, 304.

77 David Novak, "Mitzvah," in *Christianity in Jewish Terms*, 116.

78 Flusser, *Jesus*, 63.

79 Ibid.

80 Rosemary Radford Reuther, *Faith and Fratricide: the Theological Roots of Anti-Semitism* (New York: Seabury Press, 1974), 230.

81 Ibid., 84.

82 Levine, *Misunderstood Jew*, 111.

83 Ibid., 10.

84 Ibid., 19.

85 Dennis Prager and Joseph Telushkin, *Why the Jews: The Reasons for Antisemitism* (New York: Touchstone Books, 2003), 11–12.

86 Ibid., 24–25.

87 James Carroll, *Constantine's Sword: The Church and the Jews* (Boston: Houghton Mifflin, 2001), 39.

88 Flusser, *Jesus*, 75.

89 David Bivin and Roy Blizzard Jr., *Understanding the Difficult Words of Jesus* (Dayton, OH: Center for Judaic-Christian Studies, 1994), 154.

90 Brad Young, *Paul, The Jewish Theologian* (Peabody, MA: Hendrickson, 1995), 65.

91 Philo, *On The Embassy of Gauis*, Book XXXVIII, 299–305, cited at http://en.wikipedia.org/wiki/Pontius_Pilate#cite_note-ReferenceB-34 (accessed July 10, 2013).

92 Flusser, *Jesus*, 155–156.

93 Signer, "Searching the Scriptures," in *Christianity in Jewish Terms*, 91.

94 From *Luther's Works*, Vol. 47, trans. Martin H. Berstram (Minneapolis: Fortress Press, 1971), 268–293.

95 From the article "The Delicate Diplomacy of Jewish-Christian Dialogue" in *Christianity Today*, April 24, 1981. Reprinted in *Evangelicals and Jews in an Age of Pluralism*, ed., Marc H. Tanenbaum, Marvin Wilson, and A. James Rudin (Lanham, MD: University Press of America, 1990), 207.

96 Josephus, *The Wars of the Jews*, VI.9.3.

97 Joseph Telushkin, *Jewish Literacy* (New York: William Morrow and Co., 1991), 127.

98 See Isaiah 43:8, Isaiah 44:1, Isaiah 44:21, Isaiah 45:4, Isaiah 48:20, Isaiah 49:6.

99 Hoffman, "Jewish and Christian Liturgy," in *Christianity in Jewish Terms*, 186.

100 Pamela Eisenbaum, annotation on Hebrews, *The Jewish Annotated New Testament* (New York: Oxford University Press, 2011), 416.

101 Gibbs, "Suspicions of Suffering," in *Christianity in Jewish Terms*, 228.

102 *Abraham Joshua Heschel*, "No Religion Is an Island," *No Religion Is an Island*, ed. Harold Kasimow and Byron L. Sherwin (Maryknoll, NY: Orbis Books, 1991), 20. Available at http://www.cs.auckland.ac.nz/~alan/chaplain/Heschel.html (accessed June 27, 2013).

103 Ibid., 4.

104 George Lindbeck, "Postmodern Hermeneutics and Jewish-Christian Dialogue," in *Christianity in Jewish Terms*, 108.

105 David Ellenson, "A Jewish View of the Christian God," in *Christianity in Jewish Terms*, 74.

106 Abraham Joshua Heschel, "No Religion Is an Island," *No Religion Is an Island*, 5.

107 Hans Küng, *The Church*, trans. Ray and Rosaleen Oekenden (London: Burns and Oates, 1967), 138.

ABOUT PARACLETE PRESS

Who We Are

Paraclete Press is a publisher of books, recordings, and DVDs on Christian spirituality. Our publishing represents a full expression of Christian belief and practice—from Catholic to Evangelical, from Protestant to Orthodox.

We are the publishing arm of the Community of Jesus, an ecumenical monastic community in the Benedictine tradition. As such, we are uniquely positioned in the marketplace without connection to a large corporation and with informal relationships to many branches and denominations of faith.

What We Are Doing

Paraclete Press Books | Paraclete publishes books that show the richness and depth of what it means to be Christian. Although Benedictine spirituality is at the heart of all that we do, we publish books that reflect the Christian experience across many cultures, time periods, and houses of worship. We publish books that nourish the vibrant life of the church and its people.

We have several different series, including the best-selling Paraclete Essentials and Paraclete Giants series of classic texts in contemporary English; Voices from the Monastery— men and women monastics writing about living a spiritual life today; award-winning poetry; best-selling gift books for children on the occasions of baptism and first communion; and the Active Prayer Series that brings creativity and liveliness to any life of prayer.

Mount Tabor Books | Paraclete's newest series, Mount Tabor Books, focuses on liturgical worship, art and art history, ecumenism, and the first millennium church, and was created in conjunction with the Mount Tabor Ecumenical Centre for Art and Spirituality in Barga, Italy.

Paraclete Recordings | From Gregorian chant to contemporary American choral works, our recordings celebrate the best of sacred choral music composed through the centuries that create a space for heaven and earth to intersect. Paraclete Recordings is the record label representing the internationally acclaimed choir Gloriæ Dei Cantores, praised for their "rapt and fathomless spiritual intensity" by *American Record Guide*; the Gloriæ Dei Cantores Schola, specializing in the study and performance of Gregorian chant; and the other instrumental artists of the Gloriæ Dei Artes Foundation.

Paraclete Press is also privileged to be the exclusive North American distributor of the recordings of the Monastic Choir of St. Peter's Abbey in Solesmes, France, long considered to be a leading authority on Gregorian chant.

Paraclete Video | Our DVDs offer spiritual help, healing, and biblical guidance for a broad range of life issues including grief and loss, marriage, forgiveness, facing death, bullying, addictions, Alzheimer's, and spiritual formation.

Learn more about us at our website:
www.paracletepress.com, or
call us toll-free at 1-800-451-5006.

SCAN
TO
READ
MORE

You may also be interested in